To Find a Pasqueflower

A BUR OAK BOOK

Holly Carver, series editor

TO FIND A PASQUEFLOWER

A STORY OF THE TALLGRASS PRAIRIE

Greg Hoch

UNIVERSITY OF IOWA PRESS | IOWA CITY

University of Iowa Press, Iowa City 52242

Copyright © 2022 by the University of Iowa Press

uipress.uiowa.edu

Printed in the United States of America

Design by April Leidig

Printed on acid-free paper

Library of Congress Cataloging-in-Publication Data
Names: Hoch, Greg, 1971– author.
Title: To Find a Pasqueflower: A Story of the Tallgrass Prairie / by Greg Hoch.
Description: Iowa City: University of Iowa Press, 2022. | Series: Bur Oak Books |
    Includes bibliographical references and index.
Identifiers: LCCN 2021032857 (print) | LCCN 2021032858 (ebook) |
    ISBN 9781609388256 (paperback) | ISBN 9781609388263 (ebook)
Subjects: LCSH: Prairie ecology—Great Plains. | Prairie ecology—Kansas. |
    Prairies—Great Plains. | Conservation of natural resources—Great Plains.
Classification: LCC QH541.5.P7 C63 2022 (print) | LCC QH541.5.P7 (ebook) |
    DDC 577.4/4—dc23
LC record available at https://lccn.loc.gov/2021032857
LC ebook record available at https://lccn.loc.gov/2021032858

For us of the minority, the opportunity to see geese is more important than television, and the chance to find a pasque-flower is a right as inalienable as free speech.
—Aldo Leopold, *A Sand County Almanac*

To Pete
and
To John and Brent

Contents

Acknowledgments

FIRST, I thank Dave for that first visit to Smith Pioneer Cemetery in western Indiana the summer between my freshman and sophomore year. That one trip set my life on a trajectory. And also thanks for the almost daily friendship and mentorship in the three decades since.

This book is the culmination of thousands of conversations with hundreds of people over the last thirty years. I've tried to capture as much of that as possible. However, there are far too many to try to name individually and not leave just as many out. I thank everyone at Konza Prairie—faculty, post-docs, staff, fellow graduate students, and everyone else. My years there built on and helped refine the interest that developed in Indiana. Next, I thank everyone in the conservation community in Minnesota. Everyone. That includes friends and colleagues at the Department of Natural Resources, the US Fish and Wildlife Service, The Nature Conservancy, The Prairie Enthusiasts, and all the other agencies and organizations that work across Minnesota and across the Midwest to benefit prairies and grasslands.

Earlier versions of several of these chapters appeared in the magazine *Upland Almanac*.

Last, I thank everyone at the University of Iowa Press who helped make this book possible: Allison, Meredith, Karen, and especially Holly.

Disclaimer

THOSE WHO CLAIM to understand the tallgrass prairie often speak loudly and use strong declarative sentences. It's usually pretty easy to tune them out. There are also those who understand that the prairie is so complex that no one person will ever comprehend all of it or even fully grasp the small segment of the prairie they have spent their life studying, formally or informally. These people speak softly and end many of their comments with question marks. They can be fascinating to converse with. In "Coda: Wilderness Letter," one of the foundational essays of the conservation movement, Wallace Stegner (1969) quotes Sherwood Anderson, who wrote about the prairies: "I can remember old fellows in my home town speaking freely of an evening on the big empty plains. It had taken the shrillness out of them. They had learned the trick of quiet." The people who best understand the prairie understand quiet and the art of listening.

This book is a summary of my conversations with many people much smarter and more experienced than I, as well as my own education, research, experiences, and observations. It is a reflection of my own interest in and passion for the prairie.

None of the statements that I make in this book is carved in stone and almost everything is debatable. In fact, many of the topics I cover, such as the very nature of what a plant community is, have been vigorously debated for many decades. There are no final answers to these questions or any winners in the debates. I don't ask any reader to agree with everything in this book. I do hope this book sparks thought and discussion. What I am trying to portray is the ever-changing nature of scientific perspective as it studies a dynamic ecosystem, the tallgrass prairie.

I rely heavily on the long-term data set from Konza Prairie in eastern Kansas in this book, simply because it is one of the few long-term prairie data sets out there. Cedar Creek, just south of my current home in Minnesota, is another valuable source of information. Both are founding members of the National Science Foundation's Long-Term Ecological Research program. I stand by the validity of my graphs and think I crunched the numbers correctly, but they were designed to be descriptive, not definitive. They would not stand up to the statistical rigor and peer-review process of a research journal. However, that isn't the intent of this book.

The modern Midwest is a human-dominated ecosystem. Humans have largely destroyed or replaced a diverse mix of grasses and wildflowers with monocultures of corn or beans. Even before the plow, humans played a large role in structuring the very nature of the tallgrass prairie.

Over my writing desk at home is a watercolor of prairie-chickens titled "Prairie Foghorn" by Ross Hier, my friend and favorite artist. Next to that is the following quote from Edward Abbey from his book *The Journey Home* (1977). Although written about Abbey's southwestern deserts, the idea translates to other ecosystems such as the tallgrass prairie. "The moral I labor toward is that a landscape as splendid as that of the Colorado Plateau can best be understood and given human significance by poets who have their feet planted in concrete—concrete data—and by scientists whose heads and hearts have not lost the capacity for wonder. Any good poet in our age at least, must begin with the scientific view of the world; and any scientist worth listening to must be something of a poet, must possess the ability to communicate to the rest of us his sense of love and wonder at what his work discovers." This book is one person's attempt to communicate the science as he understands it as well as his love and wonder for the tallgrass prairie.

Introduction

Grass is the forgiveness of Nature — her constant benediction. . . . Forests decay, harvests perish, flowers vanish, but grass is immortal. — *Ingalls 1905*

You must not be in the prairie; but the prairie must be in you. That alone will do as qualification for a biographer of the prairie. . . . He who tells the prairie mystery must wear the prairie in his heart. — *Quayle 1905*

Prairie, to most Americans, is a flat place once dotted with covered wagons. — *Leopold 1942a*

Newcomers to the prairie are at first disconcerted by its nakedness. Later they will wish it were not so private. — *Gruchow 1985*

Only grass is eternal. — *Erdrich 1994*

[T]he Great Plains are more notable for what they are not than what they are. — *Johnsgard 2003*

HAVE YOU EVER visited two or more prairies and noticed that each one is just a little different than the others? Have you ever visited the same prairie twice and noticed it was a little different than the last time you were there, whether that last trip was a day, month, year, or decade ago? If you can answer yes to any of those questions, then you have the tools to be a prairie ecologist. Or maybe you already are a prairie ecologist and just didn't know it.

The prairie will always reveal something new to the careful observer. Your hundredth trip should be just as eye-opening as the first. In fact, it should be far more eye-opening since you'll know much more about what to look for.

One topic I want to emphasize is the idea of uncertainty. What will happen when we burn this prairie? What will the prairie look like the spring after it was grazed? We have a good general idea what will happen, but even today we often have to wait to see how some of the details work themselves out.

The prairie itself is hard to define. What is a prairie? Where are its boundaries? Is it prairie, singular, or prairies, plural? The tallgrass prairie may be the youngest ecosystem in North America. Before the Wisconsin glacier retreated, there wasn't anything a modern observer would recognize as prairie. Because it's so young, no species have had time to evolve in the prairie setting. The prairie is a mixed-up mishmash of plants and animals from other ecosystems.

The prairie has played a strong role in the life of this country. The oaks of the eastern forests, the pineries of New England and the Great Lakes region, metals from Minnesota's iron range, and the coal seams of the Appalachians built this country. The tallgrass prairie region became the breadbasket of the country and of the world.

> The energies of our other black fuels, coal and oil, are rather modest, short-term sources of power when compared to the great black loams of the American midlands. (Madson 1982)

Americans were so eager to mine this fertility that the prairie plants and animals that created the soil were gone in a generation, a blink of the eye geologically. It's interesting to note in the literature how early some regretted this loss.

> The Terre Haute [Indiana] prairie, however, has been all reclaimed, or rather, botanically speaking, desecrated by the hand of man, and no portion of it now remains in a state of nature. (Short 1845)

> When I first came here in 1843 . . . the great abundance of wild plants, most of them new to me, made a deep impression on my mind, but during those thirty-two years a large number of our

plants have gradually become rare and some even completely eradicated. (Kumlien 1876)

Once a forest is cut over, it can regrow because all of the roots, seeds, fungi, and bacteria remain in the soil. The forest looks different after harvest, but it is still a forest. Once settlers broke the prairie, they plowed and planted every year until the original prairie wasn't even a memory. Especially in its eastern reaches, native prairie exists only as an old cemetery here, the edge of a railroad grade there, and a few lost and forgotten out of the way corners. The eastern tallgrass prairie is the only ecosystem in North America that people have driven to functional extinction.

The prairie is unique in other ways. Geology and climate initially created the tallgrass prairie. People and their fires maintained and expanded the prairie for millennia. Indeed, it's easy to argue that without people, there may not have been a tallgrass prairie as we think of it. People then destroyed the prairie across much of the Midwest. The current generation is responsible for bringing it back. People have played a strong role in every stage of the prairie's history.

Our role in the tallgrass prairie challenges us to rethink the human–nature dichotomy. Is it people versus nature, people and nature, people in nature? Are people a part of the natural world? Are people dependent on nature? Is nature dependent on people? Are people only a destructive force when it comes to nature or can they be constructive? In North America we can modify this question even further. Are people who walked to North America from the west across the Bering Land Bridge thousands of years ago more natural than people who arrived in North America from the east by boat, willingly or unwillingly, after 1492?

Although I cite dozens of historians, ecologists, and other prairie experts, there are two women who have had a disproportionate and positive effect on the prairies. Lady Bird Johnson strongly influenced Americans across the country, but especially those living in the grasslands, in her advocacy for native wildflowers (Johnson and Lees 1998). The role the other woman played is best illustrated in the title of her biography, *Katherine Ordway: The Lady Who Saved the Prairies* (W. D. Blair 1989).

This book is not a how-to on prairie restoration and management. My intent with this book is to give the reader the historical, scientific, and perhaps philosophical background to understand the whys and hows of management and restoration. Second, the reader will understand the role prairies play, and still play, in developing basic ecological theories that scientists apply to other ecosystems. Third, the reader will gain an appreciation for the complexities and dynamics of the tallgrass prairie, both over the last several thousand years, the last century, and the last year. Numerous factors influence the prairie, directly and indirectly, and these factors all interact with one another and have different feedback mechanisms. The prairie changes depending on how we look at it, at what scale, or over what period of time. See the following quotes.

> Thus, the effects of fire on grassland N [nitrogen] budgets were modified by grazing, and the effects of grazing on the patch structure of grasslands were modified by fire. (Hobbs et al. 1991)

> Species richness is inversely related to grazing intensity, but relative density increases proportionately to grazing intensity. (Zimmerman 1993)

This is just a sample of how complicated things are out there on the prairie. While these statements might not make sense to you at the beginning of this book, they will by the end. This book should both answer some questions you've always had and stimulate more questions with your next prairie visit.

Finally, I offer a word of caution and suggestion on how to view both the prairie and our opportunities to do good works in the future. Conservationists in general have maybe not always had the best communications strategy. We can be downright negative in many cases. Leopold (1991) warns us that "conservationists have, I fear, adopted the pedagogical method of the prophets: we mutter darkly about impending doom. . . . But do people mend their ways for fear of calamity? I doubt it. They are more likely to do it out of pure curiosity and interest."

Much of that doom comes from our experiences. While we sometimes win a few little skirmishes, we all too often lose the larger battles. Battles often result in wounds. I hope this book educates and informs you, but a result of information is that "one of the penalties of an ecological education is that one lives alone in a world of wounds" (Leopold 1949).

That said, there's nothing as satisfying as a day in the prairie. I always feel happier and more relaxed leaving a prairie than entering it. Frederick and Fran Hamerstrom were famous prairie-chicken researchers in Wisconsin and graduate students of Leopold. One of Frederick's favorite sayings was, "good works don't have to be done in a sepulchral atmosphere" (Corneli 2002). If walking through, sitting in, studying, or sharing the prairie with others doesn't bring you joy, then something is wrong.

I started writing this book as a continuation of my trying to understand the science and ecology of the tallgrass prairie. Although my understanding did grow, my love grew even more.

> After certain principles and facts become clear, however, one comes not only to know and understand the grasslands but also to delight in them and to love them. (Weaver 1954)

There are reasons to be despondent about the history of the tallgrass region. This book should excite and inspire your curiosity and interest, your delight and love, when it comes to the future of the prairie. Describing the short-grass prairie of his youth on the Montana-Saskatchewan border, Wallace Stegner wrote, "I may not know who I am, but I know where I am from" (1962). I am from the prairie, and so are many others.

CHAPTER 1

Prairie, People, and Perceptions

[T]he utter impossibility of producing any just impression of them by description. They inspire feelings so unique, so distinct from anything else, so powerful, yet vague and indefinite as to defy description, while they invite the attempt. — *Van Tramp 1868*

[T]his utter negation of life, this complete absence of history, has struck him with a loneliness oppressive and sometimes terrible in its intensity. Perhaps so; but, for my part, the prairies had nothing terrible in their aspect, nothing oppressive in their loneliness. — *Butler 1872*

Loneliness, thy other name, thy one true synonym, is prairie. — *Quayle 1905*

They were afraid of the prairies; they looked empty and lonesome. Instead of water they held only marshes; there were rattlers and ague there and nothing over your head, nothing at your back. — *Peattie 1938*

Human intervention helped create, eliminate, and shape what we know as eastern tallgrass prairie. — *Howe 1994a*

A good test of "education" would be to ask a hundred people what is meant by prairie. . . . Most, I fear, would answer that a prairie is a flat monotonous place good for sixty miles per hour. — *Leopold 1999*

ONE OF THE MOST common phrases in the historic, modern, and scientific literature is "presettlement prairie" or some variation on that idea. There never was a time on the prairie before people. Native Americans were here when the ice sheets receded. "Presettlement prairie" is at best uninformed, ignoring the role of Native Americans on this continent. Our views of the roles of people in nature has changed over the decades as seen in the following quotes; note the dates of each.

More than a century ago when Lewis and Clark set out upon the
memorable journey across the continent of North America
(1803–6), they were the first to traverse the great climaxes from
deciduous woods in the east through the vast expanse of prairie
and plain to the majestic coniferous forest of the north-west.
(Clements 1936)

When Lewis and Clark headed west from the eastern edge of the
central grasslands, they were exploring not a wilderness but a vast
pasture managed by and for Native Americans. (Lott 2002)

The vegetation and vegetation pattern that the earliest European explorers
and Euro-American settlers found were the result of thousands of years of
intensive manipulation by Native Americans. Were the prairies "pastures"
Transeau (1935) or "prodigious game farms" (Mann 2005)? Were the prairies a wilderness? Before 1492, was the tallgrass prairie an untamed wilderness or a highly manipulated environment?

As Euro-American settlers moved west from the forested east, they occasionally came to what they called openings or barrens. These were fragments of tallgrass prairie and oak savanna embedded in the eastern forest. A couple hours or couple days more travel brought them back to the safety, security, and familiarity of the forest.

However, once they crossed the Wabash River in western Indiana, many would not see a continuous forest until they made it to the foothills of the Rocky Mountains, literally half a continent away. Several early accounts mention the Wabash River as a somewhat arbitrary jumping off place from forest to prairie (Volney 1804; Birkbeck 1817; Thomas 1819).

If the traveler from the coast of the Atlantic Ocean to this point
has grown weary of the endless journey in the forests, then he
believes himself transferred to another region of the world as soon
as he crosses the Wabash [River] and beholds these great prairies.
(Ernst 1819)

[B]ut it was not until the white man crossed the Wabash River in his westward advance that he beheld the prairies in all their splendor, and all their monotonous magnitude. (Shimek 1911)

For some, emerging from the shadows of the eastern forest was like a great awakening, moving out of the darkness and into the light.

Yet, the view of that noble expanse was like the opening of bright day upon the gloom of night, to us who had been so long buried in deep forest. (Birkbeck 1817)

There is always an expansion of feeling in looking upon these boundless and fertile wastes; but I was doubly conscious of it after emerging from our "close dungeon of innumerous boughs." (Irving 1835)

Once they moved out from the edge of the woods into the prairie, attitudes changed quickly. A few pages after the previous quote, Washington Irving writes the following.

[T]here is something inexpressibly lonely in the solitude of the prairie: the loneliness of a forest seems nothing to it. There the view is shut in by trees, and the imagination is left free to picture some livelier scene beyond: but here we have an immense extent of landscape without a sign of human existence. We have the consciousness of being far, far beyond the bounds of human habitation. (Irving 1835)

The latter quote seems to be more typical of the loneliness people wrote about on the prairie. When they arrived on the prairies, some found only a "hopeless hopefulness" (Shimek 1911). The words lonely or lonesome are a recurring theme throughout the literature of the prairie.

If human loneliness can be defined as a bleak desolation of spirit—a sort of gray hopelessness unrelieved by any color or

> joy—then winter prairie on an overcast evening is surely one if its embodiments. (Madson 1993)

What did they find when they arrived on the prairie? Some would say they found nothing or a great nothingness.

> One saw here the world as it had taken shape from the hands of the Creator. (Butler 1872)

> There was nothing but land: not a country at all, but the material out of which countries are made. (Cather 1918)

Some people didn't even think God or the angels could help them out, out there on the prairie, out past . . . well . . . everything.

> [T]he unpathed spaces where no stars light their lamps nor any angels happen by. (Quayle 1905)

> Between that earth and that sky I felt erased, blotted out. I did not say my prayers that night: here, I felt, what would be would be. (Cather 1918)

> [E]ven angels proceed at their own risk. (Norris 1993)

With no reference point for the eye, determining relative distances and sizes on the prairie can be a challenge. This is another theme in the prairie literature.

> I could now understand why a bear had been mistaken for a buffalo; for it seems that upon these immense prairies, where there is nothing to interrupt the general level, any object, however small, is, for want of something to compare it with, invested by the imagination with dimensions that do not belong to it. (Featherstonhaugh 1847)

> Another peculiarity is the great difficulty a person unaccustomed to the prairie finds in ascertaining the relative distance of objects, and

consequently estimating their size. I have frequently made, myself, and seen others make the blunder of mistaking a buffalo bull for a crow, or more frequently a crow for a buffalo bull. (Palliser 1853)

Perceiving distance is a large part of travel. Travelers in the forest have mileposts to mark time and distance traveled, even if they are only counting the trees. Travelers in the mountains can always notice peaks becoming larger and closer. On the flat prairie of the 1800s, there were only grass and cloud to mark the passing of time and distance.

He may travel from morning until night, and make good speed, but on looking around him, he fancies himself at the very spot whence he started. (Atwater 1818)

In a perfect circle the sky curved down the level land, and the wagon was in the circle's exact center. All day long Pet and Patty went forward, trotting and walking and trotting again, but they couldn't get out of the middle of that circle. . . . Next day the land was the same, the sky was the same, the circle did not change. (Wilder 1935)

That bigness assaults multiple senses, including sound, which it simply absorbs. There's nothing out here to hear, except our own thoughts, for better or worse.

[O]ne feels the stillness, hears the silence, the wail of the prowling wolf makes the voice of solitude audible, the stars look down through infinite silence upon a silence almost as intense. (Butler 1872)

Silence, so deep, that it roared in the vacuum. (Aldrich 1928)

There's nothing out there for sound to bounce off, nothing to return an echo.

It is truly remarkable how greatly the sound of objects becomes
absorbed in these extensive woodless plains. No echo answers the
voice. (Nuttall 1821)

[W]here a man could call and call but there was nothing to send
back an echo. (Peattie 1938)

It is quiet out there. It's quiet if you can ignore the howling winter winds
and yipping coyotes, the crackle and roar of a spring fire and booming of
prairie-chickens, the call of meadowlarks and bobolink or the awesome
mid-summer crack of thunder that can shake a person's soul with its
violence, the buzz and drone of countless insects, the hiss of grass blade
rubbing blade, and the whirring explosion of a quail covey.

Explorers who could pass through and know they didn't have to stay
will have different impressions than settlers who know they are going to
be marooned out there . . . somewhere . . . or nowhere.

I had the feeling that the world was left behind, that we had
got over the edge of it, and were outside man's jurisdiction.
(Cather 1918)

She did not regard her present situation as romantic; her family
had simply chosen to move far out into loneliness. (Peattie 1938)

That said, many writers and poets had a favorable view of the prairie compared to other habitats.

The spacious prairie is a helper to a spacious life. Mountains shut
us in; prairies let us out. Mountains are barrier builders; prairies
are barrier destroyers. Prairies make level roadways for the soul to
walk. (Quayle 1905)

A river closes in, rounds the bend, runs between banks. . . . The
Plains, on the other hand, open out, unfold, beg the long and
trackless view. The river draws a line; the Plains reveal a space.
(Gruchow 1988)

Probably the ecosystem that most people reference when discussing the prairie is the ocean. Allusions to ocean in the prairie literature are "almost universal in the early accounts" (Curtis 1959). One of the most famous books on the prairie, William Quayle's *The Prairie and the Sea*, directly compares the two right in the title. Grass blowing in the wind does invoke the same feeling as waves in the ocean.

> To the north, as far as I could see, the land billowed like a russet ocean. . . . I cannot say that I liked or disliked it. I merely marveled at it. (Garland 1917)

> As I looked out about me I felt that the grass was the country, as the water is the sea. . . . And there was so much motion in it; the whole country seemed, somehow, to be running. (Cather 1918)

I approached writing this book from a scientific perspective, wanting to study prairie plants and animals. I think the most interesting parts of my research were the personal and emotional responses people had to the prairie as well as the role people had in expanding and maintaining the prairie. In my own life, a walk in the prairie, alone with the pup, always provides me with whatever I need that day, intellectually and emotionally.

A Prairie Education

I T STARTED about three decades ago, in the summer between my freshman and sophomore year at Wabash College. One of my professors, Dave, said he was visiting a remnant prairie that afternoon. He asked if I wanted to come along. Although I didn't know it at the time, that innocent question and afternoon trip set my life on a new trajectory. One afternoon at Smith Pioneer Cemetery, just south of Covington, Indiana, and I was hooked.

Three years later I was taking my final field exam at The Nature Conservancy's Spinn Prairie. My notes from that day mention puccoons and shooting stars, both still among my favorite prairie wildflowers. In between were many other trips to Indiana remnant prairies.

Dave also took students each fall to his undergraduate field station, Green Oaks, just east of Knox College in western Illinois. Green Oaks is probably the second large-scale prairie restoration in the world after Curtis Prairie in Madison, Wisconsin. There he introduced me to Pete, his undergraduate professor. Three decades have passed. I visited Pete for a day earlier this summer and periodically call him to catch up. Dave and I have contacted each other daily to weekly for all these years. Directly and indirectly the two of them have had a profound effect on my entire adult life.

Wabash College is a liberal arts school where students spend just as much time studying a wide range of other subjects as they do studying for their major. Without a doubt, the part of my education that was and still is the most valuable is the focus on connections within my biology major, as well as connecting those courses to classes in many other departments on campus. I received a unified and interconnected education, not a collection of disparate facts. The other skill I developed in those four years is learning how to learn.

In 1942, Aldo Leopold gave a presentation titled *The Role of Wildlife in a Liberal Education.* He stated, "The objective is to teach the student to see the land. . . . I say land rather than wildlife, because wildlife cannot be understood without understanding the landscape as a whole. . . . Perhaps the most important of these purposes is to teach the student how to put the sciences together in order to use them."

As a naïve young college student, I assumed I needed to know the science to fully understand the prairie. I pictured my future, mid-career self with a pair of binoculars and a clipboard, in the field with a good dog by my side, counting birds and plants. I was wrong. Today I find myself sitting in a cubicle in a downtown office building going to lots of meetings about policies, testifying or presenting proposals to councils and legislators, budgeting, and dealing with dozens of competing interests.

To know the prairie, it's not enough to be a good botanist, entomologist, or ornithologist. Those skills are good to have, and hopefully they help inform decisions, but they just aren't enough.

Prairie conservation is complicated. Protection could include a landowner selling their land in a fee title to a wildlife agency or conservation group such as The Nature Conservancy, or putting an easement on the land. Conservationists need to understand the range of programs, program options, and funding mechanisms. Effective conservationists need to have an understanding of local politics and economic concerns as well as an effective communication strategy and sales pitch when discussing conservation.

Conservationists need to understand not only the science of grazing but also how to safely conduct prescribed burns. They also need to understand the politics and perceptions of prescribed fire and public lands grazing.

To effectively implement conservation programs in the Midwest, a conservationist needs to understand land values, farm economics, and the concerns of farmers. Those are influenced by farm policy, commodity markets, international trade policies, tariffs, embargoes, or how a war or natural disaster halfway around the world affects corn and soybean prices here.

My education gave me a firm base to start from, but my career took me in directions I never anticipated. Writing this book showed me quite clearly that, even after all these years, I've barely scratched the surface. Am I smarter than that college student? I know a lot more facts, but for every fact I have ten, or a hundred, new questions.

CHAPTER 2

Where the Prairie Begins

The advance of the forest would have given a continuous forest covering to the Middle West, except on those limited habitats where tree growth is impossible for edaphic reasons. . . . This advance came to a sudden conclusion with the arrival of the American Indian and the consequent introduction of prairie fires. — *Gleason 1922*

It is not necessary to assume that all prairies originated under the same conditions; in fact, it seems certain they did not. — *Woodard 1924*

In the natural sciences the explanation of the geographical distribution of the original grass vegetation has long been an enigma. This is particularly true of the Prairies. — *Borchert 1950*

The relative shortage of endemics in the grassland vegetation is a significant fact, inasmuch as it bears on the recency of tenure of grasslands in the Central Plains region. — *P. V. Wells 1970*

[C]limate is not a determinant of grassland. — *Axelrod 1985*

Temporal variability in the fire record illustrates not only the dynamic nature of anthropogenic fire regimes but also the importance of humans in culturing presettlement barrens communities. — *Guyette et al. 2003*

MY CURRENT JOB TITLE includes the word "prairie." That implies I know what a prairie is. At the very least, I should know it when I see it. The last three decades generally and research for this book specifically destroyed those calm and comfortable self-assurances.

What is a prairie? Central Asia has its steppes, Africa its veldts, and South America its pampas. North America has its central grasslands in three wide north-south bands through the middle of the continent. Short-grass steppe backs up against the eastern foothills of the Rocky Mountains.

The Central Plains form a band through the middle of the continent. The tallgrass prairie stretches from the Central Plains into the eastern deciduous forest. But one question that doesn't have a satisfactory answer is what exactly "prairie" means.

> Our mid-west prairie was a mystery. It remains such to this day. (Quick 1925)

> While most botanists and ecologists know fairly well what prairie is and can easily recognize one, there is no agreement on a definition. (Betz 1972)

Is prairie only the eastern tallgrass prairie? Does tallgrass prairie have to include at least one of the two dominant grasses, big bluestem and Indian grass as the name tallgrass implies? Does prairie encompass all the central North American grasslands? Some use prairie to describe the Palouse prairie of southeastern Washington state. Is "prairie" a generic term that can be applied to grasslands or does it refer to a specific region in the American Midwest? With research studies titled "Unraveling the enigma of the Atlantic prairie" (Hamilton 2012), or similar, there clearly seems to be some confusion on exactly what a prairie is.

Roland Harper titled his 1911 paper "The Hempstead Plains: A natural prairie on Long Island." In his 1918 publication he lists the grasses and forbs at this site. (A forb is any nonwoody plant, non-grass, or essentially a more scientific term for what most call a wildflower.) Likewise, R. B. Livingston titles his 1952 research paper "Relict true prairie communities in central Colorado." Most of the species listed in these studies would be very familiar to a midwestern botanist.

From these studies we might conclude that prairies once had a larger and maybe patchier distribution than just being in the Midwest. Second, it points to the idea that many prairie species have a wide distribution.

The most distinctive feature of the major grassland divisions in North America is the height of the grass. In eastern Colorado, the grass is often about ankle height. In central Nebraska, the grass can be about knee to waist high. In western Indiana, the grass in a wet year can stretch well over your head.

North American grasslands formed when the Rocky Mountains rose roughly 135 million years ago during the Mesozoic era. The mountains largely eroded away by the time of the Oligocene, thirty million years ago. Wind and rivers spread the product of that erosion, what would eventually become soil, out across the middle of the continent. There was a second uplift in the Miocene, creating the Rocky Mountains we know today (Risser et al. 1981).

In North America, weather patterns generally move from west to east. Warm, humid air blows east from the Pacific Ocean. The coastal mountains and the heights of the Rocky Mountains force the air up. The air cools as it moves upward. Cool air holds less moisture than warm air. The moisture falls out of the air as rain or snow on the western mountain slopes. The air coming over the peak of the mountains is now cool and dry. This cool, dense, dry air flows down the eastern slopes of the Rockies onto the Great Plains. This is the rain shadow effect.

As the air continues eastward it slowly accumulates moisture and rainfall increases. This explains why there is short-grass steppe in the eastern Great Plains at the eastern foothills of the Rockies, mixed-grass prairie in the middle of the Great Plains, and finally tallgrass prairie on the eastern side of the Great Plains. The eastern prairies can also add Gulf moisture coming from the south to their rainfall. Taller grasses follow increased rainfall. East of the tallgrass, there is enough rain to support trees and forests.

Within the eastern tallgrass prairie region there are three general types of grasslands. Xeric, or dry, prairies occur on hilltops, sandy soils, or other places with little soil moisture. Hydric, or wet, prairies occur in the lowest areas and often have saturated soils. Mesic prairies, those with moderate soil moisture levels, occur on the flatter prairies between the other two.

Across the tallgrass region, there are two steep gradients. The western part of the tallgrass region, Kansas, is much drier than the eastern part of the region in Indiana. In the north, Minnesota prairie is much cooler and has a shorter growing season than Oklahoma prairie.

To explain the origins of the tallgrass prairie we only need to go back as far as the Wisconsin glaciation. This was the last of four major glaciations named after the present-day states where they stopped their advance; Nebraskan, Kansas, Illinoian, and Wisconsin (Risser et al. 1981). The Wisconsin glacier retreated just eight to ten thousand years ago, the blink of an eye in geologic time. Before that, there was nothing in North America that closely resembled what we think of as the tallgrass prairie. Some state that the tallgrass prairie is the youngest ecosystem in North America.

However, we can't simply say that as the glaciers retreated northward, prairie moved into the Midwest. The pattern of prairie development is "more complicated than previously thought" (Nelson et al. 2006), and the tallgrass region has "gone through more stages than any other since the disappearance of the ice" (Pielou 1991).

It's difficult to make any universal statement about the establishment of the prairie after the glaciers retreated. The glaciers disappeared from the central latitudes of the tallgrass region about 12,500 years ago and only 9,500 years ago in the northern tallgrass region. Rain and snowfall have fluctuated dramatically since the retreat of the glacier. The hypsithermal, an especially dry period, stretched from 9,000 to 3,000 years ago.

In the western regions of the prairie, spruce forest followed the glacier and prairie followed spruce forest. In the east, spruce forests gave way to birch, alder, or pine dominated forests. Deciduous forest followed. Prairies then became dominant. Forests encroached again. Finally prairie came to dominate the region when the climate became drier (H. E. Wright 1970).

An area in central Minnesota transitioned from pine forest to prairie to deciduous forest back to pine forest (Jacobson and Grimm 1986). In parts of south-central Minnesota, the landscape transitioned from boreal forest to elm and hop-hornbeam forest to prairie and finally to oak woodland and oak savanna (Camill et al. 2003). In northwest Minnesota, coniferous forest changed to mixed-grass prairie to tallgrass prairie to deciduous forest to coniferous forest (Nelson and Hu 2008). In southern Minnesota through Iowa and into Illinois there was an early pulse of prairie, followed by an expansion westward of deciduous forest, and then movement of the prairie back to the east (Nelson et al. 2006). The prairie-forest border region has been very dynamic since the last glacier and it is hard to make many generalizations about changes and patterns over time. These dynamics aren't ancient history; they are still occurring.

One area of interest for the last couple of hundred years is the underlying patterns and processes in the environment that control the distribution of vegetation across the Midwest. Some argued that the distribution of soils explained the distribution of prairie and forests across the tallgrass region (Whitney 1876; Fuller 1923; McComb and Loomis 1944). Some claimed that historic flood patterns delineate the boundaries of grasslands. Indeed, much of the Midwest was once an inland sea, explaining the limestone found in many parts of the region (Atwater 1818). Another popular explanation for the distribution of prairie is climate. Grasslands are hotter, drier, and windier than forests. Together, these factors create a lot of water stress on plants. Grasses are better able to cope with these stresses than trees are. The observations were most confusing when prairie and forest were intermingled in complex patterns.

Climate is one of the most often cited explanations for grasslands around the world, or not:

> The more the prairies are studied, the less one will feel disposed to adopt any theory for their origin dependent on climate. (Whitney 1876)

> Neither geological formation, topography, nor soil determines the character of the flora which develops under the master hand of climate. (Weaver 1968)

Most grasslands around the world are in the center of large continents. These areas have a continental climate. Coastal areas have oceans to buffer their temperature. The centers of continents have no water bodies to moderate temperatures. On the west coast seasons are warm and cool. In the center of North America, summers are hot and winters are cold. In addition to these annual seasonal changes, these areas are also susceptible to climate extremes.

Periodic drought may help to explain the shape of the eastern prairie. There is more variability and more frequent droughts in the prairie region than surrounding forested regions (Changnon et al. 2003). This may explain the eastern "prairie peninsula" (Transeau 1935) in Indiana and Illinois, where there is forest to the north and south of the grassland, and a peninsula of grassland bulging into the forested region. Note the word "extreme" in the two following quotes.

> One of the axioms of plant ecology is that the extremes of the factors are vastly more important than the means. (Transeau 1935)

> These extremes of seasonal moisture variation combined with the low summer humidity and irregularity of precipitation seem to be the dominant factor in the prairie peninsula. (Whitford 1958)

It's not that the average climate, temperature or precipitation, are on average different, but the extremes are more extreme in the prairie (M. D. Smith 2011). Still others rely on a combination of factors to explain the distribution of prairie.

> No single explanation has yet been advanced that adequately accounts for the actual distribution of grasslands and forests, nor can it ever be hoped for because the very complex nature of both communities clearly implies a multifactorial relationship with the environment. (Curtis 1959)

Although the eastern tallgrass prairie can probably best be defined by multiple factors, perhaps the dominant factor is fire.

I think it must be evident to every one who will view the barrens attentively, that their present appearance was caused by fires. (Bourne 1820)

Fire has been considered the cause of the treelessness of the prairies more frequently than any other factor. (Shimek 1911)

One issue that has been debated by scholars is the cause-and-effect relationship of fire and prairie. Are prairies the result of fires, or are fires a product of prairies?

We may therefore consider fire as the cause of the continuance, if not the original existence, of prairie. (Keating 1823)

Prairie fires were an effect rather than a cause, and where acting as a cause were local. (Shimek 1911)

The origin of the prairie as a type of vegetation cannot, however, be referred to prairie fires as a cause. . . . A prairie fire presupposes a prairie. (Gleason 1912)

Fire and climate may have interacted to control the prairie-forest boundary. However, that interaction itself may be a bit counterintuitive. It makes sense that fires would be more destructive of woody vegetation in drought periods when the fuels are very dry and the trees are water-stressed. John Weaver wrote at length in multiple studies about the destruction of trees during the Dust Bowl years when droughts were severe and prolonged.

However, there are alternative views. In what Shuman et al. (2009) report as an "ecological surprise" (their quotes), they found there were more fires during the wettest periods over the last four millennia. Wet periods promote the greatest growth of grasses and the highest accumulation of the fine fuels—dried grasses—that produce the most intense fires. Even in wet periods, not every day is wet. There will still be hot, dry, windy days capable of carrying intense fires. During droughts, the prairie produces less grass, or fine fuels, which reduces the intensity of

FIGURE 1. Bur oaks often grow on hilltops. The shorter grasses that grow on hilltops may not provide enough fine fuels to support the intense fires that kill trees in other areas of the prairie. Photo courtesy of the author.

fires. They found that the repeated droughts starting around 1265 reduced grass biomass, leading to less intense fires, and an expansion of trees. This is the opposite of what researchers saw during the Dust Bowl. Nothing in the prairie is as it seems.

We can look at topography, river courses, and other features to explain where those fires went and stopped. We generally think of trees as growing in riparian forests along waterways. However, if the hilltops are dry (Figure 1), grass short, and fuel load low, then these areas will provide refugia from fires (R. W. Wells 1819; Gleason 1912; Petty and Jackson 1966).

At broader scales, wetter regions, especially to the east, favored trees, while at smaller local scales drier areas favored trees. In the prairie, the answer to any question can be completely different depending on the scale.

If high hills had one effect on the vegetation, then low wetlands had another effect. Tree groves were often on the eastern or southeastern side of wetlands or lakes. With prevailing westerly winds, the water would form a natural firebreak (Gleason 1912; Vestal 1914). The flames would eventually creep around the lake and burn the east side, but the flames would be cooler and less intense.

Where did our "tallgrass prairie plants" come from? They didn't come from the tallgrass prairie region (Axelrod 1985; Reichman 1987). The plants in the prairies of Ohio have "decidedly western affinities, with a strong southern mixture." (Braun 1928a). The prairie flora is "derivative," as in derived from other regions of the continent (P. V. Wells 1970). Likewise, there are few species "belonging distinctively to the prairies" (Coulter and Thompson 1886). Even the dominant tallgrass prairie grasses "are all of eastern origin" (Gleason 1922). If prairies are only a few thousand years old, that's not a lot of time for evolution to develop new species.

> The mingling of species of different origins and the persistence of relics of earlier migrations results in a fascinating botanical crossword puzzle for anyone interested in the dynamics of vegetation. (Costello 1969)

The plants that we know today as tallgrass prairie species, even species such as big bluestem, *the* tallgrass species, evolved in other areas of North America and then moved into the Midwest. We see this pattern over and over with many so-called prairie plants.

To add to the confusion, not all the plants arrived in the Midwest at one time. Species gradually moved in over millennia. The plant community shifted, adjusted, and changed. Some species were quickly outcompeted and went locally extinct. Others persisted and thrived (Costello 1969). We can say this about entire plant communities as well as individual species.

> Thus, it appears reasonable to believe that the expansion of prairies in Wisconsin was not a single, unified movement of a homoge-

neous plant formation, but rather a gradual entrance of a variety of elements, with each arriving during separate climatic regimes. (Curtis 1959)

Today invasive species are one of the greatest threats to ecosystems. Typically, we think of an invasive species as a plant or animal that people transported to this continent from another continent or a distant part of the same continent. For better or worse, this information gives a new, long-term perspective to the idea of what an invasive species is in the tallgrass region. If no species evolved in the Midwest and all species moved into the tallgrass region from surrounding parts of the continent, can we say that all prairie plants are invasive species, from a certain perspective?

To summarize, prairie plants don't come from the prairie. Wetter areas favor trees at some scales but drier areas favor trees at other scales. And we aren't even to the confusing chapters in this book yet.

The Next Prairie Visit

S EVERAL YEARS AGO the pup and I spent a few mornings looking for prairie-chickens where others had said there weren't any. In a week and a half, we found nineteen new leks, or booming grounds. Of course, they weren't new. It's just that no one had looked in this area before. So much for conventional wisdom when it comes to the prairie.

There was one last prairie I wanted to check. It sure looked good on the map and there were other booming grounds in the area. The birds just had to be there. It was the last day of "our surveys" and the season was starting to wind down. Birds were much less active than they were just a couple weeks ago and would be hard to hear. We needed to get there right at dawn if we had any hopes of hearing and then finding them.

We pulled up, stopped the truck, and I rolled down the window to listen. Silence. We got out, one of us standing silently, listening intently to the horizon. The other dancing around with pent-up energy ready for our morning walk. More silence. After surveying prairie-chickens for several years and many mornings over the last four weeks this year, it just felt right. They had to be here.

A gentle ridgeline headed north from where we were standing. Maybe the birds were on the far north side of the unit and the wind was working against us that morning. It was a good morning for a hike. We set off, the pup fifteen feet in front of me. After a couple minutes the ridge flattened. We kept walking. Suddenly I stopped walking. Hearing nothing in the grass behind him, the pup stopped and turned to look at me. Neither of us were sure why I stopped. We started again and thirty seconds later, I just stopped again. He stopped to look at me again. And again, I didn't know why I stopped.

Then I saw them. There were two wolves directly ahead of us, sitting on the edge of a brushy swale maybe one hundred yards away. Seeing wolves in northern Minnesota doesn't happen every day, but it happens. Usually I see only the tail end heading away from me at a fast pace. This pair sat in stony stillness. After the wolves and I stared each other down for twenty or thirty seconds, which seemed like an eternity, they silently stood up and ghosted into the brush. Somehow, one part of my brain must have seen those wolves and told me to stop but the rest of my brain was unaware. That sensation had never happened before and hasn't since.

I whistled quietly, turned around, and we headed back to the truck. I really want to say I saw a fierce green fire in their eyes, but that would be a stretch for this story. Thinking there might have been a den with pups in that draw, we didn't go back that year as I was afraid of disrupting them.

A year later in mid-summer we jumped a fisher out of the prairie. If you've never seen a fisher, imagine an otter with long luxurious fur. These are animals of supposedly northern forests. Yet we saw one out in the bluestem. I wouldn't have guessed what the animal was as it darted through the waist-high bluestem, but we'd seen a roadkill fisher last winter just a quarter mile from this prairie. The fisher ran up a nearby cottonwood tree, and once at a safe height, turned to stare up down. That long look allowed me to confirm my earlier identification.

While we don't see wolves or fishers or prairie-chickens or orchids on every prairie visit, we do always see something new. That's what people miss as we lose prairie and society becomes less interested in being outside or out there. Not only is it seeing something new or different, but almost as important is the chance or possibility of seeing something. Will we stare down a wolf the next time we visit a prairie? Probably not, but the chance to see something is what will get us out for our next visit, hopefully in the very near future.

In one of my favorite lines in all of literature, Annie Dillard (1974) wrote, "The answer must be, I think, that beauty and grace are performed whether or not we will or sense them. The least we can do is try to be there." The pup and I want to be out there as often as possible, just so we don't miss something.

CHAPTER 3

Where the Prairie Ends

When the white people settle on the barrens or near them, the Indians recede, fires are seldom seen, a young growth of trees, healthy and vigorous soon spring up, far superior to the stinted growth which the frequent fires have scorched, and the barren assumes the appearance of a timbered country. — *Bourne 1820*

Thus the prairie-forest conflict probably has continued for many centuries, though the scene of action has shifted. — *Cowles 1928*

[T]he exact limits of the several prairies can never be set, and the boundary lines drawn on any map can be general approximations. — *Weaver and Clements 1938*

In the pioneer days the eastern boundary of the grassland was a broad belt in which patches of prairie and forest formed a great mosaic. — *Gleason and Cronquist 1964*

Within the transitional zone [tallgrass prairie] no single set of environmental factors explains the mosaic pattern of vegetation. The environmental factors influencing the vegetation operate in concert, with the relative importance of each factor and the interactions of these factors varying in time and space. — *R. C. Anderson 1983*

Almost everyone who has tried to map the grasslands has provided a somewhat different set of terms and mapped boundaries. — *Johnsgard 2001*

IN ALMOST EVERY PRAIRIE I know today, the edges and boundaries are clear, sharp, and distinct. There's often a fence or a line of signs stating that the prairie is owned and managed by a state Department of Natural Resources, the US Fish and Wildlife Service, The Nature Conservancy, or similar entity. In one step I can go from prairie to something else, usually corn or soybean stubble.

Likewise, we know exactly what the state of Iowa looks like. By itself or shown in the context of surrounding states, Iowa has a unique shape.

We can say the same thing about Minnesota, Wisconsin, Indiana, Illinois, Missouri, and Kansas. Each state has distinct and easily recognizable boundaries. On Iowa's north and south, the boundaries are arrow-straight lines running east and west. On the east side there is the Mississippi River while the western border is delineated by the Missouri and Big Sioux Rivers.

In contrast, if it's hard to define the prairie itself, it may be even harder to define the boundary on a map. While researching this book, I found scores of maps of the tallgrass prairie. Unlike Iowa, where every map is the same, each map of the tallgrass prairie is a little different because the maps were drawn at different times, at different scales, or with different assumptions.

To complicate the issue even more, grasslands have an image problem. Most mapmakers come from forested regions. Their maps of forests are often detailed: oak-hickory forest, maple-basswood forest, riparian forest, etc. Grasslands are simply labeled "grasslands." Many mapmakers describe grasslands as treeless, but almost no one describes forests as grassless (Kuchler 1954; Malin 1967).

This is where mapmaking comes in. Mapmakers like hard, thin, and preferably straight lines, such as the border between Illinois and Wisconsin. The maps ecologists make rarely have straight lines and it's really hard to draw a hard thin line on a map of habitats or ecosystems. Most ecologists would probably draw broad, fuzzy, wiggly lines instead of thin, hard, straight lines.

To an ecologist, those lines separating one type of vegetation from another are called ecotones. An ecotone is the area where two habitats come together, such as the prairie-forest ecotone. How to draw that ecotone, how wide to draw it, whether it should have hard or fuzzy edges, whether the line is straight or wiggly, are perennial problems for both ecologists and cartographers.

Some have argued that the entire central grasslands are just a boundary between the dry deserts of the west and the humid forests of the east.

Others argue that the tallgrass prairie is a boundary or dynamic tension zone between the grasslands of the Great Plains and the eastern deciduous forest.

> It is here [Iowa and Illinois] that the tension line between grassland and woodland is more in evidence and that the prairie problem is most acute. (Cowles 1928)

> The climatic region coincident with the prairies is actually a broad boundary zone between steppe and forest. (Borchert 1950)

Some maps don't show any prairie to the east of the Mississippi River. Wisconsin, Illinois, and Indiana are labeled "prairie-and-oak transition" (Savage 2004). Likewise, we can describe western Indiana, almost all of Illinois, western Wisconsin, and much of Missouri as the "prairie-forest transition" (R. C. Anderson 1983). According to these descriptions, Illinois, the Prairie State, doesn't have much prairie. Others will say that Illinois and Indiana are where the grasses reach their tallest heights and where the name tallgrass prairie is most deserving.

Probably the two most recognized vegetation maps of the tallgrass prairie are from Transeau (1935) and Kuchler (1964). These two maps don't line up well at all. First, they are basing their maps on two different assumptions. Transeau's goal is to "locate more accurately the eastern extension of the prairie at the time of settlement." Transeau's map famously describes the "prairie peninsula," which was a broad grass intrusion into a forested region with the areas to the north and south of this region covered in forest.

Alternately, Kuchler's goal was to map "the vegetation that would exist under the present climate if man were removed from the scene and if the resulting plant succession were telescoped into a single moment." Much of what Transeau labels "Prairie Peninsula," Kuchler labels "Mosaic/ Bluestem Oak–hickory." In essence, he's saying that most of what others map as the eastern tallgrass prairie is a transition or ecotone between grassland and forest. Note that Savage (2004) and R. C. Anderson (1983) also refer to the peninsula as a "transition." Is the eastern tallgrass prairie an ecosystem or just a meeting and mingling of other ecosystems?

Perhaps the most interesting words in those statements are Kuchler's "if man were removed from the scene" and Transeau's "at the time of settlement." Transeau explicitly captures a snapshot in time, the beginning of the Euro-American settlement period. Kuchler's removal of humans from the scene is probably a reference to fire, implying that without Native Americans there might not have been a tallgrass prairie, or at least it wouldn't be as extensive as it was. One of the themes of this book is that there was or is no point in time when humans were not actively involved in the tallgrass region. Another theme is that the prairie and prairie boundaries are very dynamic.

Figure 2 is an imaginary landscape where dots represent trees across the prairie-forest border. Imagine you're a mapmaker and you're allowed to draw one straight line dividing prairie from forest. Where do you draw that line? Next, you can draw one line, but it can have a gentle curve. Last, you can draw a line and make it wiggle as much as you want. Where did you draw the lines? Let's now say that we can identify an oak savanna, scattered trees, in the boundary between the open forest and closed canopy forest. Now you can draw two lines, dividing prairie from savanna and savanna from forest. Where do those lines go? Imagine showing several people this diagram and asking each to draw a line on it. What are the chances everyone's lines perfectly agree? What does that say about how easy it is to identify the prairie-forest border?

Can a prairie be defined as a grassland with "less than one mature tree per acre" (Curtis 1959)? Doesn't that seem arbitrary? What about one tree per hectare, or per forty acres? Clearly, mapmaking and defining boundaries require some judgment calls.

There are a couple openings in the eastern side. Are these small enough that they are just gaps in the forest or are they large enough to be considered prairie openings? There is a small gap in the northeast and a larger

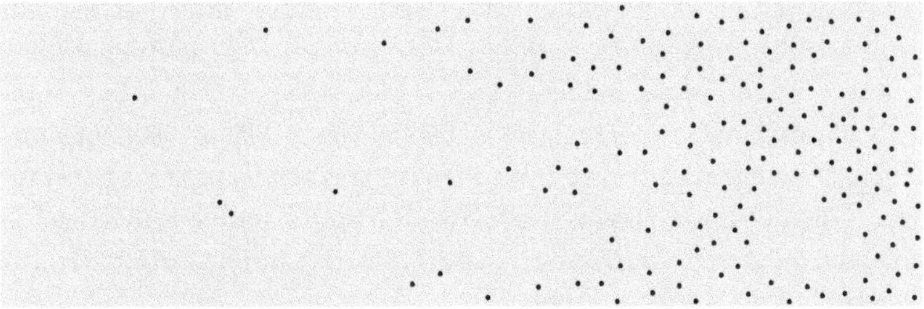

FIGURE 2. In this representation of a prairie-forest border each dot represents a tree. Where is the best straight line that divides the prairie from the forest? Is there a definable savanna between the prairie and the forest?

gap in the southeast. Do you include one but not the other? How many trees does it take before a prairie becomes a savanna? When does a savanna get so dense it becomes a forest? How big does a gap in the forest have to be before it becomes a prairie opening?

Figure 2 could represent an area one hundred yards wide or one hundred miles wide. Transeau (1935) described the prairie-forest boundary as "these borders are often miles in width" and two pages later as "at most a few rods in width." Within the same sentence, Gleason and Cronquist (1964) write "individual boundaries between forest and grassland were commonly sharp . . . but the boundary between the two provinces as a whole was not." So, the boundary between prairie and forest is both wide and narrow, sharp or not. As we'll see throughout this book, the answers to many questions about the prairie depend on a person's perspective.

The question of scale is also important. Imagine you are mapping vegetation while orbiting the earth in 1800. You would probably draw a fairly general southwest-northeast running diagonal line through northwest Indiana dividing prairie from forest. Now imagine flying over Newton County, along that border, at fifteen thousand feet. You could draw more lines and they would curve and wiggle much more. You see more detail than from orbit, but you're still missing a lot. Now imagine walking across

The Nature Conservancy's Kankakee Sands Preserve. You could map the vegetation in great detail. Each of those maps is valid, although each of those maps will be quite different.

If the eastern boundary against the trees was difficult to define and fluctuated dramatically over time, then the western boundary against the mixed-grass prairie was very difficult to identify and very dynamic. In fact, the differences between grassland types may just be "arbitrarily designated" (R. C. Anderson 2006).

> A series of dry years shoves all boundaries eastward, and wet years push them west again. (Gleason and Cronquist 1964)

> The Great Plains thus end as they begin, not with a sudden bang but with a quiet whisper. (Johnsgard 2003)

Chapter 2 demonstrated how dynamic the prairie vegetation was since the glaciers retreated. The boundaries of the prairie have been and continue to be very dynamic. Over the last several thousand years, the prairie probably stretched much farther east than Transeau's map describes. One problem with trying to draw a line between the prairie and the forest, or prairie and plains, is that the line is always shifting. These shifts didn't happen at millennial time scales, they were fast enough that people saw them over the course of decades. Note that people were describing these changes in the early and mid-1800s, long before most Euro-American settlers reached this region.

> The ravages of fire amongst it has been very considerable; and in this part, the prairie, was visibly gaining on the woods.
> (Thomas 1819)

> That the annual conflagrations have prevented the growth of timber on the prairies, is clearly proved by the very vigorous growth of young wood which takes place along their margin, wherever the fire has been kept out for a few years. (Oliver 1843)

In many cases, as this prairie-forest boundary fluctuated over time, some species were left behind. Thus, we have prairie species left behind as the forests moved west and forest species left behind as the prairies moved east. Are prairie openings in the forest indicators of a once larger prairie or are forest groves in the prairie indicators of a once larger forest? The answer is yes . . . probably . . . it depends.

> The occurrence of scattered colonies of prairie species beyond the eastern limits of the province may indicate a former more extensive range of the prairie. (Gleason 1909)

> [T]he prairie groves may be in many cases remnants and not recent invaders. (Bray 1957)

When anyone draws any map of the Plains, prairies, and forests, it needs a time stamp. It doesn't make sense to draw a line dividing prairie from forest, or plains from prairies. It does make sense to say that this is the prairie-forest boundary in 1492, or 1836, or whatever reference point you choose.

We have a valuable tool for reconstructing historic vegetation patterns in the Midwest, but that tool can be misleading. That tool is the General Land Office Survey that mapped vegetation across the Midwest, county by county, township by township, square mile by square mile in the first half of the nineteenth century. Some of the most useful data the surveyors collected were witness trees at the corners of each square mile. Surveyors recorded the size and species of these trees and wrote general descriptions of the vegetation. However, they were catching only a snapshot in time.

Some of the earliest French explorers left accounts of the vegetation and wildlife in the 1630s and earlier. In the 1830s and 1840s, surveyors measured and described the vegetation. In those two centuries, diseases decimated Native American populations while other tribes were displaced from the eastern part of the continent into the Midwest. At least eighteen different tribes moved into or through Iowa during the historic period

(Mutel 2008). We can't just say Native American. There were dozens to scores of tribes and cultures in various times and places within the tallgrass prairie region. Presumably all of these changes would have had dramatic effects on the amount of fire Native Americans were using (Mann 2005). Changes in fire probably led to changes in land cover, presumably more trees with less fire. If there can be noticeable land cover change, forests invading prairie, over a couple decades as described earlier, how much change could happen between the 1630s and 1830s?

If you watched television in the late 1970s, the word "prairie" probably evokes images of a little house and people named Pa, Ma, Mary, Laura, and Carrie. However, the first book in Laura Ingalls Wilder's series was titled *Little House in the Big Woods*, which was near the city of Pepin along the Mississippi River in the Driftless Region of southwestern Wisconsin. The Driftless Area today is well known for its extensive forests (Swenson 2009). An analysis of the General Land Office Survey records concluded that the region was "a landscape dominated by savanna and a variety of oak communities" (Shea et al. 2014).

In 1766 Jonathon Carver described the land just south of Pepin near today's Prairie du Chien, Wisconsin, as "the country round me appeared like a meadow full of hay cocks all covered with grass" and "neither trees nor stones except a few elms and maples on the banks of the river." He described the area around Pepin as "these mountains are covered with grass with here and there a small tree. The valleys have some groves of trees" (Parker 1976).

When describing the land along the Mississippi between the Wisconsin River and the modern-day Twin Cities, Featherstonhaugh (1847) frequently mentions prairie and tall grasses. Traveling that same route, Catlin (1844) describes "the whole face of the country is covered with a luxuriant growth of grass . . . a carpet of grass, with spots and clusters of timber."

Are the General Land Office Survey records providing an accurate account of the vegetation? Yes, for the arbitrary point of time the survey was conducted in each township and county. That's not to say that the area always looked like that. Clearly the landscape and prairie-forest border could change relatively quickly and quite dramatically. Was the Driftless Region an open grassland, an oak savanna, or a big woods? Obviously, we can't take some anecdotal historical accounts about specific locations and reach grand conclusions about entire regions. However, these accounts do paint three very different pictures of this region. Perhaps the next interesting question is "should we be managing these areas for prairie, savanna, or woodland, and what is the justification for our decision?"

Personal Geographies

CHEMISTS OR MICROBIOLOGISTS will disagree with this statement, but I just don't see how anyone can become emotionally attached to a beaker of chemicals, fuzz on a petri dish, or lines of DNA spread out on a gel. Granted those may be connected to a disease they are trying to cure, which is obviously important, but that's a step removed.

However, it's hard not to feel an emotional tug when opening your fingers and watching a songbird fly from the palm of your hand with a new band on their leg. It's hard not to feel something when watching an upland sandpiper land on a fencepost and fold their wings, defining the word grace. It's hard not to feel you're in a special place when you're staring through a camera lens at a western prairie fringed orchid.

Even more important is a connection to place, specific spots on a map. Every conservationist has these spots. In "Wilderness Letter," Wallace Stegner talks about a geography of hope. Although he was referring generally to "wild country," every dedicated conservationist has a personal geography. These are special places for any reason or number of reasons. There may be a unique geological feature. It may be especially scenic. It may be a place where you first found or have only found a particular wildflower. It may be memorable for the person or people you were with on the first or subsequent visits. By middle age, most of us should have a catalog of these places. Some we share with others, such as a state or national park. Some are circles on our personal maps we like to show to friends. And some places are so personal and special we don't share them with anyone.

I first visited Smith Pioneer Cemetery the summer between my freshman and sophomore year of college. That will always be my first prairie remnant. Shiloh Pioneer Cemetery and Spinn Prairie, both in west-central Indiana, are special in their own way and I have specific memories of both. Those memories include people I visited the sites with, as well as plants.

The following fall semester I visited Green Oaks Prairie. It's been almost three decades since I was last there, but the map in my head still has plenty of details. It's as if the last visit was last weekend.

From there it was Konza Prairie in the Flint Hills of eastern Kansas. And while Konza itself is special, there are also special places there, special for a number of reasons and probably special only to me.

After eight years in Kansas the dog and I moved to the Agassiz beach ridges of western Minnesota. Within a ten-minute drive from the house there were at least ten publicly owned and protected tracts of grassland that contained native prairie. I moved away from there almost a decade ago and don't get back enough.

Next, we lived in south-central Minnesota. Here the pup and I found a number of small hillsides, most less than an acre, some much less than an acre, on public lands that weren't mapped as being native prairie. Although heavily dominated by brome, the forbs we found in these places told us they had never seen a plow. Now we live well into the forest side of the prairie-forest border. Yet we still know a number of roadsides and railroad rights-of-ways where prairie species have hung on.

I've only been back to Kansas once in twenty years. We still get back to our prairies in northwest Minnesota ever year or two. And I still know within inches where the clumps of ladies slippers orchids are in each of the wet prairies and which hilltop prairies have the most prairie smoke.

At the same time, I can list several sites that used to be covered with high quality prairie. These days those acres just produce corn, gravel, or trophy homes. From Indiana to Kansas to Minnesota, the geography of my life has been a rough triangle that approximates the tallgrass region. My life is bounded by bluestem.

Graduate students are taught that scientists must be these cold, rational beings. Impossible. Conservationists are people with lives and relationships and loves. Some of those loves are locations, and if you've been doing this long enough some of those locations are losses.

CHAPTER 4

Historic Prairie Fires

[A]nd the grass of which is yearly burnt down by the Indians. — *Beltrami 1828*

It is good testimony in favor of my opinion that all the prairies watered by the Mississippi and the Missouri are the work of the Indians who destroy by fire the rich vegetation to assure themselves of animal food. Let the vast and unshorn prairies that we cross remain untouched and the forests, with time, will appear. — *Nicollet 1838*

They are magnificent spectacles. I have stood upon the roof of our large hotel in the evening, and looked into a sea of fire which appeared to be unbroken for miles.
— *Farnham 1846*

All the country in every direction, having been burnt over, was perfectly black.
— *Featherstonhaugh 1847*

To still others the Prairie Peninsula represents a pyropyrrhic victory of the Indians and pre-Indians attempting to enlarge native pastures, or to capture their grazing meat supply. — *Transeau 1935*

To a limited extent, the results could have been obtained by lightning fires, but the known incidence of dry lightning in Wisconsin is totally incapable of explaining the huge areas influenced by fire. — *Curtis 1959*

IN ONE OF MY PREVIOUS JOBS, we used to discuss a loose cluster of a few bur oak trees in the center of a certain prairie in northwest Minnesota over lunch. Some of us argued that this area should be managed as prairie and that those trees needed to go, even if they were bur oaks. Others argued that those oaks were indicative of a former forest or savanna at that site and therefore needed to stay.

After a couple months, I stopped on my way home and cored several of the largest and presumably oldest trees. We then looked up the approximate time period when the prairie sod in that part of the county was first plowed under. Presumably this was when fires became smaller and less frequent. Those years roughly correspond to the age of these oaks. Are those oaks a vestige of a former woodland or oak savanna? Or are they a product of plowing the surrounding prairie and a resulting reduction in fire frequency? We'll probably never know.

There are two primary sources of fire: lightning and people. One question for both historians and ecologists is the relative role of each in prairie fires. Did lightning or humans ignite more fires in the tallgrass prairie? Lightning starts a large percentage of western forest and grassland fires. These western regions often have what are called dry lightning storms. There's lots of rain and lightning, but the air is so dry the rain evaporates before it gets to the ground. In the humid Midwest, if there's lightning it's usually raining buckets.

Lightning could hit a tree, smolder, and a couple days later a branch falls off, igniting the now dry grass at the base of the tree. We can also imagine a strike in an area with thick thatch, the thatch smoldering, and then igniting the grass after the storm passes. There are occasional instances of lightning-started fires in the tallgrass prairie region. However, occasional fires and the historic references to frequent or annual fires don't match up (McComb and Loomis 1944; Curtis 1959).

It may be stated that the writer has no record of a prairie fire produced by lightning. (Gleason 1913)

That leaves people as the primary ignition source for prairie fires. Using fire, Native Americans had dramatic impacts on the vegetation (Grimm 1984; Mann 2005), and indirectly on the wildlife. People affected the prairie with their fires from the very beginning. There's no such thing as a presettlement tallgrass prairie (Costello 1969). There may be few other ecosystems in North America more directly affected by people.

With this one tool, the Indians changed a very large portion of the entire vegetational complex of Wisconsin. . . . The presence of nomadic hunting tribes throughout the state in the entire postglacial period means that man-made fires were an important if not sole cause of the fires. (Curtis 1959)

What this may mean is that the distributions and locations of people controlled the locations and frequency of fire. That in turn may have affected regional vegetation patterns. If that's the case, would there have been a prairie, especially an eastern prairie, without people?

Inasmuch as Indians controlled the probability and location of fire ignitions in the study area (Minnesota prairie-forest border), they strongly controlled the fire probability. (Grimm 1984)

The vegetation pattern of the study area was closely associated with Indian sites of the agricultural Potawatomie and Winnebago tribes. Soil associations, climate and topography appeared to have little effect on the vegetation pattern. This leaves Indian-caused fires as the likely cause of the vegetation patterns. (Dorney and Dorney 1989)

Fires exerted strong constraints on vegetation composition and patterns. Historical patterns of Native American occupancy in the region are consistent with the reconstructed vegetation and fire histories. (Batek et al. 1999)

Without the very frequent burning that the Native Americans conducted, the tallgrass prairie region would be a forest. This was recognized by some of the earliest observers (Freeman and Custis 1806; R. W. Wells 1819).

The [Illinois] soil is well adapted to the growth of timber, and, when protected from fire, is soon covered with a vigorous growth of young trees.

But here, as in other parts of the west, when the prairies are protected from fire, a growth of young timber soon springs up. [Minnesota] (Van Tramp 1868)

Not only were there changes with the disruption of the fire cycle, the changes happened over the course of a couple decades. The earliest Euro-American settlers noticed the rate of change just as modern prairie managers notice trees invading today's prairies.

Native Americans and early European explorers used fire for a number of reasons, including offensive and defensive warfare (Bradbury 1810), to make travel easier (Bourne 1820), to attract game animals to the tender new grass after a fire (Featherstonhaugh 1847), and to signal others (Nicollet 1838). Hunting was the most common use of fire. Most of these fires were in the fall, especially October. In the fall, game animals are at their fattest and healthiest after feasting on nutritious food all summer and early fall. Fall is also when people are looking to store up food for the long cold winter.

The historical records reveal some interesting patterns in prairies. First, fires occurred very often. Many accounts describe the "annual" or "yearly" fires.

> Every autumn the Indians within the entire circuit of their possessions hold a grand hunt. They set fire to the dry grass of the prairie, and the flame with incredible rapidity spreads over all the country. (Ernst 1819)

One point of caution is that it's easy to interpret this as every acre burned every year. Clearly that couldn't have been the case or the abundant wildlife so often described would have no place to nest. We can imagine a scenario where people see fires every year. However, they may see fires to the north one year, to the south the following year.

Fires in prairie leave few traces in the long term. However, when intense fires reach the trees on the edge of the forest, they can do enough damage to the tree trunk to form fire scars. Dendrochronologists, scientists who study tree rings, study the frequency and intensity of these fires by studying scars within the rings. Studies from Oklahoma found a fire return interval between two to six years (S. L. Clark et al. 2007; DeSantis et al. 2010; Allen and Palmer 2011). Parts of Missouri had an average fire frequency of 2.8 years between 1740 and 1850 (Cutter and Guyette 1994). Put another way, fires were frequent.

Most studies find scars in any one year on only a small percentage of the trees (Guyette et al. 2003). This means that fires weren't intense enough to cause scarring on every tree or that fires were patchy in nature. Fire scars are a minimum estimate of fire return intervals as not all fires leave scars.

Another issue with making inferences about prairie fires, especially pre-Euro-American settlement fires, is the age of the trees in the study. Most studies go back only to the late 1700s and early 1800s. That leaves at least two centuries of disease spread, conflicts with European expansion in the east, and displacement of local Native American communities where we don't have any records.

Along with frequency, there are questions about the size of historic fires. Before a modern prescribed fire, managers spend significant amounts of time cutting or mowing firebreaks to control the perimeter of the fire. Historically, no one was cutting any firebreaks anywhere and there was unlimited fuel to the horizon to carry the fire. Individual fires could have been immense (Beltrami 1828; Farnham 1846).

> The plains are burned almost everywhere; only a few small spots have escaped the fury of the flames. (Henry and Thompson 1799)

> Every acre of these vast prairies . . . burns over during the fall or early spring leaving the ground of a black and doleful color. (Catlin 1844)

In many cases, streams and rivers provided natural firebreaks. But during a drought or with high winds, it's pretty easy for a fire to jump a creek. Humidity might have limited some fires. In the Flint Hills of Kansas, many ranchers like to burn in the evening when humidity levels are higher and, as a result, flames are shorter. One could imagine some fires being completely extinguished on a night with heavy dew. But it would take only a few embers to survive the night in deep thatch and get caught in the following day's wind to start the fire again.

In addition to size, frequency, and seasonality, many early settlers recorded their impressions of fire at night. Night fires were both a source of terror and fascination for many early settlers (Brunson 1835; Featherstonhaugh 1847; Catlin 1844; Palliser 1853).

> Few sights can be grander than that of the prairie on fire during the night; the huge body of flame spread far and wide, leaping and plunging like the waves of the sea in a gale against a rocky coast. (Oliver 1843)

> When night came, the whole sky and countryside were lighted up. One could lie in bed in a curtainless room and read by its light. (Quick 1925)

We often blame the plow for much of the destruction of the prairie. However, there were also indirect effects of plowing. The bare soil left behind the plow provided a very good firebreak. Without fire, trees quickly expanded. So, with the aid of the plow many acres of prairies were lost directly to row crops, and the plow stopped fires that indirectly led to further loss of prairie to forest.

> As soon as the oak openings in our neighborhood were settled, and the farmers had prevented running grass-fires, the [oak] grubs grew up into trees. (Muir 1913)

> In the 1840s a new animal, the settler, intervened in the prairie battle. He didn't mean to, he just plowed enough fields to deprive the prairie of its immemorial ally: fire. Seedling oaks forthwith romped over the grasslands in legions. (Leopold 1949)

What did the prairie peninsula look like in the 1400s before diseases ravaged Native American populations and probably changed the use of fire? It's hard to imagine continuous prairie all the way to the Hempstead Plains (Harper 1911) along the East Coast. However, we can imagine the peninsula extending much farther to the east. Were the patchy oak openings and barrens that dotted Ohio and nearby areas connected into one much wider prairie before European settlement (Braun 1928b)?

After frequency and size, the last issue to consider with historic fires is their seasonality. They are out there, but it's difficult to find references to spring fires in the historic literature. References to autumn fires, especially during October, are common. This is simply because many fires were related to hunting and most hunting occurs in the fall. What's more interesting, and still not perfectly answered, is why we switched to April burning (McClain and Elzinga 1994).

Historically researchers just couldn't believe that Native Americans were able to have significant impacts on the landscape. While they may have been able to affect a localized area, the view for much of the early twentieth century was that Native Americans couldn't "be responsible for a plant cover of such a tremendous area" (Stewart 1955). Native Americans in New England (Cronon 1983) and Yellowstone (MacDonald 2018) had profound, large-scale impacts on the land well before Europeans arrived. It's hard not to read some racist undertones into the ideas that Native Americans had no impact or weren't capable of altering the environment (Callicott 1994; Krech 1999).

So where does that leave us? Fires maintain the tallgrass prairie. We know from the frequency and seasonality that people controlled the fires. So what does that say about the prairie and humans' role in the prairie?

> These relics are still being invaded by the forest and unless some of them are acquired and the forest succession halter artificially, the prairie will disappear from Wisconsin. (Thomson 1940)

> When the annual burning ceases, then the trees may invade the artificially maintained prairies. (Thomson 1940)

Was the Prairie then "unnatural"? If so, when was it natural?
(Kuchler 1951)

Is the prairie artificial or unnatural? Why or why not? Is the tallgrass prairie a legitimate plant community or ecosystem? Was it artificial simply because people played and still play as much a role in the prairie as the bison or any other animal? Does human involvement have a place in the natural world? What human actions are or aren't natural? Is a person with a herd of cattle natural but a person with a plow unnatural? What about a person with a drip torch? Or is all human involvement or intervention always unnatural?

The prairie asks a lot of tough questions of both ecologists and historians. And who knew prairies were so philosophical?

Prairie Wilderness

I T HIT ME when I opened *Testimony* by Stephen Trimble and Terry Tempest Williams to pages 113 and 114. There was a map of the US with designated wilderness areas. The intermountain West was heavily dotted and the eastern forest lightly stippled. But in the middle of the country, there was a giant blank triangle of emptiness, the land of the tallgrass prairie.

Looked at another way, there are no blank spots in the Midwest. Every inch of land has been measured, mapped, gridded, plotted, and labeled. And plowed. Most of the year, the land is blank of vegetation or wildlife, bare earth blowing and washing away. All the lines are straight and meet at right angles at section corners. It's hard to walk a mile and not hit at least a gravel township road.

Most of the writing and philosophy around wilderness focuses on the idea of a landscape untouched or unaffected by human hands. Section 2c of the 1964 Wilderness Act begins, "A wilderness, in contrast with those areas where man and his works dominate the landscape, is hereby recognized as an area where the earth and its community of life are untrammeled by man." Later, the act defines wilderness in part as a place "primarily affected by the forces of nature, with the imprint of man's work substantially unnoticeable."

Of course what was meant by this was by Euro-American hands. Today we can include American hands of all skin colors and nations of origin. Before 1492, the tallgrass prairie was very much a hands-on landscape, well-trammeled by dozens of cultures. Especially in the east, these prairies were largely created, or at least expanded, by fire. The prairie is itself an imprint of "man's work," not to mention woman's work.

With less than 1 percent left, there just aren't places within the tallgrass prairie region to establish a prairie wilderness based on the remaining tracts of native prairie. So, this begs the question of whether we can create wilderness. Is that question a statement of hubris or a way to try to give back? If wilderness is defined as a place without people or evidence of people, can people create a wilderness? Leopold (1949) states that "the creation of new wilderness in the full sense of the word is impossible." However, Stegner (1969) writes "better a wounded wilderness than none at all."

Because we can restore a reasonable facsimile of the prairie in only a few years, prairie gives us one of the few opportunities to actually create habitat, and when large enough, an experience that at least has some of the components of true wilderness. We can't create a mountain, grow an old-growth forest, or build a cascading waterfall, at least within anyone's lifetime. We can plant a prairie.

The language of the Wilderness Act continues with itemized points further defining wilderness as a place with "opportunities for solitude," "at least five thousand acres," and "may contain 'features . . . of value.'" The five thousand acres will be a stretch in most places, but even forty or eighty acres can provide some solitude, at least for a short period of time, and provide value.

A trip to a prairie may not be the same as a two-week paddle in the Boundary Waters or a trip into the Bob Marshall Wilderness, but we don't always need that experience every day. Sometimes we just need to go and sit and watch and listen, even if only for a few minutes.

CHAPTER 5

A Stable, Balanced, Cooperative Equilibrium

We even enter the domain of philosophy, and speculate on the fundamental nature of the association, regard it as the basic unit of vegetation, call it an organism, and compare different areas of the same sort of vegetation to a species. — *Gleason 1926*

As an organism, the formation arises, grows, matures, and dies. . . . The climax formation is the adult organism, of which all initial and medial stages are but stages of development. — *Clements 1936*

The ordinary citizen today assumes that science knows what makes the community clock tick; the scientist is equally sure that he does not. He knows that the biotic mechanism is so complex that its workings may never be fully understood. — *Leopold 1949*

The grassland is complete in itself, a relatively stabilized product of nature, the outgrowth of climate, soil, vegetation, animals, and microorganisms, all interacting together. — *Malin 1967*

It appears fairly certain that there can be no final victory for either, there can only be periods of varying duration in which prairie or forest holds the ground won by the favor of the changing climate cycle. — *Weaver 1968*

A first principle is that chance and change are the rule, the future is as unpredictable to other organisms as it is to us, and natural disturbance is too frequent for equilibrium models to be useful. — *Drury 1998*

EVERY TIME THE PUP AND I visit a prairie, even ones we think we know like the back of our hand, or paw, we see something different. Every trip is unique for any of a dozen different reasons. While I can generally predict that there will be a lot of sunflowers and asters blooming in the late summer, I don't know exactly how many or exactly where they will be.

I have no idea what birds we might flush from the grass. There's a lot of uncertainty at the beginning of every prairie visit.

Previous chapters provided a longer-term historical context for how dynamic the prairie landscape was, and still is. The prairie is also very dynamic over short time periods and small areas. Researchers in the prairies in the first half of the twentieth century largely influenced how scientists around the world thought about ecosystems. It still influences how many non-scientists perceive ecosystems today.

The three factors that largely determine the diversity and productivity of the prairie are fire, grazing, and weather extremes, especially periodic drought. Ecologists call these events disturbances. One of the most often cited definitions of an ecological disturbance is "any relatively discrete event in time that disrupts ecosystem, community, or population structure and changes resources, substrate availability, or the physical environment" (Pickett and White 1985). The disturbance would destroy or damage much of the existing vegetation and would be especially destructive of the most dominant species. (Think about a forest fire killing mature pine trees in the Intermountain West.)

"Disturbance" definitely has a different context in social and scientific settings. Disturbance may have a negative social context, such as hearing on the news about a domestic disturbance. In his landmark book *Man and Nature*, George Perkins Marsh (1864) wrote, "But man everywhere is a disturbing agent. Wherever he plants his foot, the harmonies of nature are turned to discord." In this mindset, humans and nature are separated. Only humans were able to disrupt things, and only humans caused problems in the natural world.

> Kansas and the great plains were largely in their primeval state, one hundred years ago. A balance among plants and animals, between each species and its parasites and predators, has been established through the ages, which was, until the coming of man, but little disturbed. (R. C. Smith 1932)

Man alone can destroy the stability of the climax [plant community].
(Clements 1936)

In the past, and often still today, we wanted nature to be a peaceful, harmonious place. Bambi, Thumper, Flower, and Friend Owl all dance and frolic together. We wanted processes and ecosystems to be at equilibrium and for all things to be in balance and stable. We wanted nature to be predictable. We wanted nature to be simple enough that we can understand it and predict what will happen next. That's all comforting. It gives us at least a little sense of control. This mindset probably expresses itself most clearly in the phrase "balance of nature" (Edgerton 1973; Simberloff 2014).

Unlike "disturbance," the word "balance" has a positive connotation. However, nature isn't in balance, well-balanced, out of balance, unbalanced, or imbalanced. Nor can we through our actions or inactions get nature back into balance. We just shouldn't use the words "nature" and "balance" together.

Modern ecologists are more of the view that "the idea of 'balance' has had a cultural and religious connotation rather than a strict scientific foundation" (Wu and Loucks 1995). That said, a quick search of titles shows a number of books published relatively recently with some version of "balance of nature" in the title or subtitle. This seems to be an idea we don't want to let go of culturally.

The "balance of nature" term and concept may have been one of the areas where Aldo Leopold, and many others, struggled. At various times he wrote that ecologists "accept it only with reservations" (1939), and that "this figure of speech fails to describe accurately what little we know" (1949). That said, Leopold used phrases such as "internal processes must balance" and "an internally balanced community" (1949).

Along with the idea of balance are the ideas of stability and equilibrium. And here we can connect back directly to the prairie. Frederic Clements was one of the leading plant ecologists of the early 1900s and did much of his work in the prairies of Nebraska. He interpreted his research findings to show that undisturbed prairies were stable. John Weaver, another well-known ecologist, was a student of Clements and also conducted his research in Nebraska grasslands.

> It can still be confidently affirmed that stabilization is the universal tendency of all vegetation under the ruling climate. (Clements 1936)

> The great stability of the prairie . . . denotes a high degree of equilibrium between vegetation, soil, and climate. (Weaver 1968)

Stability leads up to the concept of ecological succession, or what happens to the plant community over time after a disturbance. In theory, there is a predictable and orderly sequence of species that dominate the disturbed area over time. Eventually, the original, pre-disturbance, or climax plant community once again dominates the area, and the vegetation becomes stable and at equilibrium. Henry Cowles first described this process in 1901 from his work at the Indiana Dunes in northwest Indiana.

In Clements's view, Plant Community 1 is composed of Species A, B, and C and develops immediately after a disturbance. After a period of time, it is replaced by Plant Community 2, composed of Species D, E, and F. Eventually the site will reach a point where the Plant Community is dominated by Species X, Y, and Z. From then on, Species X, Y, and Z will replace X, Y, and Z when a plant dies. This is the stable climax plant community that is at equilibrium. As importantly, the timing and sequence of species and formations after the disturbance should be somewhat predictable.

Clements took the idea of plant succession and the sequential replacement of one plant community by another one step further. He stated that plant communities functioned as a superorganism.

> Like other but simpler organisms, each climax not only has its own growth and development in terms of primary and secondary succession, but it has also evolved out of a preceding climax. (Clements 1936)

Hence prairie is much more than land covered with grass. It is a slowly evolved, highly complex organic entity, centuries old. It approaches the eternal. (Weaver 1954)

Not everyone bought into the ecosystem as organism viewpoint. One can hear the tension some of these ideas created within the scientific community. Comparing a plant community to an organism is a "flight of the imagination" (Braun-Blanquet 1932). Put another way, "there is no need to weary the reader with a list of the points in which the biotic community does not resemble the single animal or plant. They are so obvious and so numerous" (Tansley 1935). That said, writers such as Aldo Leopold and others make frequent use of the "land organism" or related wording as a metaphor for ecosystems.

The next related concept is cooperation. Again, cooperation is a social construct. There are examples of the elements of nature seeming to work together such as a fungi and algae living together to form a lichen or *Rhizobium* bacteria in the root nodules of legumes.

Charles Darwin made it clear that life was about struggle, against both the elements and other organisms. Is the prairie a cooperative effort or a bloody field of battle? Compare the following quotes from Aldo Leopold.

This biota, through ten thousand years of living and dying, burning and growing, preying and fleeing, freezing and thawing, built that dark and bloody ground we call prairie. (Leopold 1949)

Any prairie is a model cooperative commonwealth. (Leopold 1999)

Likewise, we can compare the following quotes from John Weaver's *Prairie Plants and Their Environment.*

The beauty and quiet calm of the grassland should not obscure the fact that the prairie is both a field of battle that is centuries old and a field in which the conflicting species, never wholly victorious nor entirely vanquished, each year renew the struggle.

> The great stability of the prairie, resulting in part from the long lifespan of many species, denotes a high degree of equilibrium between vegetation, soil, and climate. (Weaver 1968)

Is the prairie a dark and bloody ground or a cooperative commonwealth? Is the prairie a field of battle or a place of stability and equilibrium? It doesn't seem like it can be both. We can most easily see that battle between forests and prairies, but each grass and forb on the prairie fights its own battle with neighbors.

> One may see in the oak openings of Wisconsin the area in which the fight is still doubtful, where in some spots the forest is advancing on the prairie, in others receding before it. (Quick 1925)

> The grass and trees went to war, and they are still fighting for the land. (Peattie 1938)

> The average battle line between prairie and forest was about where it is now, and the net outcome of the battle was a draw. (Leopold 1949)

Leopold's quote almost makes it seem like the battle is over and each side signed a truce. The other two quotes give a more evolutionary and ecologically more accurate description of a battle that continues on.

It's interesting how many times words like fight, battle, and war show up in the prairie literature. That doesn't sound very cooperative. That historic struggle can lead to patterns that are sometimes difficult to understand today.

> [T]he prairie species practice "team work" underground by distributing their root-systems to cover all levels. (Leopold 1949)

Species don't practice teamwork in rooting depths, or anything else. We're all familiar with the phrase "nature red in tooth and claw," which was actually written by the poet Alfred, Lord Tennyson. If nature is red in tooth and claw, it is also dark of shade and deep of root. Charles Darwin gave us the phrase "struggle for existence" and his contemporary Herbert Spencer coined the phrase "survival of the fittest."

Over evolutionary time, fighting tooth and claw, or leaf and root, each species finds the best ways they can avoid competition for light, nutrients, water, and pollinators. Each species has diverged in these characteristics to avoid or minimize competition from other species. This is called the "ghost of competitions past" (Connell 1980). The two species aren't competing today, because they've already fought those battles and figured out how to avoid each other. Today, it may look like they aren't competing and are cooperating.

Donald Worster (1990) wrote, "We look for cooperation in nature and we only find competition. . . . We hope for order and discern only a mishmash of conjoined species, all seeking their own advantage in utter disregard for others." Battle line, battle, fight, war, mishmash, and utter disregard do not sound like the plant community behaving as an organism or cooperating together. Nor does it make the natural world seem stable, balanced, or at equilibrium.

The following quotes perfectly illustrate two different strategies. There is no ideal situation in the natural world. Species can avoid competition by living in a harsh environment. Or a species can avoid a harsh environment by living in a competitive environment.

Only gravel ridges are poor enough to offer pasques full elbowroom in April sun. They endure snows, sleets, and bitter winds for the privilege of blooming alone. (Leopold 1949)

In June as many as a dozen species may burst their buds on a single day. (Leopold 1949)

Pasqueflower grows and blooms when it is cold, when there's a good chance of late spring snowstorms, when there aren't a lot of pollinators, and on hilltops with poor soils and low water availability. Those aren't ideal conditions, but it allows this species to escape competition. In contrast, in June there's still moisture from the spring rains, it's warm but not yet hot. However, these plants face intense competition for pollinators. These plants have a benign climate, unlike pasqueflower, but face intense competition that pasqueflower doesn't have to deal with. These are two strategies, but neither is perfect or ideal.

Henry Gleason was a midwestern prairie plant ecologist in the early 1900s. He developed what became the Individualistic Hypothesis. According to Gleason's theory, each point in space and each time period along a successional sequence is a far less predictable sequence of species or communities than what Clements hypothesized.

Gleason's theories conclude that the natural world is less predictable than it is according to the Clementsian view. After a disturbance, there will be a sequence of species at a location, but the exact order of species isn't always predictable. Each species comes and goes individually without close association with other species. Much of Gleason's world was based on probabilities and randomness, not comfortable ideas if one is looking for stability, equilibrium, and predictability in the world.

> The vegetation of every spot of ground is therefore also continually in a state of flux, showing constant variation in the kinds of species present, in the number of individuals of each. (Gleason 1939)

Although academic debate goes back to the 1930s, there was a small revolution in ecology in the 1960s and 1970s. Ecology became much messier, fuzzier, and unpredictable, with a lot more uncertainty. Scientists started to see ecological disturbances as driving and maintaining ecosystems, not disrupting them. Imagine an area with no disturbance. The most competitive and aggressive species will crowd out the others and diversity will be low. Imagine another area that is facing frequent, intense, large-scale disturbances. Only the weediest, most ruderal species will be able to survive all those stresses and diversity will be low. (Typically "weed" is equated to an invasive species. A ruderal species is a native species that does well in highly disturbed environments, such as Canada goldenrod in a road ditch.)

Now imagine an area where there are some disturbances, but they aren't too frequent, too large, or too severe. There's just enough disturbance to knock back the dominant plants that crowd out other species, but not enough disturbance to eliminate a large number of species. These areas will have a higher level of diversity than undisturbed or heavily disturbed areas. This is known as the Intermediate Disturbance Hypothesis (Connell 1978).

Then add a spatial component. One area hasn't been disturbed in ten years; one area burned five years ago; and in one area cattle grazed last year. Now each area has a different disturbance history, type of disturbance, and time since disturbance. Each area will have a slightly different plant community or dominant species due to those disturbances. Added together, the diversity across the larger area should be relatively high.

This probably describes the prairie before Euro-American settlement. Bison grazed the prairie, but they moved around and didn't graze every area every year. Fires were common, but not every acre burned every year. Floods periodically disturbed areas along creeks and rivers. Droughts occasionally affected entire regions. At the smaller scale, badgers and ground squirrels made burrows and dirt mounds. All of these are unpredictable in both space and time.

Much of the research conducted historically was designed with a more Clementsian, balanced viewpoint. In more recent decades things have changed. The following quotes demonstrate just how complicated and intricate all the interactions on and in the prairie are.

Within the transitional zone [tallgrass prairie] no single set of environmental factors explains the mosaic pattern of vegetation. The environmental factors influencing the vegetation operate in concert, with the relative importance of each factor and the interactions of these factors varying in time and space. (R. C. Anderson 1983)

Their [Wu and Loucks 1995] argument, that the classical equilibrium view in ecology has failed to provide a useful predictive model of most natural systems because of the rarity of equilibrium conditions in nature, is certainly true for grasslands. In contrast, elements of the nonequilibrium models they reviewed—such as the focus on transient dynamics, stochastic processes, fluctuations in environmental variables as dominant processes, the important role of historical factors, nonlinear interactions, sensitivity to critical changes that cross threshold boundaries, and inherently low predictability—are the features that make nonequilibrium models ideal for interpreting grassland dynamics. (Knapp and Seastedt 1998)

That all seems complex, unpredictable, and full of jargon, but that's the idea. It's complicated. In other words, the more (we think) we know, the less we can predict. If all that wasn't confusing enough, they go on a few pages later to state:

Put another way, what truly makes the tallgrass prairie a challenging system to study is the high frequency of switching between limiting factors during and among years. Fire, herbivores, and climatic extremes all influence, and their effects are influenced by, this variation in supply and demand for essential resources. (Knapp and Seastedt 1998)

Each of those factors, fire, grazing, and climate extremes, are disturbances. It's these, and other, disturbances acting at different times, different frequencies, different intensities, and different sizes that makes the prairie so complex and dynamic.

To make the prairie more complex than most ecosystems, the limiting factor is frequently changing. Deserts are hot and dry. Tundra is cold. The understory of coniferous forests is dark. However, in the prairie, light, water, temperature, and other factors can vary from spot to spot and year to year, so the limiting resources are constantly changing in space and time. Frequently, it's the history of disturbance and the most recent disturbance that determine the limiting factor at that spot at this time. Taking this one step further, studying the changes in the vegetation, and the reason behind those changes, may be more useful and informative than studying the vegetation itself.

> [V]egetation is constantly undergoing various kinds of change, but the increasing habit of concentrating attention on these changes instead of studying the plant communities as if they were static entities is leading to a far deeper insight into the vegetation. (Tansley 1935)

> Currently, ecological interests have shifted from seeking similarity for the purpose of classification to understanding variability within the context of natural disturbances. (Collins and Glenn 1995)

Today, most ecologists think that we live in a more Gleasonian than Clementsian world. However, that's not to say that ecologists have completely abandoned Clements's ideas (Tansley 1935). Although the superorganism idea has led to criticism, Clements's ideas still have many positive influences on how modern scientists understand plant communities (Collins and Glenn 1995). So let's go back to Leopold's land organism. He was drafting these chapters through the late 1930s and into the 1940s. Gleason's work and the research of Shimek, Tansley, and others, demonstrate that there were different viewpoints out there.

Was Leopold out of touch with science when he wrote about the land organism? Did he get this wrong? No, he was not wrong, but he wasn't right either.

Although Gleason's ideas were present in the 1940s, they weren't widely adopted. Through the 1940s scientists were still taking an equilibrium view of the world. When it came to Gleason's theory, "most simply ignored it" (McIntosh 1975) and "few American ecologists publicly agreed with it or even seemed to notice it" (Barbour 1995). However, Barbour also states that "prior to the 1950s nature was simplistic and determin-istic; after the 1950s nature became complex, fuzzy-edged, and probabi-listic." Likewise, "ecology was basically a study of equilibrium, harmony, and order; it had been so from its beginning. Today . . . it has become a study of disturbance, disharmony, and chaos" (Worster 1990). So, Leo-pold was reflecting mainstream science, at the time. It's just that the times have changed.

Things are changing all the time and there's a lot we don't know or understand. How do we develop policies and management plans built on change, uncertainty, unpredictability, disturbance, and chaos? No matter how much or how long any person or group studies an area, there's still a lot to learn. Indeed, at the end of a career studying or managing the prairie, most have far more questions than answers. And every time we think we have something figured out, the prairie will do something to confuse us.

> I have looked for a prairie remnant that I could manage, where I
> could apply unfettered what I think I have learned. (Drobney 1999)

Note the phrase "think I have learned." Every time you think you know something, the prairie is going to surprise you.

Conversing with the Dead

I'VE NEVER UNDERSTOOD WHY, but people like to know other people's favorites. What's your favorite color, or song, or movie? Who's your favorite Beatle? What's your favorite bird? What's your favorite prairie flower? When asked this, I always say I'll have to think about it and then try to change the subject.

I suppose that if threatened with bodily harm, I could name two or three of my favorite birds and flowers. Really, they are all pretty interesting in their own way. Two of those flowers would probably be pasqueflower and shooting stars, and another would be hoary puccoons. I like them all for personal and probably irrational reasons, but they are my reasons.

In writing about the Illinois and Iowa prairies, Leopold describes "a narrow thread of sod" between the road and toppling fences. He also describes a cemetery that "flashes by," presumably due to its small size. He writes that the cemeteries' borders were "alight with prairie puccoons." However, across the rest of the landscape other species, mostly invasive, provide a splash of yellow that puccoons once provided. He ends the paragraph with a sorrowful "puccoons converse only with the dead."

There may be two possible ways to interpret this line. First, puccoons are found only in native prairie and much of the native prairie left in Illinois and Iowa is in pioneer cemeteries. The second interpretation is a little more complicated. Cemeteries, especially older cemeteries, are rather static. They don't change much.

It's relating puccoons to a static prairie that I would like to politely argue with Leopold about. Puccoons are a species that are difficult to restore and therefore seeing them almost always indicates a remnant of native prairie.

Even in the highest quality native prairies, puccoons often do best at small disturbances, such as the bare ground left from small mammal burrowing. When it comes to ditches, the place I often see puccoons is right on the edge of road, where gravel meets grass. After snowy winters when the township snowplows have been out in force, puccoons are often most common in spots where the plow blade scraped off the top bit of soil.

So, while puccoons do indicate either a high-quality plant community, or at least an area where a few species have hung on, relating them to the relatively static conditions found in old cemeteries may do a disservice to the natural history of this species. This is a species that is often dependent on some level of disturbance. This also tells me that puccoons may not be the best competitors and hang on best where they have a little elbow room. Puccoons are dependent on disturbance and change, and don't do well in any static or stable situation, where they are soon crowded out.

This is not to argue that snowplows are a prairie's best friend. However, it is an attempt to show that burrowing animals, grazing, and in some cases human mechanical disturbances can be beneficial to some species and can help maintain the overall diversity and dynamics of the prairie.

Puccoons were abundant at my undergraduate research site, a sandy area along the Wabash River. I still remember checking small mammal traps at dawn and seeing the dew glistening on the puccoons. I recorded them at Spinn Prairie on my last trip to an Indiana prairie as a college student.

Since I moved to Minnesota, puccoons have always been one of the species I most rely on to show me where there might be some remnant prairie in a field corner or ditch. If I see puccoons, I stop and look. More often than not, I'm rewarded with some prairie violet, blue-eyed grass, pasqueflower, prairie smoke, and other prairie species hanging on in that narrow thread of sod.

CHAPTER 6

Prairie Flora

It should be noted that these [dry, mesic, and wet prairies] intergrade, passing into one another gradually, instead of alternating sharply, and that many species tolerate a wide range of soil moisture and of other environmental conditions, so that some species are found abundantly in more than one association. Some species, too, reach greatest abundance in transitional growths intermediate between two associations. — *Vestal 1914*

Are we not justified in coming to the general conclusion, far removed from the prevailing opinion, that an association is not an organism, scarcely even a vegetational unit, and merely a *coincidence?* — *Gleason 1926*

[M]ost "associations," regardless of the magnitude of their conception, contain only a few species which are regularly or even usually present. Rather, they are mixtures of many species, most of which occur rarely or occasionally. — *Curtis and Greene 1949*

The over-all composition of a large area of prairie may remain stable and constant, but any small area within it would show violent fluctuations over time. — *Curtis 1959*

The concept of a climax tallgrass community is deeply rooted in historical views of stable, self-replicating communities. In modern terms, such a perspective may predict a single equilibrium community under given climatic conditions, quite likely represented in restoration and conservation biology as a "Prime Directive" that unconsciously imposes a sentimental monotony on a community that otherwise would take many forms. There are overwhelming theoretical and empirical reasons to doubt the sufficiency of a static image of tallgrass ecology. — *Howe 1994a*

For prairies . . . annual changes in community composition were rapid and unpredictable. — *Collins and Glenn 1995*

IF YOU'RE LOOKING AT downy gentian, it's probably in a matrix of little bluestem and there's a good chance that a showy goldenrod, rough blazingstar, and silky aster are somewhere close. If you see these species, you're probably on a hilltop or an area with very sandy or gravelly soils. If you walk downhill, you may see a bottle gentian. The gentian will most often be found in a stand of big bluestem and there's a good probability that there is some Canada goldenrod, prairie blazingstar, and smooth blue aster nearby. If you continue walking and get to the edge of a wetland, you may find fringed gentians. They are typically found in wetter areas dominated by sedges or cordgrass, and there's usually some Riddell's goldenrod, marsh blazingstar, and New England aster in the area.

Walking from hilltop to wetland edge, you might see scattered prairie blazingstar, then an area with a high density of prairie blazingstar, and then fewer prairie blazingstar until they disappear. You would see the same pattern with Canada goldenrod and smooth blue aster, but each of the three species would appear, have peak densities, and disappear at different points along that walk. As prairie blazingstar becomes less common along this path, marsh blazingstar might become more common. Some species you may see almost the entire length of your walk. Other species may appear and disappear rather quickly. You will see thousands of flowers of some species while other species you may only see one or two individual plants.

While there are some very general patterns we can describe, you probably won't find downy and fringed gentian growing next to each other. However, the words "often," "typically," "usually," and "might" in the writing sound somewhat fuzzy, while "chance" and "probability" sound like gambling. That said, prairie botanists are always muttering to themselves something like "that plant isn't supposed to be growing there."

In the 1950s, plant ecologists developed the idea of the continuum (Whittaker 1951; Curtis 1955). Like Frederic Clements's and Henry Gleason's work in the prairies, John Curtis's work in Wisconsin tallgrass prairie made significant contributions to our understanding of many ecosystems. Curtis's continuum is essentially what was described at the beginning of this chapter, where a person walking across a prairie would see "a continuously changing series of species" (Curtis 1955), especially if that walk crossed soil types or elevations. It's not radically different from Henry Gleason's Individualistic Hypothesis, perhaps more of a variation on a theme.

There are analogies between space and time. If you stand on a hilltop and walk downhill to the edge of wetland, you would see a sequence of plant species. Likewise, if you visit a heavily disturbed area within the prairie and revisit that same spot every year for a decade or more, you would see a similar pattern of a series of species appearing, becoming abundant, and fading away. You would see different species in your annual visits than you saw on that hilltop to wetland walk. However, the patterns would be similar, one in space and one in time. While it is often hard to identify a boundary in the plant community in space, it can be equally "impossible to distinguish accurately the beginning or the end of an association in time" (Gleason 1926).

To take the continuum to extremes, we would never be able to draw a sharp line in the prairie dividing plant community A from community B. There are no distinct communities or plant associations and every group of plant species just fades and grades into any other group of plants. However, it is not all one smooth continuous transition on the prairie. There are boundaries and distinctions at several scales that can often be related to soils or disturbance patterns. Nested within the continuum is the idea of patches and patch dynamics. A short walk in the prairie would show a number of discontinuities, or sharp edges.

> At a time when the vegetation stands quietly, or is only slightly ruffled by the breeze one may perceive in the mosaic pattern of the prairie recurrent strips, patches, or spots whose various shades of green mark the boundaries of different communities of plants composing the vegetation. (Hayden 1945)

These patches can be quite dynamic in space and time and can be different sizes. They are often related to disturbance; a grazing patch, a patch of prairie that burned, a small patch of loose soil created by a gopher mound, or a patch where a cow urinated and added nitrogen to the soil. In other cases, changes in soil types may create distinct boundaries in the plant community, such as a small area that holds water and is dominated by cordgrass instead of big bluestem. There can be dramatic differences in the prairie over just a few feet. No two spots of prairie, no matter how small or close, are the same.

> More careful examination of one of these areas, especially when conducted by some statistical method, will show that the uniformity is only a matter of degrees, and that two sample quadrats with precisely the same structure can scarcely be discovered. (Gleason 1926)

I was able to generally test Gleason's statement about similar quadrats using data from Konza Prairie Biological Station in the Flint Hills of Kansas. These data illustrate patch dynamics very well. Researchers at Konza Prairie record plant species presence and cover in a series of five circular plots that are each ten square meters in size equally spaced along a fifty meter long transect. There are four of these transects in upland and four in lowland soils within several watersheds at Konza.

First, we need to pause to define a few words. Diversity and biodiversity are commonly used words. To most people, this probably means the number of species in a given area. To an ecologist, species richness is a count of the species. Diversity is an index that combines the number of species and their relative abundance.

Imagine three plant communities each with one hundred individuals of ten species, Species A through J. In the first community, there are ninety-one individual plants of Species A and one individual plant of species B through J. In the second community, there are fifty-five individuals of Species J and five individual plants of Species A through I. In the third community, there are ten plants of each of the ten species. Each community will look very different, but the richness is ten in each plant community. However, diversity, dominance, evenness, and other indices would

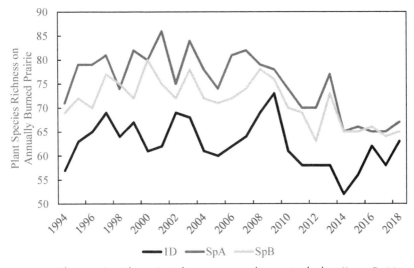

FIGURE 3. Plant species richness in eight transects on three watersheds at Konza Prairie Biological Station in Kansas over twenty-four years. Data courtesy of Konza Prairie Long-Term Ecological Research program.

be quite different. Ecologists have a number of simple and complicated ways to measure plant communities. Often, they use different measures together to understand a plant community or to compare multiple communities. Now, let's get back to our storyline.

I looked at the plant species data from one year in a watershed that is grazed by bison and burned every four years. Along one transect on the upland soils, species richness in the five plots was 35, 38, 33, 30, and 25 species. That seems like a fair amount of variability between plots only a few feet apart. Comparing the adjacent plots with 35 and 38 species, only 28 species occurred in both plots.

There is also a lot of variability from year to year. Figure 3 combines the total number of plant species among all eight transects in three Konza Prairie watersheds and clearly illustrates that the number of species fluctuates, sometimes quite dramatically, from year to year. That fluctuation is fairly random and unpredictable. All three of these watersheds are burned annually in the spring. Given the same management and disturbance history, species richness not only fluctuates, but fluctuates asynchronously. These watersheds are all within a mile or two of each other at the southern end of Konza Prairie.

The length of time covered by this graph is important for a couple different reasons. First, it shows that there is lot of year-to-year variability in the number of plant species and that variability is unpredictable. Look at any four-year period on any of the lines on Figure 3. Is there a way to predict the number of species recorded in the fifth and sixth year?

Imagine several graduate students studying plant species richness in watershed 1D, Figure 3, which is annually burned in the spring. Graduate student projects typically last two or three field seasons. One graduate student studies the watershed from 2007 to 2009 and concludes that annual spring burning increases plant species richness. The second graduate student studies the same watershed from 2009 to 2011 and concludes that annual burning decreases plant species richness. The third student studies the period from 2011 to 2013 and concludes there is little to no effect of burning on plant species richness. A fourth graduate student does a retrospective analysis of all twenty years and concludes that over long periods of time, richness doesn't change under annual burning although there are annual fluctuations. Who is right?

Just as interesting, the ups and downs in plant richness aren't parallel. There are many years when one watershed increases in richness and the other two decrease, and vice versa. So we can't just point to the weather and say something like "plant species richness declines in wet years" since each watershed seems to respond independently. It's really hard to find any patterns or predictability in this graph.

Why do short-term versus long-term studies of fire often result in conflicting results? (Knapp et al. 1998)

Next, I looked at prairie turnip in watershed N4D, burned every fourth year and grazed by bison, at Konza Prairie within each of the four upland transects and the five plots along each transect, twenty total plots, over a twenty-year period. Prairie turnip wasn't recorded in six plots over those two decades. In the remaining plots, turnip showed up between four and seventeen of the twenty years. What's even more interesting is that turnip seems to appear and disappear randomly in both plots and transects. There are no good years where turnip is in almost every plot or bad years where it's rare.

The presence of turnip in each plot and transect seems to be almost random and independent of other nearby plots and transects. Sometimes turnip appears and disappears almost annually. In other plots, turnip is present for a number of years and then seemingly disappears. Or, after being absent for several years, turnip suddenly appears in the plot, sometimes for just a year and sometimes for several years in a row. This is the combination of spatial and temporal variability that ecologists deal with daily, which makes their data so complicated.

> [F]or there are variations in the abundance of many of the species from year to year, some apparently disappearing for a time, and different (even closely contiguous) parts of the same prairie show variations which may result in part from differences in topography or which may be due to the accident of distribution. (Shimek 1911)

> [W]e must conclude that stands of any major community are highly variable, differing widely from place to place within the stand and, to a considerable extent, from year to year in the same place. (Curtis 1959)

The real world is much more complicated than Figure 3 shows. The graph just shows the total number of species. We can imagine many species following patterns similar to prairie turnip's, and then we would need to do this same exercise with seventy or more species within a prairie. Each species will act independently of every other species and independently of individuals of the same species in different plots only a few meters away. Species appear and disappear individually in both space and time, making for an incredibly dynamic plant community at even very small scales.

We can probably trace many of the fluctuations in the prairie to different disturbances. Disturbances in prairies aren't just one-time events. Imagine monitoring a small plot of prairie over ten years after a disturbance that you witnessed, such as a gopher mound. Over your ten years of monitoring there were a couple fires, it was grazed one year, and there was a three-year drought at the end of the decade. Each area on the prairie, each patch, has been subjected to a different history or combinations of disturbances, different intensities of disturbance, different times between disturbances, and different last disturbances. Then there are the fluctuations that cannot be tied to any disturbance.

Even in well established climax flora, there is a great fluctuation in the relative number of both individuals and species. (Shimek 1931)

Any given spot of mature prairie is likely to be destroyed and replaced by pioneer plants at any time. (Curtis 1959)

[S]mall patches of tallgrass prairie vegetation were highly variable in space and time in the absence of disturbance. (Collins and Glenn 1995)

In addition to showing year to year fluctuations, Figure 3 demonstrates that the history of the prairie may be as important as modern management. In theory, these three watersheds have been managed the same way with annual spring fire, no grazing, had the same rainfall and temperature patterns over time, and are a short distance apart. One would think they would be overlapping and always be on the same trajectory. They aren't.

[D]ifferential competitive advantages are likely to result in changes in species composition . . . if management is continued for a sufficiently long time. (Hoover and Bragg 1981)

Tallgrass prairie is resilient to change, and although cover of some indigenous perennial forb species eventually increased in response to autumn and winter burning, that effect required repeated fire. (Towne and Kemp 2003)

At the start of this graph, researchers had been burning each of these watersheds annually in the spring for almost two decades. Is that not enough to push the plant communities to be more similar?

Plant associations are contemporary expressions of historical events and processes. (Sauer 1950)

Differential management in the past may be reflected in the current composition of the prairie, and may to some extent still override current management. (Gibson 1988)

Overlaid on these short-term fluctuations are long-term patterns that often don't change. As a graduate student at Konza Prairie, I remember looking at satellite images of the southwest corner of the research station in watershed 20A. Researchers managed this watershed as a single unit for over two decades, but there was still a visible line through the middle in some images. I never saw this line when I was walking around the edge of the watershed. In the couple dozen other satellite images I worked with at Konza, this line isn't visible. This happens to be the boundary between Riley (north) and Geary (south) Counties. It is also the boundary between the initial acquisition of Konza in the mid 1970s, south of this line, and the acquisition of the rest of Konza Prairie in the early 1980s.

The prairie has a long memory, and it can take a significant push to make it change its mind. In some ways it's hard to understand these observations in the context of invasive species. While it can take significant time to change the native species composition, anyone who has spent time managing these areas has unfortunately seen invasive species expand quickly and dramatically.

Before 1950, mid-summer haying was the primary management at Kaslow Prairie. Since 1950, spring fires have been the most common management tool. It's hard to say when in that fifty-year period the shift in species occurred, but "this practice may have also exerted strong selection pressures on the native community" (Dornbush 2004). There was a change in plant communities with changes in management over a fifty-nine-year period in Wisconsin prairies (Rooney and Leach 2010). Shorter-term studies concluded that changes over a nine-year study were "relatively small" and that those changes were dependent on the starting conditions of the site when the management program started (Ahlering et al. 2020).

The studies cited set up contrasting views of the prairie. On one hand, prairies show a "constant flux of arrivals and departures," species are "destroyed and replaced," and the plant community is "highly variable in space and time." By contrast, the prairie is also "resilient to change" and we must manage "for a sufficiently long time" to see changes.

We can go back to scale. Find a hilltop in a rather large prairie. Look to the horizon. Across that prairie, change is relatively slow. Standing in the same spot, look down at your feet. At that scale, things may change quickly. In yet another apparent paradox, the prairie is both unchanged and always changing.

Historically, ecologists thought that succession was the predictable series of weedy or ruderal species through to climax species. Today, many scientists think succession is driven as much by the remaining or surrounding vegetation as by any all-encompassing process. If there are a lot of remaining roots of Species A and B in the soil, Species A and B will probably be dominant after the disturbance. If the disturbance is intense enough that it kills many of the plants in that area, then the resulting plant community may be largely affected by the nearby plant community. If Species C and D are nearby and rain a lot of seed into that area, Species C and D will probably be dominant after the disturbance.

> In summary it may be stated that environment varies constantly in time and continuously in space; environment selects from all available immigrants those species which constitute the present vegetation, and as a result vegetation varies constantly in time and continuously in space. (Gleason 1939)

Given this backdrop of randomness and unpredictability in plant communities, is it even worth trying to develop some classification system? It's human nature to want to name and classify things, even if nature can be hard to label and categorize. Still, most scientists feel the need to come up with some general way of organizing ecosystems and plant communities.

Some ecologists have classified prairies based on soils (Curtis and Greene 1949; Betz and Lamp 1989; Corbett and Anderson 2006), but each study identified a different number of plant communities from those soils and used different soil categories. Other studies classify prairies based on moisture levels, which are often related to soil types. These classifications based on moisture level can include wet, wet mesic, mesic, dry mesic, gravel, and sand (White and Glenn-Lewin 1984), or dry sand, transitional 1, hill prairies, transitional 2, mesic, and wet-mesic to wet (Corbett and Anderson 2001). Note that these studies have almost as many transitional plant communities as they do distinct plant communities.

Other studies categorize prairies based on the dominant grasses (Weaver 1954; Bliss and Cox 1964; Smeins and Olsen 1970). Again, each came up with a different number of plant communities. Others include forbs such as "most noticeably characterized by the Silphiums [primarily compass plant and prairie dock]" (Shelford 1913) or included big bluestem and prairie dock as the dominant plant species (Braun 1928b). This points to the bias observers can introduce into science. There were probably few prairies where compass plant or prairie dock dominated by either biomass or number of individuals. However, *Silphiums* like compass plant and prairie dock are such impressive plants, it's easy to see why someone's eye would be immediately attracted to some species over others.

Researchers clearly struggle with how to classify plant communities within the prairie. How many communities should there be? Should the communities be based on moisture level, soil type, or the dominant plants? Should there only be distinct names, wet and mesic, or are transitional areas, wet-mesic, distinct enough to have their own label? How different does a collection of species have to be before it is deserving of its own distinctive classification? In describing the boundaries between the major grassland types in the center of North America, short/mixed/ tallgrass prairie, there may be "no sharp divisions between these arbitrarily designated grassland regions" (R. C. Anderson 2006). Is this true at large regional scales? If so, is it also true at small local scales? Why or why not?

> Now, when all these features of the plant community are considered, it seems that we are treading upon rather dangerous ground when we define an association as an area of uniform vegetation, or, in fact, when we attempt any definition at all. (Gleason 1926)

Are all plant communities "arbitrarily designated" human categories and are we on "dangerous ground" when we try to classify different prairies into different types or groups?

One of the first steps in classifying a prairie is coming up with a list of species at that prairie. That can be easier said than done. I looked at the cumulative number of plants in surveys in three watersheds at Konza Prairie over a two-decade period. The watersheds were 1D, burned annually, 4B, burned every four years, and N4D, burned every four years and grazed by bison. In the first year I looked at there were 63, 73, and 104 species sampled across uplands and lowlands in each watershed. After two decades of surveys, researchers found a cumulative total of 94, 145, and 184 species respectively. Put another way, a one-year survey found only 67, 50, and 57 percent of the species in each of those watersheds. A one-time survey of any prairie may tell us little about the total species richness of the site, or the dynamics of those species and communities.

If a plant community is a collection of populations of different species, a population is a collection of individuals of the same species. Therefore, populations should be much simpler and understandable. If only that were true.

In the savannas along the prairie's eastern border we can simply count the number of oak trees. Then we get to the aspen forests on the northern edge of the tallgrass prairie, and the issue gets more confusing.

Here we have to introduce new botanical terms, genet and ramet. A genet is a genetically unique organism. A ramet is a stem of a plant. In many plant species, the genet is the ramet. Each tree in an oak forest is a genetically unique and identifiable individual, at least most of the time. However, in an aspen forest, all the stems over a large area can be connected by an underground root system. They are, collectively, a genetically unique individual, a clone or genet. Each tree trunk of that genet is a ramet.

The largest plant identified so far is an aspen clone in Utah that is made up of 47,000 trunks and covers 106 acres (Grant 1993). Many of the sod-forming grasses probably act like aspen trees. Clones of big bluestem in Kansas average about six to seven feet in diameter (Keeler et al. 2002).

The contrast of genet and ramet may be easiest to see in some of the goldenrods, especially showy and Canada goldenrod. These two species often grow in clumps, frequently large clumps. Each clump is not many goldenrods, it is one genetically unique goldenrod (genet) with many stems and flowering heads (ramets).

All this information gives us a new way to look at the prairie plants. Imagine looking at a spring prairie a few weeks after a burn. There is a thick carpet of grass, probably big bluestem, that is dotted with a few puccoons. Viewed from above, one could conclude that there is a lot of big bluestem and a few puccoons. In reality, there could only be a couple bluestem genets and the puccoons actually outnumber the grasses, if we count genetically unique individuals.

Whenever we talk about populations, we have to talk about both the plants and the seeds. Seeds are genetically unique and identifiable individuals, even if they haven't germinated yet. Surely all those flowers producing all those seeds must be important in the prairie. Actually, the seed bank, seeds sitting in the soil waiting to germinate, is rather small in the prairie (Rabinowitz and Rapp 1985; Rapp and Rabinowitz 1985; Johnson and Anderson 1986). The prairie does have an extensive bud bank. A bud is an underground meristem, the actively growing part of a plant.

Life on the prairie isn't much fun for a seed. First the seed falls off the parent plant and lands in the thatch of the previous years' growth. Some seed will get caught here and never reach the soil. Some seed will fall through the thatch and make contact with the soil. Prairies look bright and sunny to us, standing four to six feet tall above the prairie. However, at the soil surface, the prairie is a very dark environment with typically about one third of 1 percent of the light penetrating through the thatch layer (Knapp 1984). The seeds down there in the dark and damp are under constant threat of attack from fungi, bacteria, insects, small mammals, and birds.

In the following spring, the seed must germinate, grow a shoot up and a root down. The seedling is competing against plants with deep roots that may be a decade or more old with a significant amount of energy stored in the roots from last summer. The shoots must be able to get to light and not be overshadowed by the surrounding plants.

If the seedling does survive the first few weeks, it has to worry about summer's heat and wind. Deep-rooted plants can take a fair amount of stress. Seedlings with small root system can't handle the water stress of a hot, dry, windy summer. Then the seedling has to escape being grazed by animals, stepped on, buried in the loose dirt generated by burrowing animals, or overshadowed by neighboring plants.

Seedlings make up less than 1 percent of the stems at the end of growing season (Benson and Hartnett 2006). Seedling establishment is a "rare event" (Rapp and Rabinowitz 1985) or an "extreme rarity" (Benson et al. 2004).

By contrast, a new shoot, or a new ramet from an existing genet, can tap into an existing root system and use those resources. The disadvantage is that the plant isn't able to disperse its genes any distance. Because the prairie is such a competitive environment, most "new" plants are probably just new ramets from old and established genets. In the prairie, it's the bud bank, not the seed bank, that drives the plant community (Dalgleish and Hartnett 2009; Ott and Hartnett 2015).

Let's get back to the idea of disturbance and diversity. If seedlings can't compete in soils and plant communities that haven't been disturbed recently, do they do better on soils that have been recently disturbed such as gopher or badger mounds, or any other disturbance that loosens soil and at least temporarily removes the competing vegetation?

An Iowa study found that plant communities on gopher mounds were different from the surrounding area (Wolfe-Bellin and Moloney 2001) . In contrast, research from Kansas found that the vegetation on gopher mounds was simply a subset of the plants in the surrounding prairie (Rogers et al. 2001). Vegetative regrowth may be the primary way soil disturbances were recolonized and "the seed rain was considerably less important in maintaining diversity of forbs and annuals than previously believed" (Rogers and Hartnett 2001).

This brings up yet another paradox of the prairie. The prairie in mid and late summer is a riot of color from all the flowers. The sole purpose of a flower is to produce seeds. However, if seeds are rarely successful, why do prairie plants invest so much energy into producing flowers and ultimately seeds if the seeds rarely survive?

What do we know about plant communities and populations in the prairie? First, the scientific theories developed from studying the prairie have become fundamental to many of the basic principles of plant ecology in other ecosystems. Second, there's a large amount of variation, often over short time periods and short distances. Third, all that variation makes the prairie an incredibly dynamic ecosystem.

Let's end this chapter by thinking about ecological studies that have been done and will be done in the future. This chapter used a couple of examples from Konza Prairie that looked at two decades worth of data.

Ecology is largely the study of processes and patterns that developed over hundreds to thousands to hundreds of thousands of years. However, ecologists often work on the time scale of a two-to-four–year graduate student project or research grant funding cycle.

The other emerging idea with modern research is that scientists can collect data from many sites and conduct large analyses that cover entire continents or hemispheres (Kratz et al. 2003). Combining data from a number of Long-Term Ecological Research sites across North America revealed more about these sites than a set of individual projects done in isolation (Knapp and Smith 2001).

Likewise, researchers studied tallgrass prairie at 130 management units across western Minnesota, southeastern North Dakota, and eastern South Dakota (Ahlering et al. 2020). What's just as interesting as the scientific data collected is the number of people who collaborated on the project. The authors of this study work for The Nature Conservancy, Minnesota Department of Natural Resources, US Fish and Wildlife Service, Chicago Botanical Garden, US Geological Survey, and University of Minnesota. While there are still numerous smaller questions that can be addressed at a few sites in a couple years, many of the emerging questions of prairie management are going to rely on these large-scale, in both time and space, research projects, which will require cooperation, coordination, and collaboration across organizations, agencies, and universities.

What We Know

THERE ARE SEVERAL LEVELS of "knowing" when it comes to the tallgrass prairie. With so little left, most people don't even know what a prairie is or what one looks like. In *A Sand County Almanac*, Aldo Leopold wrote that "we grieve only for what we know. The erasure of Silphium from western Dane County is no cause for grief if one knows it only as a name in a botany book."

People know forests and mountains. They know lakes and rivers. Individual species, the cuter or nobler looking the better, will generate interest. However, because there is so little left, prairie may be a bit of an abstraction for some. It's just grass. And any plant that isn't grass or a crop is just a weed.

When writing about trying to dig up the enormous taproot of a compass plant, Leopold said the "Silphium first became a personality to me" (1949). Conservation and environmentalism are too often too abstract. For people to care, to be connected, to become engaged, the prairie, or even one or two plants or animals in the prairie, need to become a personality to us.

There's a second level of knowing for those who are familiar with the prairie. What will I see on that next visit to a familiar prairie? Undoubtedly it will be something different than I saw on the last visit, and if I look hard enough, I'll find something I've never seen at that prairie.

How and why do we restore and manage prairies? Or what are the effects of our management actions? Those questions may best be answered with the phrase *it depends*. Was this area originally forest, savanna, or prairie, and what should we manage for today? *It depends*

on the timeframe you have for "originally." What is the effect of spring
burning? *It depends* on whether it's an early or late spring burn, whether
it's followed by a dry or wet summer, and whether the prairie is grazed
soon after the fire. What are the effects of grazing? *It depends* on how
long the prairie is grazed, by how many animals, and whether there's
a drought that year. What happens after a disturbance? *It depends* on
the type, size, and intensity of the disturbance, the remaining roots and
buds, and nearby seed sources.

That's not to be flippant or dismissive. It does point to the idea that
there is no balance of nature, no equilibrium or stability, nothing nature
is supposed to be. More importantly, it shows that there is so much that
we don't understand and can't predict about the prairie.

What will happen if we burn this prairie this year? The only conclu-
sive answer to that question is that the result won't be exactly the same
as the last time we burned this prairie.

This is where scientists often have issues when communicating with
the public. The public and politicians want clean and clear answers
to even the messiest questions. We want to know that if we do this,
then that will happen. If we spend these dollars, we will have this
result. When scientists are asked questions, they often use words like
"probably" or "there's a good probability . . ." They aren't trying to be
evasive; they simply understand that there are many things we can't
predict precisely, and just as many we can't predict at all.

Perhaps, in the end, all we can know is that, in the words of Leopold,
"biotic mechanism is so complex that its workings may never be fully
understood" (1949). However, I don't think he meant for that to be a
reason to give up or quit trying, but as a challenge to all of us to spend
more time looking, listening, and learning.

CHAPTER 7

Modern Fires, Plant Community, and Productivity

[S]o tall that an army of men on horseback might easily be concealed amongst them.
— *Oliver 1843*

The vegetation in this part of the prairie was very rank, and in some places gigantic, the grass growing over thousands of acres from five to eight feet tall. — *Palliser 1853*

Everywhere, as far as the eye could reach, there was nothing but rough, shaggy red grass, most of it as tall as I. — *Cather 1918*

Our data indicate that only 3 weeks difference in timing of spring burning has a dramatic long-term influence on the vegetation. — *Towne and Owensby 1984*

[D]ormant-season burn management that favors tall late-season competitors could reduce the overall species diversity over that expected under management regimes that permit early-flowering species to persist. — *Howe 1994b*

The inability of a single factor, such as precipitation to explain a large portion of the interannual variability in NPP [net primary productivity] is consistent with the concept that patterns of NPP in tallgrass prairie are a product of spatial and temporal variability in light, water, and nutrients, driven by a combination of topography, fire history, and climate. — *Briggs and Knapp 1995*

IF PEOPLE KNOW anything about the tallgrass prairie, they know that it's tall. They probably heard stories about herds of cattle hidden in the grass or children being lost in it (Catlin 1844; Peattie 1938). As described earlier, equating the prairie to the ocean is so common in the early prairie literature, it almost becomes expected of anyone writing about the prairie. However, almost all of these oceanic references are from the perspective of looking out to the horizon over the waving stalks of grasses that are similar to the waves of the ocean. That's never been the reference that stuck with me from my experiences in the prairie. I finally found one person who felt the same way.

> To walk in a stand of big bluestem or Indian grass is to be submerged. It is an enclosing element, differing in feeling both from forest and from conventional pasture land. (Berry 1981)

Being in the tallgrass prairie in late summer on a wet year really can leave you feeling like you are drowning in grass. On a few visits, I've been within four feet of my friends and not been able to see them. The feeling becomes even more vivid if you kneel on the ground to inspect something close up. There's no scary sense of drowning. There is a peaceful sense of immersion.

However, it wasn't all tall everywhere every year. There are gradients in productivity or biomass production in the tallgrass prairie. The drier edge of the tallgrass region in the Flint Hills of Kansas is less productive than the wetter edge of the tallgrass region in northwestern Indiana. Within a site, the grasses on hilltops are significantly shorter than grasses at the base of the hill. An area with sandy or gravelly soils will have shorter grasses than deep, loamy soils. Wetter areas will have taller grasses than drier areas. While there were areas in the prairie that could hide a person on a horse or a herd of cattle, it would be misleading to think that the grass was that tall everywhere in the prairie region.

> [Illinois] On the untouched prairie, the grass grows to a height of three or four feet, mixed, on the rich flats, with weeds, which sometimes usurp nearly the whole surface, and are so tall that an army of men on horseback might easily be concealed amongst them. (Oliver 1843)

> [Kansas] It ordinarily attains to the height of three feet, toward the close of summer; but where the land is moist, it grows more luxu-

riantly, and is said to become "tall enough to hide from view horse and rider." (Van Tramp 1868)

Prior to Euro-American settlement, prairie fires were frequent and occurred primarily in the fall. In modern times, most prescribed fires are in the spring and aren't nearly as frequent. McClain and Elzinga (1994) reviewed historical accounts from the 1670s to the 1850s and were able to document this switch in burning practices with the arrival of Euro-American settlement. However, it's still not perfectly clear why there was a shift in the cultural practices over this time period.

How do modern springtime prairie fires differ from fires at other times of the year? The year can be roughly broken into several periods, from a plant's perspective. There is the latter half of the growing season when the plants are sending a lot of their energy down to the roots. This allows them to store energy through the winter and use that energy to emerge the following growing season. There is the dormant season, fall through winter into early spring. Then there is the period of time in late spring and early summer when plants are moving energy from the roots up to the shoots, using energy captured by photosynthesis last year to supplement this year's growth. That's an oversimplification, but that's generally how plants work.

How plants respond differently to fire and other disturbances during those periods is important. We can't simply say spring, summer, and fall fires (R. A. Henderson et al. 1983; Lovell et al. 1983). An early spring fire, when plants are dormant, may be more similar to a fall fire, when plants are dormant, than to a late spring fire when many plants are starting to actively grow. Burns three weeks apart in the spring can produce different responses from the plants (Towne and Owensby 1984).

There are a number of native cool-season grasses and forbs such as prairie smoke, pasqueflower, shooting star, the prairie violets, and others that emerge early and don't do well if the prairie is only managed with mid- to late-spring burns (Glenn-Lewin et al. 1990; R. A. Henderson

1990a, 1990b). Spring fires halved the abundance of the early blooming common golden alexander, but abundance almost tripled following an August burn (Howe 1999a).

Mid-summer burns usually damage the dominant grasses such as big bluestem and Indian grass. This should reduce their competitive abilities and favor the sub-dominant plants (Howe 2000). Overall richness, native prairie richness, and richness of early, mid, and late-season flowering species were all higher after the late-summer burn compared to spring burns in Illinois prairie. Early flowering species richness can increase over 650 percent with the late-summer burns (Copeland et al. 2002). Overall perennial forb cover can increase in winter and fall burns compared to spring. Purple prairie clover increased the most in autumn and spring burn treatments, while white prairie clover increased the most in the winter burn (Towne and Kemp 2003). The fact that the two closely related prairie clovers have different responses shows that every species responds differently to fire, or any other management activity or disturbance.

Within the grasses, big bluestem and Indian grass respond most positively under late-spring burning, while little bluestem did best with an early or mid-spring burn. June grass did best with a winter burn. Perennial forbs as a group did best with an early spring or winter burn (Towne and Owensby 1984).

All that said, no one can simply say that burning at a particular time is "good" or "bad." It all depends on the species or suite of species under consideration and what plant species a manager wants to promote or suppress. With any management, we are benefitting some species and hurting others by directly damaging the plants, altering the environment, or suppressing competing species (Hoover and Bragg 1981; Copeland et al. 2002).

When talking about plant richness or diversity, we tend to focus on the forbs. Talking about productivity, or the biomass of the prairie, moves the conversation largely to the grasses. In most ecosystems, there is a significant carryover of aboveground plants from one growing season to the next. Trees in the forest or cacti in the desert don't completely die back to the soil surface and emerge from the ground again the next year. However, that's exactly what happens in prairies and most other grasslands. The height of the living grass in spring is essentially zero. By late summer, the grass can be well over the heads of most people. That's a significant change in just a few summer weeks. Because so much of the prairie is grass, and because so much of grass is meristem tissue, the actively growing part of a plant, prairies will respond to changes in rainfall, temperature, and other aspects of climate and weather more dramatically than most other ecosystems.

One of the most studied parts of the prairie is the variability in the height or biomass of the vegetation, mostly grasses, from year to year. In a desert, forest, or tundra it can be hard to tell the difference between a wet and dry year. In the prairie the grass during a dry year may not make it halfway to your knee. In a wet year, the grass in that same spot may be over your head. The range of annual variability in productivity is much greater in tallgrass prairie than other grassland, forest, desert, and tundra ecosystems (Knapp and Smith 2001). Figure 4 shows the variability in the average height of little bluestem and big bluestem on annually burned upland prairie in watershed 1D at Konza Prairie.

Average height of big bluestem ranged from 1.7 to 4.1 feet, more than a two-fold change between wet and dry years. The average height for little bluestem is 1.1 to 2.7, again more than a two-fold change in grass height. Just as interesting, in some of the wetter years little bluestem is taller than big bluestem is in the drier years.

In most ecosystems, there is a single dominant factor in most seasons of most years that limits productivity. Alpine and arctic ecosystems are limited by cold temperatures that in turn limit water availability. Deserts are limited by hot temperatures and low rainfall. The understory of most forests is light-limited during the growing season. The prairie is perhaps unique in that different limiting factors dominate in different years or under different management regimes.

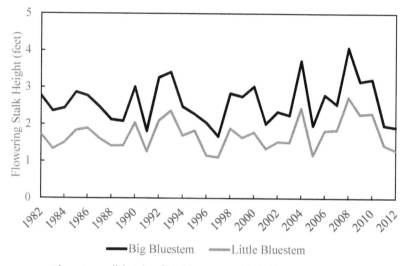

FIGURE 4. Flowering stalk height of big bluestem and little bluestem on upland soils in watershed 1D at Konza Prairie Biological Station, which is burned every spring. Data courtesy of Konza Prairie Long-Term Ecological Research program.

Picture a prairie that has burned annually for several years. Each year the fire removes all the thatch, allowing full light exposure on the soil surface and on the emerging plants. The nitrogen that was in the thatch literally goes up in smoke and is lost to the system. An annually burned prairie will have abundant amounts of light but may be limited by the amount of nitrogen in the soil.

Another prairie hasn't burned for several years. There is a build-up of thatch that covers the soil surface several inches thick. This keeps the soil surface darker and cooler. As that thatch decomposes, it releases nitrogen back into the soil. This prairie may have more nitrogen than the annually burned prairie, but it will be limited by the amount of light at the soil surface.

Now, imagine a prairie that is burned every fourth year. Burning removes the thatch, allowing plenty of light onto the soil surface where the emerging plants can use it. Nitrogen has accumulated in the soils for several years. Now, neither soil nitrogen nor light on the soil surface is limiting. In this case, there will be a pulse in the productivity of the vegetation with more growth than in either of the other two scenarios. This is called the Transient Maxima Hypothesis. In the following quotes, notice how many different factors the scientists bring up, all of which control, directly and indirectly, the productivity of the prairie. How those factors interact is just as important.

> Productivity is higher during a transition period when the relative importance of an essential resource is changing than during an equilibrium interval generated by a single resource limitation. These "transient maxima" are both characteristic and easily measurable in the tallgrass prairie because of the unpredictable climate and ecological constraints such as grazing and recurrent fires that modify water, nitrogen, and light availability. (Seastedt and Knapp 1993)

> Thus, patterns of productivity in tallgrass prairie are best explained within the context of a nonequilibrium system where the relative limitations of N [nitrogen], energy, and water vary across multiple scales in both space and time. (J. M. Blair 1997)

If all those dynamics sound complicated, they are. And they once again point to the nonequilibrium conditions in the prairie. The limiting factor for productivity changes from place to place and year to year. A lot of those dynamics are driven by disturbances from fire, grazing, and fluctuations in the weather.

With this as the background, we can look at the range of factors that affect plant growth and productivity. As we walk around on the prairie, one of the first things we notice is the sometimes harsh, even blinding, sunlight. That's a human perspective with our eyes several feet off the ground. At the soil surface, underneath the thatch, only about one third of 1 percent of the light reaches the soil surface (Knapp 1984). It's very dark for plants trying to emerge from the soil.

Soil temperature is another factor. The thatch forms an insulating layer of the soil, keeping the soil that was frozen all winter cool into spring. Many times I've found a thin layer of snow under some of the thickest grass well into late spring.

Fire itself doesn't warm the soil. The fire moves quickly, and heat goes up. It's not unusual to walk through a recently burned prairie and find plastic tools, plastic trash, or shotgun shells that are barely damaged.

However, the black, ash-covered soil absorbs sunlight in the days following the fire and that does warm the soil and stimulates plant growth. Surface temperatures were seven degrees Fahrenheit higher in burned compared to unburned prairie (Hulbert 1988). At a half inch, four inches, and eight inches deep, the soil can be nine to ten degrees warmer under a burned prairie (Ehrenreich and Aikman 1963; Hulbert 1969) well into the spring. By mid-June, there is enough shading from the growing plant canopy that the differences between the soil under burned and unburned prairie are smaller.

Thatch continues to build up each year until about year four. Four years after a burn, thatch accumulates and breaks down at about the same rate (Ehrenreich and Aikman 1963). Therefore, a prairie that burned four years ago and fourteen years ago will have about the same amount of thatch.

Thatch isn't bad. Birds use thatch as nesting material. Among the insects, there are hundreds to thousands of species who live in and feed upon this thatch. In drought years, unburned prairie is sometimes more productive than burned areas (Knapp et al. 1998), possibly because the thatch layer reduces water loss from the soil.

Legumes are an interesting family of plants to study in relation to fire. Unlike most other plants, legumes can fix their own nitrogen in a symbiotic relationship with *Rhizobium* bacteria in root nodules. If annual or frequent fires lower soil nitrogen, then legumes should have a competitive advantage. Indeed, legumes in an annually burned prairie are 25 percent of the plant biomass, but legumes were only 11 percent of the plant biomass in unburned prairie (Towne and Knapp 1996).

Another effect of fire is that it stimulates flowering and seed production. Big bluestem increases flowering by up to 3,700 percent, little bluestem by up to 1,200, and Indian grass by 660 percent (Glenn-Lewin et al. 1990). Anyone who has walked through a recently burned prairie knows how much fire can stimulate flowering among the forbs. This can be especially handy when land managers plan harvests for future restorations.

Let's circle back to one of the themes of this book, ecological disturbance. Is fire a disturbance in tallgrass prairie? One of the issues with this question is "more in semantics than in ecological substance" (Evans et al. 1989), and the answer is "exacerbated by terminological baggage in which the word *disturbance* has a strictly negative connotation" (Collins 1990). A robust definition of fire in tallgrass prairie as a disturbance "has proved elusive" (Evans et al. 1989).

Fire does recycle nutrients and creates a much different light environment at the soil surface. Altering resources is one common effect of disturbances. Fire alters the habitat for and populations of many animal species. Fire probably doesn't lead to much mortality, at least among grassland plants.

Following the Intermediate Disturbance Hypothesis described in Chapter 5, it makes sense that a high level of disturbance lowers diversity. The only species that survive the frequent disturbances are the weedy, ruderal plants. In a typical ecological scenario, disturbances have the greatest impact on the dominant species. Hurricanes and tornadoes often do the most damage to the largest trees in the forest. However, in prairie, the opposite is true. With more disturbance, greater fire frequency, the dominant grasses become more dominant (Glenn-Lewin et al. 1990; Knapp et al. 1998). Tallgrass prairie never follows the rules.

Looked at another way, if fire is needed to maintain the diversity and productivity of the prairie, can it be a disturbance? If this is the case, is the lack of fire the disturbance?

> [F]ire-induced disruptions and alterations can maintain the status
> quo. (Evans et al. 1989)

> Investigators now realize than an unnatural habitat is one in
> which disturbances have been reduced, altered, or eliminated.
> That is, disturbance—in its common usage as an alteration with
> a detrimental effect—may in fact be the absence of such pertur-
> bations while regular disruption of the status quo may be the
> norm. (Reichman 1987)

Without fire, most prairie will convert to shrubland or forest. Therefore, we could see fire as a factor that keeps grasslands from becoming forests. Is the eastern tallgrass prairie a forest disturbed by fire or a grassland maintained by fire? Where else but the tallgrass prairie does disturbance or disruption equal status quo? The prairie is a constant and perennial source of confusion.

Today fires and the well-trained people who set those fires play a strong role in the conservation and maintenance of the remaining remnants of prairie as well as other midwestern grasslands. Unfortunately, prairie managers cannot ignore that fire has a strong cultural component to it. News coverage of western fires every summer includes words like destruction, catastrophic, devastation, etc. And, unfortunately, these fires can cause catastrophic property loss, and too often loss of life. However, no one ever mentions fire renewing or rejuvenating the ecosystem and that the historical policy banning fires largely caused many of today's issues.

One of the first lessons children learn is "don't play with matches." (In no way is this book advocating that children *should* play with matches!) Then add Bambi and Smokey the Bear as cultural icons who strongly reinforced a "fire is bad" mindset. Some have called Smokey the Bear the best public relations campaign ever invented. Prairie advocates may not buy into that line of thinking.

Smokey the Bear has perhaps been the worst enemy of the prairie chicken. (Hamerstrom 1980)

Today most prairie managers burn in the spring. There are at least a couple reasons for this. From a ranching perspective, spring burns stimulate growth of the grass for summer pastures. Wildlife agencies, whose primary clientele are often hunters, burn in the spring so that there are stands of cover by the fall hunting season. In larger prairies, managers can burn different parts at different times of the year and still leave plenty of habitat for hunting and overwinter cover for the birds.

Often managers simply rotate their management within a large prairie. For instance, they may try to burn a different quarter of the prairie every fourth spring. However, this is giving the entire prairie the same treatment, spring burn, just done in different years. Could this homogenize the prairie after a time?

Would it be better to always burn one area in the spring and always burn other areas in the late summer or fall? This would give a somewhat "predictable" area for species that thrive under each type of burn. For instance, the area burned in spring will have a high density of warm-season grasses and late summer asters. The area burned in the fall will have a high density of early-blooming forbs, which would be beneficial for a number of pollinators.

In this way, would the plant community in each part of the prairie start to diverge and overall diversity increase? Early-season and mid-season blooming species "virtually disappeared" in plots burned in the spring. These species made up 32 percent of the cover in the summer-burned prairies (Howe 1995). Likewise, the dominant late-flowering species made up 92 percent of the cover in the March-burned prairie but only 47 percent of the cover in prairie burned in summer (Howe 1994b). Would having areas dominated by these different groups of plants because of varying fire season increase overall diversity across the whole site?

Biologically, managers should probably mix up their burning seasons. However, there are some practical considerations. It takes a lot of specialized equipment and staff to conduct prescribed fires. If a crew burned yesterday, it's pretty easy to burn today because all the equipment is ready to go. It may be a challenge to get all the burn equipment and crew together for a small number of summer or fall burns.

Alternatively, spreading a fire season out into late summer and fall may allow managers to get more acres burned. In some cases, they can bring in specialized equipment and staff from outside their region for an off-season burn. Those crews are often busy during the regular burn season. (Off-season and regular season vary by location.)

In addition to the when, managers think about how much to burn. In a perfect world, managers would cut firebreaks in the middle of every prairie and burn only half or less of the prairie at any one time. This leaves some nesting cover for birds and protects populations of pollinators and other invertebrates that overwinter aboveground.

However, nothing in life is ever ideal. Managers don't want to mow firebreaks during the burn season, that's for burning. If they want to burn a prairie in the spring, they will usually mow firebreaks in the fall. That means a truck, trailer, tractor, and mower, and staff have to drive out to the prairie, mow the breaks, and drive back. Depending on the distance, that can be an entire workday for multiple staff. Then in the spring, a crew has to drive to the prairie to burn it. They now have to burn along a firebreak with fuel—grass—on the other side. This requires a lot of time, equipment, and staff.

Alternatively, they can burn the entire unit at once. They don't need to visit in the fall. Because midwestern prairies are often bordered by agricultural fields, there's less need to defend or protect any grass during the fire. The fire can be done faster, with fewer people, less equipment, less expense, and often more safely.

In the firebreak scenario, a crew could be doubling their time while halving their acres. Many times accomplishments are totaled by acres, or the quantity of burn, instead of the quality of burn. More is always better when reporting accomplishments, especially if next year's funding is tied to this year's accomplishments. There isn't a right or wrong answer in the shared scenarios. In a time of shrinking budgets and fewer staff, land managers often have to make difficult decisions.

Without Native Americans frequently using fire over the millennia there may not have been an eastern tallgrass prairie in the past. Without well-trained fire crews today there will be no prairie in the future.

Ashes to Ashes

YESTERDAY WAS ALL ABOUT meteorology, physics, and chemistry. And noise. There was the roar and crackle of fire, the further roar of several pumps and engines, and although there was good radio discipline, there was some chatter. We kept our eyes up, looking at smoke and wind, always thinking about the next stage of the fire, always thinking about how we would react if the fire escapes.

Today it's about botany and ornithology as the pup and I walk through a blackened landscape. It's somewhere between quiet and silent, not even the sounds of dead grasses rubbing against denim. Each boot and paw print raises a small black cloud. Although there is a beautiful sky overhead, our eyes look down. Once cloaked in knee-high thatch, the prairie is stripped bare by the flames.

There's so much to learn in this landscape. There are tightly woven nests that the fire raced over. If the eggs are still there, it's not hard to tell if the nest was successful or not last year. Eggs that hatched versus those that were bitten into look quite different. There are the runways of voles. Ideally, we'll spot an ivory-white antler against the black and have a souvenir for the day.

What I hope I don't find is one of this year's nests. However, prairie birds are champion re-nesters. While we may sacrifice a few nests that will quickly be replaced by the same hens, we've created better habitat for all birds to nest in for the next couple years. The balance sheet is in our favor.

Three hundred years ago any bison in the area might have been immediately attracted to the area, first for the minerals in the ash and later for the first tender, young, succulent, nutritious green shoots of grass. In another day or two, these blackened acres will green up. We won't see green in the adjacent unburned grassland for another couple of weeks.

Today there are scores of birds in the ash and flying overhead. They are probably feasting on roasted insects, insect eggs, and plant seeds that are now exposed on the soil surface. What's most interesting is that the adjacent grassland is silent. The fire seems to have attracted everyone over here.

The black ash left after the fire will quickly warm the soil in a few sunny days, jump-starting the metabolism of all eggs or larvae under the soil's surface. In a few more days, there will be even more insect protein hopping around in the ash. To demonstrate the point, we watch a whirlwind run across the burn, picking up the finest ash particles and launching them scores of feet into the air. The little tornado clearly sprang from the heated air just above the ash.

The wetlands are full of ducks, little bothered by all the heat and excitement of yesterday. The cattails still release the occasional puff of smoke, probably from some long-dead smoldering cottonwood. I've seen fire crash into one side of a wetland, flushing the ducks, who then circle once and settle back on the water before the fire has completely wrapped around the cattails.

In a few weeks we'll find pheasant chicks, able to forage on the abundant insects and move around freely without crawling through all the thatch. The hen probably nested in the unburned grass across the road, but she knows where to take her chicks to find the most food.

Today the overwhelming color of the landscape, from a distance, is black. Black is an oversimplification. Headfires move fast and leave coarse black ash behind. Backfires burn slower and cooler, leaving a fine gray ash. It's easy to see patterns in the colors once you know what to look for. Where did the headfire rush forward on a gust of wind? Where did an eddy in the wind cause a brief backfire? On the downwind side of the burn, where did the backfire meet the headfire? On the flank fire, how often did the wind direction shift just a couple degrees, slowing or speeding the fire and changing the resulting ash? Up close there are almost as many colors and patterns as the mid-summer prairie, just a different palette of shades and tones.

In a few weeks, black ash will be a memory and these acres will be blanketed with flowers that cover the spectrum of the rainbow. Unlike the phoenix, prairie birds are not reborn from the ashes of fire . . . but their habitat is.

CHAPTER 8

Prairie Remnants

Grass heals over the scar which our descent into the bosom of earth has made, and the carpet of the infant becomes the blanket of the dead. — *Ingalls 1905*

I never came upon the place without emotion, and in all that country it was the spot most dear to me. — *Cather 1918*

This old flora, like an old book, should be preserved for its historical associations. We can hardly understand our history without knowing what was here before we were. — *Leopold (1942a)*

Along railroad rights-of-way, and here and there in small patches throughout the state [Iowa], virgin prairie sod is still to be found. — *Hayden 1945*

It is perhaps appropriate that the best assemblages of prairie species are often found today in cemeteries which date from settlement. . . . This prairie, which occupied approximately 13% of the Indiana landscape of 1816, is known to us only through such remnants and from imperfectly formed memories. — *Petty and Jackson 1966*

Local prairie remnants served as our model for species composition and proportion. — *Schulenberg 1970*

MOST OF THE TRIPS the pup and I take to Minnesota prairies today are reminiscent of that first prairie visit three decades ago. It's a long drive through monotonous monocultures of corn or beans to get to a small patch of diverse prairie. Oddly, we probably see more plant species in our first couple steps into the prairie than we saw on the couple hours of driving through the modern agricultural landscape.

Today the prairie is like the sea, but opposite of the way that the metaphor has been used historically. Remnant prairies are small islands of native diversity in an ocean of exotic monocultures. Across a study of Illinois and Indiana prairies, thirty of forty-five prairies were smaller than an acre and only three were larger than five acres (Betz and Lamp 1989, 1992). These prairies were spread across forty-two counties in Illinois and twenty counties in Indiana. Prairies are islands in a sea of corn.

The prairie had two inadvertent saviors. Pioneer cemeteries figure prominently in the tallgrass literature (Figure 5).

> [W]hen the open-grazing days were over, and the red grass had been ploughed under and under until it had almost disappeared from the prairie . . . so that the grave, with its tall red grass that was never mowed, was like an island. (Cather 1918)

> It is an ordinary graveyard. . . . It is extraordinary only in being triangular instead of square, and in harboring, within the sharp angle of its fence, a pin-point remnant of the native prairie on which this graveyard was established in the 1840s. (Leopold 1949)

The other factor was the railroad. First the railroad acquired wide rights-of-way along the tracks that settlers didn't plow. Historically, locomotives would have scattered sparks igniting the prairies each fall that protected them from encroaching woody vegetation.

> The purest remnants of the prairie are often found along the right of way of the older railways which entered the territory before the original prairie was broken. (Shimek 1925)

> The outstanding conservator of the prairie flora, ironically enough, knows little and cares less about such frivolities: it is the railroad with its fenced right-o-way. (Leopold 1949)

Whether along the railroad or in the historic cemetery, these prairies never fail to fill a knowledgeable person with emotion or bring out the poet in the writer.

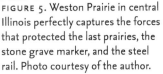

FIGURE 5. Weston Prairie in central Illinois perfectly captures the forces that protected the last prairies, the stone grave marker, and the steel rail. Photo courtesy of the author.

Certainly it saw the successive funerals of the local pioneers as they retired, one by one, to their repose beneath the bluestem. (Leopold 1949)

How ironic that the long steel road which carried the freight of destruction to the prairie should be a refuge for its scattered remnants and that those who turned their lives against a wilderness of grass should sleep in its last few shadows. (Petty 1973)

One way of looking at plant communities that is especially relevant to small, fragmented prairies is the Core-Satellite Hypothesis (Hanski 1982). This hypothesis states that there are some species that are common, the core species, and species that are rare, the satellites. While it was Hanski who formalized this theory, the basic idea had been around for over a century in the prairies.

> Its leading feature is rather the unbounded profusion with which a few species occur in certain localities than the mixed variety of different species occurring everywhere. (Short 1845)

> Thus the extreme importance of a relatively few species stand in great contrast to the relative infrequency of the great majority of the total flora. (Curtis 1959)

Multiple studies found this hypothesis to hold up with prairie plants (Gotelli and Simberloff 1987; Collins and Glenn 1991). The dominant grasses and a few dominant forbs such as some of the goldenrods are abundant and widely distributed. These are the core species and show up at almost every site or every plot within a site. Many of the forbs are loosely scattered at low densities through this grass matrix. These are the satellite species and rarely or sporadically occur, usually at low densities, and usually occur only at a few sites or few plots within a site.

In Wisconsin, 62 percent of the plant species occurred in 20 percent or fewer of the remnant prairies (Curtis and Greene 1949). In a survey of 26 Michigan remnants, 24 percent of species were found in three or fewer sites (P. W. Thompson 1983). In Illinois and Indiana surveys, 42 and 68 percent of the species were found in three or fewer sites (Betz and Lamp 1989, 1992). We can summarize all these studies up with the simple phrase "most species are rare." If we would lose an entire remnant, or a species within that remnant, we may be looking at a regional extinction, not just a local extinction.

This isn't just theory. It has some real, practical implications for managing prairies. The smaller the prairie, the greater the probability of losing species just by bad luck or random events. Imagine a population of a few shooting stars in the corner of a small prairie remnant. A juvenile ground squirrel randomly finds this remnant. It randomly starts digging in this corner, uprooting and killing all the shooting stars. In a large prairie with a large population of shooting stars, the loss of a few individual plants wouldn't matter. No one random event, such as a ground squirrel arriving in an area, could wipe out all the shooting star in a large prairie. However, because this was a small population of plants in a small remnant of prairie, shooting star is now locally extinct in this scenario. If there aren't any other nearby populations, then shooting star is regionally extinct. This is a purely random event. If the ground squirrel had never found this area or had taken up residence in another corner of the remnant, the few shooting star plants would still be there.

> [D]uring the 100 years in which the relics have been isolated there may have been times in which certain species were reduced to very low populations levels, or even wiped out, by temporary meteorological or biotic influences on the particular area of the relic. (Curtis and Greene 1949)

This can lead to "unpredictable species loss to local extinction" (Howe 1994a). This unpredictability and the accidental nature of local extinctions are what keep conservationists up at night. Even with the best planning, the most careful actions, something random can still happen. That's scary when you're talking about the last few individuals of a species, within a single prairie or across a region. Unfortunately, the smaller and more isolated the prairie is, the greater the probability things like this will happen.

For example, one of the most notable species at my first prairie, Smith Pioneer Cemetery in western Indiana, is royal catchfly. There are eight populations of royal catchfly in Indiana, and it is relatively rare through the rest of its range. Smith Pioneer Cemetery contained 895 individual plants. The other seven populations consisted of 165, 64, 58, 53, 25, 6, 5 individuals (Dolan 1995). Smith Pioneer Cemetery makes up 70 percent of the population of the entire state. Fortunately this remnant prairie is protected. However, if it were ever lost, it could represent a loss of almost three-quarters of the population across an entire state. There are many similar species and locations across the prairie region.

In addition to the number of individuals in small populations, there can be genetic issues. Research shows that royal catchfly "populations in the eastern portions of the range to be genetically depauperate compared to western populations" (Dolan 1994).

What is the effect of being a small population on the plants and what are the long-term effects of a population being genetically depauperate? In populations of 150 or fewer plants, seed germination is lower than in larger populations of royal catchfly (Menges 1991). This could be from two issues. The first is inbreeding due to a loss of genetic variability in small populations. When prairies become fragmented and populations get small, the only sources of pollen are from close neighbors, which are often close relatives.

Imagine how large many prairie plant populations were before the prairies were broken. Populations were huge and pollinators could carry pollen, and genes, over long distances. Over time, genes could mix over large regional areas. In today's small, fragmented, isolated populations, plants that are near relatives may be the only plants to pollinate with.

The second issue is reduced pollinator activity (Menges 1991, 1995). A small and isolated population may not attract very many pollinators. Pollinators need to find the isolated patch, which might be a challenge, and there needs to be enough pollen and nectar in that area to make it worth their while to stay in that area. An isolated patch with few plants may not be worth the search effort, the travel to get there, or staying around to gather nectar and pollen.

If all that isn't bad enough, small prairies are actually smaller than they look. Edges are more susceptible to invasive species and other issues. The outer thirty feet of some remnant prairie is less diverse than interior parts of the prairie (Taft 2016). A thirty-foot buffer around the smallest site in this study represented 32 percent of the area. If a small site has the highest quality plant community only on the inner 68 percent of the area, small prairies become tiny prairies.

It's tempting to say that these remnant prairies are a representative of the original tallgrass prairie that once dominated large swaths of the Midwest.

> What is the importance or value of these perhaps ephemeral relicts of a long-vanished prairie? What do they signify? In a sense, I think, they serve us as "control plots." (Berry 1981)

> [T]hese cemetery prairie remnants give us a small glimpse of what the settlers of the pre-settlement Illinois-Indiana first saw when they entered the region. (Betz and Lamp 1989)

However, these remnants often represent the driest, hilliest, steepest, wettest, or rockiest grounds (Figure 6). These remnant prairies were the only places the pioneers couldn't get a breaking plow or drainage ditch. They may not always characterize the wide, flat prairies that once surrounded these remnants and that dominated the Midwest historically. Compare the following quotes to the previous quotes.

> The remnants of the prairie flora still existing along our railroad tracks give only a faint idea of the normal structure of the prairie vegetation. (Gleason 1909)

> The information obtained in this study should be used in reconstruction of the composition of the original prairie in Wisconsin only with very great caution. In most instances the relicts are on atypical sites, so far from the great bulk of the original prairie area is concerned, and have largely persisted because of this fact. (Curtis and Greene 1949)

Just as important, there may be caveats we want to consider if we use these remnants as models of restorations we want to do in the area. They

FIGURE 6. Many of the prairies that remain are those that were too steep or too rocky to plow. Photo courtesy of the author.

are probably the best models we have and the information in these prairies cannot be ignored. However, it might not be the best goal to try to exactly replicate any prairie since each one is slightly different from every other one.

That is what makes the conservation, protection, and management of even the smallest fragments of the original prairie all the more important. Each one of these remnants is unique. There isn't a plant community just like them anywhere else. Just as likely, the remnant may hold a species that doesn't occur anywhere else or only in a couple other places in the region.

With less than 1 percent left in most states, surely, we aren't still losing prairies. We are (Wright and Wimberly 2013; Lark et al. 2018, 2020). Even cemeteries aren't sacred anymore. A story on Minnesota Public Radio reported the plowing of a century-old cemetery. The state archeologist stated, "I'd say it's not unusual." The article goes on to state that people simply "removed the headstones and plowed over the top of it" and that someone "simply piled the headstones in the ditch and plowed up the cemetery" (Gunderson 2012).

Every remaining prairie is different and unique. While that one acre may not characterize the full range of prairie types in that area or region, they are incredibly valuable. Each loss is its own tragedy. In contrast, each prairie saved is a reason for celebration as there probably isn't another prairie like it anywhere in the Midwest.

Prairies I've Known

W E KNOW THIS PRAIRIE. Although the pup has only been
here a couple times, his predecessor visited scores of times
with me. We have walked this prairie many times in every
season over a decade. Although it had been a couple years since our last
visit, I can still close my eyes and map out the plants in my mind.

A decade ago I spent a summer conducting what I thought was a
fairly comprehensive survey of the forb community at this site and
twenty-seven other native prairies in this area on Waterfowl Production
Areas. I surveyed the sites four times that summer. This site came in
third with sixty-seven forb species. I know this prairie.

So here I stand, in the southeast corner of the prairie, just on the west
side of the aspen clone, scratching my head. There should be several
hundred prairie smoke right here. They should be getting their fuzzy,
wispy seedheads and be very easy to see. But I can't find any of them. I
remember so clearly because this is a fairly wet site and prairie smoke is
usually a sandy, hilltop species. I always thought it odd to find it at this
prairie.

We start to walk a tight grid across the area but can't even find a leaf.
After a very frustrating ten minutes we give up and move on to other
areas. After another few minutes we've counted fifteen species in flower.

We wander on looking for flowers to photograph and I stop dead in
my tracks. There are several dozen small yellow ladies slippers in front
of me. Once I see a few, I see more, and more, and more. This site has
always had a high density of small white ladies slippers, but the yellows
were new to me.

After snapping some photos, we move on. And we find ground plum. This makes me scratch my head even more. While abundant at some nearby prairies, I don't remember it here. Like prairie smoke, ground plum usually grows on the dry hilltop prairies, so what is it doing here in this wet prairie? We finally do find one lone prairie smoke, but not in an area I remember seeing it before.

Our next prairie is another favorite, a small hilltop prairie, a few miles to the southeast. And there were several pale penstemon right where we always walk into this prairie. I don't remember that species here, but it's a dry prairie species on a dry prairie. I'm sure I have it in my records.

On the drive home, I think back about another prairie a few miles west and a couple miles north of this one. Again, over the course of a decade the dog and I walked that prairie hundreds of times. If I know these prairies well, I knew that prairie intimately.

One summer, the area right by the parking lot, not some far back corner we rarely got to, was covered with wood lilies. These tall, fluorescent orange flowers are hard to miss. I'd never seen them there before but, on this visit, there were hundreds. The following year there were a few, and the next I couldn't find them at all. While not as distinct as their orange petals of the flower, wood lily leaves are pretty distinctive. I couldn't even find any non-flowering wood lilies in following years.

When we arrived home that evening, the first thing I did was look at my old records. Sure enough, ground plum, small yellow ladies slippers, pale penstemon were all in my records, but not for those sites. All that time and effort and I still missed several species.

Maybe I don't know these prairies? Or maybe no matter how well you think you know a prairie, the prairie always keeps a few surprises.

CHAPTER 9

Prairie Belowground

The fertility and productiveness of the country I had passed through gave me the highest idea of its capacity for maintaining a great agricultural production. It seemed to me as if I had never been in a country where agriculture could be practiced with less expense, or greater success. — *Featherstonhaugh 1847*

Often the share would go the entire "round" without striking a root or a pebble as big as a walnut, the steel running steadily with a crisp crunching ripping sound which I rather liked to hear. — *Garland 1917*

"[P]rairie soils," a secondary product rather than cause of grassed surfaces. — *Sauer 1950*

In fact, the role of vegetation in soil genesis is of such far-reaching effect that it is generally conceded that without vegetation there could be no soil. — *Weaver 1954*

The moles, skunks, and badgers also move large amounts of soil in their activities and contribute greatly to the internal instability of the prairie. — *Curtis 1959*

Out of the raw, lifeless stuff brought by glaciers and winds, rich soils were slowly formed in a complex melding of organic and inorganic agents that was monitored by the master hand of climate. — *Madson 1982*

ONE OF THE MOST interesting experiences for a prairie lover is visiting a restored prairie adjacent to a native prairie. Start in the restored prairie and walk into the native. You'll notice a difference after the first or second step into the native prairie. The soil under the restored prairie, even if the restoration is several years or decades old, is hard. The soil under the native prairie is springy. Cornfield soil is "heavy and solid" while the native sod is "soft, almost fluffy" (Madson 1982).

The prairie soils are why almost all the prairie is gone. They are arguably the most fertile and productive soils on the planet. This fertility was recognized by the early explorers, who wrote "no better soil could be found" (Jolliet 1673), "the soils, which yield bountifully" (DeGannes 1695), and "the fertility and productiveness of the country" (Featherstonhaugh 1847). Oddly, the first settlers seemed to ignore or be ignorant of that fertility "because they did not trust the grasslands" (Archer and Bunch 1953).

> These were a forest people; they had a tradition that you had to clear the trees away before you could farm. . . . They were afraid of the prairies; they looked empty and lonesome. (Peattie 1938)

> The prairies were generally a trackless waste, any man who bought and improved land out in mid-prairie, at that day, was laughed at for his folly. (Faragher 1986)

Indeed, this mistrust of the prairies and prairie soils largely shaped early settlement patterns across the tallgrass region as people continued to farm the forested areas along the edges of the prairie.

> So the early arrivals settled at the edge of the timber, or in a woodland "grove." It was nearly ten years before the first hardy souls ventured out on the prairie to live. By that time the "groves" and "points" (where the trees extended into the prairie along minor streams) were all occupied. Newer arrivals were forced to spread out and so, unknowingly, to get the best lands. (McFarland 1969)

In addition to prairie being unfamiliar to those coming from forested areas, the prairie was lacking one basic ingredient of pioneer life, wood. Houses were built of wood and heated with wood. Food was cooked with wood. Most tools were made of wood. The prairie-forest margin was the best of both worlds for many, wood for all the necessities and pasture for the livestock (Van Tramp 1868; Shimek 1911).

Breaking the prairie nearly broke many early farmers. Their horses and oxen probably fared even worse (Farnham 1846; Madson 1982), even when "five to ten yoke of oxen" pulled the plow (Faragher 1986) or "four horses strained desperately in their traces" (Garland 1917). Those roots had been in the soil for millennia and they did not give up easily.

In fact, it wasn't until John Deere invented the moldboard plow in the 1830s that they could break the prairie at all. The steel blade on the mold-board plow was self-scouring. Before that, with wooden or iron blades, the farmers had to stop frequently to scrape the soil from the plow's surface. Few of the plant roots were easy to break through and they collectively gave a new meaning to the term Gordian knot.

> The tough wirelike roots of the bluestems and prairie clovers twanged with a thousand ringing sounds as each step of the horses pulled the sharp blade forward through the sod of ten thousand years. (Costello 1969)

> As the furrow was cut, there was a constant popping sound, like a volley of tiny pistol shot, caused by the breaking of the tough roots and spurs. This incessant cracking and popping had a slight ring to it, amplified by the tempered steel of the moldboard plow. (Madson 1979)

One of today's most popular prairie plants was decidedly unpopular with those breaking the prairie. The roots of leadplant, known to settlers as prairie shoestring, broke with a "characteristic snap" (Weaver 1954) and "briefly held up the plow before they popped" (Reichman 1987). However, in the end, the prairie was no match for that much steel and muscle.

> At last the wide "quarter section" lay upturned, black to the sun and the garden that had bloomed and fruited for millions of years, waiting for man, lay torn and ravaged. (Garland 1917)

It wasn't just the vast fields soon to be planted to corn and wheat that caused problems. Even a vegetable garden tested the strength of many. If the prairie roots and sod tested twenty oxen, we can only imagination the frustration of those who wielded only a hoe.

> After selecting a garden spot in front of the cabin, on the verge of the prairie, she began to chop at the sod, only to have her garden hoe rebound as if she struck solid rock. The sod was impervious to horticultural tools. (Faragher 1986)

None of us today has seen an endless tallgrass prairie, or walked miles back and forth behind a yoke of oxen. We can assume that each evening they felt a sense of accomplishment. As the breaking continued, some began to regret what they were losing.

> I confess that as I saw the tender plants and singing flowers bow beneath the remorseless beam, civilization seemed like a sad business and yet there was something epic, something large-gestured and splendid in this "breaking" season. (Garland 1917)

> The turned turf lay smooth to the light, and the ancient roots began their rot and deep ferment. This way they broke the prairie's heart, an acre a day at the best. (Peattie 1938)

At the same time, people were beginning to see the problem that would plague the Midwest ever since, erosion.

> One day, just as the early sown wheat was beginning to throw a tinge of green over the brown earth, a tremendous wind arose from the southwest and blew with such devastating fury that the soil, caught up from the field, formed a cloud, hundreds of feet high, a cloud which darkened the sky, sending noon into dusk, and sending us all to shelter. (Garland 1917)

Many of the conservation efforts across the midcontinental grasslands over the twentieth century were focused on soil erosion. Prairie soils have a date, perhaps an arbitrary one, which we can associate with them: March 21, 1935.

On that day a black mass of blowing dirt moved across Washington, DC, blotting out the midday sun. Conveniently, and well planned out in advance, Hugh Bennett was testifying in Room 333 of the Senate Office Building on the need for more and better soil conservation practices. He procrastinated, delayed, and read reports to drag out the time. Eventually one of the Senators stated, "It is getting dark. Perhaps a rainstorm is brewing." Then Bennett began his testimony (Brink 1951).

Erosion had long marked and left its name on the midwestern landscape. Minnesota, known for its ten thousand crystal clear lakes, is actually named after a sediment-filled river (Keating 1823; Nicollet 1838). The prairie region has two Red Rivers, one on the boundary between North Dakota and northern Minnesota, and one between Oklahoma and Texas. The name Red River implies that they were rarely crystal clear. The Platte River was too thick to drink and too thin to plow, while the Mississippi River has always been famously muddy.

Lewis and Clark's journals also show numerous references to siltation or sedimentation. As the Corps of Discovery started to move up the Missouri River, they made comments about muddy water or the riverbanks falling into the water on May 15th, May 24th, May 29th, June 1st, June 10th, June 14th, and June 15th. And that was just the first month of the expedition.

Prairie soils are actually a product of erosion. The parent material for the Midwest's soils came from farther north, dragged down by the glaciers. Other material came from the west, washed down from the Rocky Mountains or blown in on the winds. These wind-blown soils were called loess, with the most well-known deposits being the Loess Hills of western Iowa. In some places, glacial deposits were over six hundred feet thick (Mutel 2008). Although locked in place by roots after the prairie established, in the late Pleistocene, some of the dust storms may have rivaled or been larger than the human-caused dust storms of the 1930s (Seastedt 1995).

Geology, glaciers, wind, and rivers create dirt. Biology, plants, animals, fungi, and microbes create soil.

We may not say that the soil of the prairie patches, which is unlike all other soils of the region, is responsible for the development of the prairie, but rather, the long occupancy by grassland has resulted in the development of this particular soil. (Braun 1928a)

Prairie grass communities preceded the prairyerths, but prairyerths once established favor the continuation of prairie. (Transeau 1935)

Virtually every terrestrial form of plant and animal, from microbe to mammal, has an impact on soil formation. (Reichman 1987)

Before we continue, our story of America's tallgrass prairie must take a brief detour to Europe in the 1640s. There a chemist named Johannes Baptista Van Helmont started the research that eventually informed us about how plants grow. In his day, people thought that plants grew aboveground by absorbing or removing material from belowground.

Van Helmont placed a willow shoot weighing five pounds into two hundred pounds of dried soil. He watered the willow and watched it grow for five years. He then carefully dug up the willow and found it weighed 169 pounds. He dried and weighed the soil and found the soil weight had only decreased by two ounces.

What Van Helmont had inadvertently discovered was photosynthesis, the capture of light by plants and the conversion of light energy into plant biomass through the process of carbon capture. Some of the carbon captured from the air in photosynthesis ends up as or in the roots. Those roots eventually die and become soil. The carbon that makes the soil black comes from the clear air and bright sunlight.

The grassland vegetation has exerted a powerful influence as a soil-builder. Plants, which introduce the living, biological factor into soil formation, return much more to the soil than they take from it. (Weaver 1968)

Belowground, the roots compete for water and nutrients in the dark as much as the leaves compete for sunlight aboveground. This is why there are so many roots at so many different depths within the soil. One of the easiest places to see this competition is in restorations. In the initial phases of the prairie restoration, managers usually try to kill off as many of the existing plants as possible. This means there's very little competition. Whatever species gets there first and gets established can quickly crowd out others. This often happens when too much grass seed is used relative to forb seed in the initial seeding, but sometimes forbs can use this to their advantage also.

Thus, when the reputedly very conservative rattlesnake master (*Eryngium yuccifolium*) was introduced in a few places in the University of Wisconsin Arboretum, it literally exploded, making a solid stand several acres in extent, almost to the exclusion of all other plants. The blazing stars, yellow coneflowers, and prairie docks have done the same. (Curtis 1959)

Burrowing through all that soil to get to deeper water takes a lot of effort and energy on the plant's part. That points to one of the differences between roots, belowground, and shoots, aboveground. When shoots grow, they move upward into air. When roots grow, they move down into rough, abrasive soil. However, soils are generally moist, and temperatures don't change much. Shoots aboveground have to deal with blazing hot afternoons, drying winds, and thunderstorms. Aboveground is a very dynamic environment, while belowground is relatively stable.

Prairies are famous for their deep roots. Prairie rose can send roots twenty feet into the soil, while dotted blazing star can send roots sixteen feet down. The primary root of compass plant can go down almost fourteen feet (Sperry 1935; Weaver 1954).

However, not all plants sink all their roots this deep; 43 percent of roots of big bluestem are in the top four inches of soil and 78 percent of the roots are in the top twelve inches. When it rains, these roots are able to absorb a large percentage of the water that soaks into the soil (Weaver

1968). Similar studies found that 59 percent of prairie roots were in the top two inches and 87 percent were in the top ten inches (Dahlman and Kucera 1965).

Roots are important to prairie plants and plants make a large early investment in their roots. After a summer's growth, button blazingstar was three inches tall but three feet deep (Weaver 1954). In the first seventy days, big bluestem roots grow 21 inches into the soil. Cumulatively, all those roots add up. After three years, there were 5.5 tons of roots per acre in a big bluestem planting (Weaver 1968).

In my own restoration efforts, I started some prairie turnip seed in peat pots. I pulled one seedling from the soil approximately six hours after it broke the soil surface. The shoot was about a quarter inch above the soil while the root had already grown almost six inches below the surface.

Some plants are able to live, directly or indirectly, off the efforts of other plants. This can have some interesting effects on plant diversity and abundance. Lousewort or wood-betony is a hemiparasite of prairie plants. Hemiparasite roots graft onto other roots and steal water, minerals, or carbon molecules while still conducting their own photosynthesis. The best plants to parasitize are the common and dominant species such as big bluestem.

Lousewort can influence the entire plant community by reducing the dominance of some grasses. Plant diversity correlates to the amount of lousewort in the prairie (Hedberg et al. 2005). In Wisconsin, lousewort reduced the flowering of the dominant grasses by 90 percent and leaf height by 50 percent. Seven years after researchers introduced lousewort, seventeen species of forbs bloomed in the area where lousewort was established and the dominant grasses were reduced (R. A. Henderson 2003). False toadflax, northern bedstraw, and pussy-toes are species that are either hemiparasitic or allelopathic. Allelopathy is when one plant secretes a chemical into the soil that suppresses nearby plants. These species "appear to be agents of change" (R. A. Henderson 2003) because of the effects they have on overall species diversity by reducing the dominance of a few species.

There's more than soil and roots under that grass. Most of us associate fungi with rot and decay. Some prairie fungi play this role. However, other fungi are vital to the survival of some plants. The roots of many prairie plants have a mutualistic relationship with mycorrhizal fungi. These are fungi that penetrate into or wrap around plant roots. They send strands out into the soil called hyphae. The plant gives the fungi carbon from photosynthesis and the fungi provides chemicals from the soil that the plant may have trouble obtaining, especially phosphorus. The fungal hyphae increase the functional surface area of the root and can aid in water absorption. Mycorrhizae may also benefit host plants by improving defenses against grazers and defending against pathogenic fungi (Wilson and Hartnett 1997).

Some species, such as certain orchids, are especially dependent on mycorrhizae. There are at least seventy-five species of fungi associated with eastern prairie fringed orchid across Illinois and Michigan (Zettler and Piskin 2011). Orchids are one group of plant that may need mycorrhizae for seed germination and plant establishment.

The ability of the dominant grasses such as big bluestem and Indian grass to exploit these symbiotic relationships may be a large factor in explaining their competitive ability. When researchers suppressed fungi, the dominant grasses declined and other species became more abundant (Wilson and Hartnett 1998; Hartnett and Wilson 1999).

They are small, but there are a lot of animals down in the soil also and they may have major effects aboveground. Invertebrates may consume up to 40 percent of the annual production of roots and there may be a greater mass of earthworms than cattle on the prairie (Joern 1995). Grazing belowground is different than grazing aboveground. Water enters plants through root hairs and leaves plants through tiny holes in the leaves called stomates. When leaves are grazed, there are fewer holes to lose water. When roots are grazed, there are fewer roots to absorb water. Losing roots may be more detrimental to the water balance in plants than losing shoots.

Flint Hills prairie has at least 228 species of nematodes in the soil

(Orr and Dickerson 1966). There are 470,000 nematodes per square foot under little bluestem in South Dakota mixed-grass prairie (Ingham and Detling 1984). Those nematodes consumed more overall grass biomass than prairie dogs and bison. In many grasslands, nematodes "constitute a major portion" of the prairie fauna (Smolik and Lewis 1982). An acre of prairie soil may contain 1.2 million earthworms; 405,000 macroinvertebrates; 202.4 million microinvertebrates; and 22.3 billion nematodes (Ransom et al. 1998).

Before Euro-American settlement, approximately 52,860,000 acres of prairie covered Iowa and Illinois (Samson and Knopf 1994). If we assume the same relative densities of soil invertebrates across those two states, that gives us 64,200,000,000,000 earthworms; 21,400,000,000,000 macroinvertebrates; 10,700,000,000,000,000 microinvertebrates; and a whopping 1,177,000,000,000,000,000 nematodes in the prairie soils within Iowa and Illinois.

Earthworms leave numerous channels that allow air, water, roots, and other invertebrates to move through the soil more easily. Earthworms will pass through their gut 10 percent of the total soil organic matter in the top six inches of soil (James 1991). Put another way, earthworms could consume and pass through their gut the entire upper layer of soil every decade.

> The surface horizons of the prairie soils are, in actuality, invertebrate fecal material, intertwined with living organisms of every trophic status. (Clearly, Mom was right when she told us to go wash our hands following any soil explorations!) (Seastedt 1995)

When roots die, they also leave channels in the soil. Earthworms and other invertebrates can follow these channels and enlarge them. This allows both air and water into the soil and provides pathways for soil organisms to move. In native prairie, approximately a quarter of the root systems are replaced each year (Dahlman and Kucera 1965). That's a lot of death and turnover and decaying roots leaving channels between the soil particles. That's also a lot of carbon added to the soil every year.

Ideally, soil should be 50 to 60 percent particles and 40 to 50 percent pore space. Depending on the soil type, time of year, and when it rained last, those pores will be taken up by some combination of air and water.

While the soils are open and porous, the soil particles are also chemically cemented together into aggregates. Much of the humus that increases aggregation of soil particles comes from decaying roots (Weaver 1947). Early settlers cut bricks from sod and built sod houses, or soddies. Some of them stood for decades. That's how well aggregated those soils used to be. It's hard to imagine forming the soil in a modern cornfield into a brick and that brick surviving a rainstorm.

Although there are dozens of other elements in soil besides the carbon derived from photosynthesis, perhaps the most important element from a plant's perspective is nitrogen. The nitrogen cycle is very complex because nitrogen can take so many forms. There is nitrate (NO_3^-), nitrite (NO^-), nitrogen (N_2), ammonium (NH_4^+), and ammonia (NH_3) to name some of the most important compounds. Denitrification is the conversion of nitrate to nitrogen. Fixation is the conversion of nitrogen to ammonia. Nitrification is the conversion of ammonium to nitrate. Mineralization is a multistep process where organic nitrogen, nitrogen in carbon containing molecules, is converted to inorganic nitrogen that can be taken up by plants. Immobilization is when soil microbes take up nitrogen compounds. Clearly, studying nitrogen requires a specialized vocabulary.

While modern society requires expensive power plants and fossil fuels to capture nitrogen for fertilizers and other uses, in the prairie much of the same work is done with flowers and bacteria. Specifically, members of the legume family have a bacteria called *Rhizobium* in nodules along their roots. The root nodules provide a safe habitat and carbon for the bacteria while the bacteria are able to break that tough chemical bond and create usable forms of nitrogen for the plant.

So why is nitrogen important to plants? First, the nitrogen atom in these compounds can have a range of electrical charges, from -3 in ammonia (NH_3) to +5 in nitrate (NO_3^-). Numerous microbes are able to use these changes from one chemical to the next and changes in the charge on the nitrogen for energy (Schlesinger 1991). Nitrogen is one of the most important elements in proteins and amino acids, critical to all forms of life.

As complex as the prairie is in the sunlight, with blossoms and bees and butterflies and bison, the unseen prairie below our feet may be as complex, and probably more diverse.

Only Gravel Ridges Are Poor Enough

W E ARRIVED AT OUR favorite gravel hilltop prairie late in the morning late in the month of April. It was a chilly 43 degrees with a stiff southern wind trying to disperse the clouds overhead. A merlin flashed off the fencepost as we pulled up. Not a classic prairie bird, but a good sign. The pasqueflowers were in bloom, so it was worth the long drive this morning.

This is a sandy, gravelly, steep-sloped hill prairie between two large wetlands. It's a tiny islet in a sea of row crops. From up here we can see for several miles in every direction. What we see is bare dirt and the little stubble that hasn't been disced under yet. There's one tractor working the fields, a rooster tail of dirt blowing away behind it.

The grasses and flowers under our feet may have once felt the hooves of bison or elk, but the roots and soil never felt the rip of a steel plow. Those roots below and blanket of leaves above have held the soil together for all these centuries.

The pasqueflowers were just beginning to open when we arrived. We drove down to another nearby prairie and oak savanna to hike and birdwatch for a couple hours. When we came back around noon, we could almost watch the flowers open as the day continued to warm. We walked a circuit, checking several flowers every ten minutes or so. There were noticeable changes with each check until the petals had fully opened.

As the air temperature warmed and the flowers open, the air becomes alive with I don't know how many bees. They seem to be buzzing everywhere and each looked different to my uneducated eye. These pasqueflowers are the only plants blooming for several miles in every direction. How does this little hilltop have enough nectar and pollen this time of year to sustain this diversity and abundance of bees? Where are they coming from, and where are they going next? Do they know the world beyond this hilltop or has this hilltop been the sole home for countless generations of these bees?

Much of this book is about change. The prairie has changed over the millennia since the Pleistocene. There were occasional floods and extended droughts. There were blazing hot summer days and bone-chilling winter nights. Sunny days gave way to afternoon thunderstorms. Blizzards came out of nowhere. Fires swept the prairie on a regular basis. Herds of wildlife grazed the grasses and trampled the soils. With the coming of the plow, the prairie was lost in a few short decades. It was gone before anyone noticed, except for a few hard to get to and out of the way places like this hillside.

In a couple days, the prairie smoke will bloom. In another couple weeks the fluffy, wispy seedheads of both pasqueflower and prairie smoke will be blowing in the wind. These are maybe the only two prairie flowers that are more recognizable as seedheads than flowers. Soon green grass will grow up through brown. Blue-eyed grass, ground plum, and puccoon will follow shortly, and by mid to late summer these will be followed by sixty or more additional species.

Today's changes occur by the hour and minute. From cool to warm, from quiet to buzzing, from closed to open. No visit to the same prairie is ever the same.

CHAPTER 10

Prairie Beasts

[T]he plains were covered with buffalo in every direction. — *Henry and Thompson 1799*

The country is devoid of game. — *Nicollet 1838*

Buffalo herds in the East were never huge, never teeming, never rivaling the truly vast herds that thundered across the Plains. — *Belue 1996*

The question of whether bison and cattle are analogous herbivores may be of less importance than asking how Great Plains plants and animals communities are influenced by . . . management activities. — *Hartnett et al. 1997*

We recommend that the focus of mixed prairie conservation be on developing ecologically sound goals and practices for grazing management, rather than on whether bison or cattle are the more appropriate grazers. — *Steuter and Hidinger 1999*

Where boundaries of warring tribes met, buffer zones of various tribes met, buffer zones of various sizes that neither side occupied became established where some hunting was allowed but was usually light. . . . The importance of these buffer zones is that they left game within them relatively undisturbed and allowed the buildup of herds. — *Flores 2001*

IF THE PUP AND I have a choice between walking a thoughtfully grazed prairie or an ungrazed prairie, it's really not a choice. We'll take the grazed prairie every time. There's more to see, more patterns on the landscape, more plants to identify, and often more birds, butterflies, and bees to see. Identifying plants in full bloom is easy. Identifying grazed grasses provides an enjoyable botanical challenge.

Well-grazed prairies open up so many new questions as we walk and observe. Why did the animals graze here instead of there? Why did they graze at different intensities in different areas? How does the wildlife re-spond to the grazing patterns?

In reading early descriptions of the North American continent, it's easy to believe that wildlife was lined up shoulder to shoulder from sea to shin-ing sea, and the sun was daily eclipsed by the vast clouds of waterfowl, passenger pigeon, shorebirds, and songbirds. While that was the case sometimes, it wasn't always like that everywhere.

> Animals were so scarce that we suffered much from hunger. (Henry and Thompson 1799)

> On the route from Chicago to Fort Crawford we saw but one deer . . . upon upwards of two hundred miles of prairie land. (Keating 1823)

We've seen how people had a strong influence on the prairie landscape and vegetation. They also influenced the distribution of wildlife at re-gional scales. Native American groups informally created wide buffers between tribal areas (Hickerson 1965). It was safe for them to travel in their area, but they would minimize travel in these buffer areas to avoid conflict with neighboring groups. Wildlife would concentrate in these areas where they received the least hunting pressure.

> On the banks of this river [Sheyenne River] I am informed they [black bears] are also very numerous, and seldom molested by the hunters, it being the frontier of the Sioux, where none can hunt in safety; so there they breed and multiply in security. (Henry and Thompson 1799)

> Toward 6:00 we pass near a pond where the buffalo come fre-quently to refresh themselves with its salt water; it is a good area for hunting, but the Sioux seldom come here for fear of meeting their enemies. (Nicollet 1838)

Mammalian diversity on the prairie lags behind other groups of ani-mals, such as birds and invertebrates. A review of the Konza Prairie mam-mal list includes American badger, two shrews, one mole, one ground squirrel, one gopher, six species of mice, two voles, one lemming, and two rats, among other species. In other parts of the prairie we can add Franklin's and Richardson's ground squirrels and a few other rodent species. Unfortunately, most of these species are hidden in the grass, out of sight and out of mind to most people. And let's face it, mice are never going to be as charismatic and generate the conservation interest and concern that warblers will.

Other species such as red fox, striped skunk, raccoon, several weasels, and white-tailed deer are more forest or forest-edge species. The coyote is probably a true grassland species, although they do well in almost any habitat.

We often think of elk as a forested species that lives in the mountains. That's because it is the only habitat we have allowed them to persist in. Reading early accounts of the prairie demonstrate that the elk is very much a grassland or grassland-forest edge species.

That said, this chapter will focus on THE prairie animal, the bison. Going back in time, bison evolved in Europe and came to North America over the Bering Land Bridge during a past glacial period 200,000 to 800,000 years ago (Dary 1974). Just like so many iconic prairie plants, the iconic prairie animal isn't originally from the prairies. They aren't even from North America. The modern bison was at least the fourth, and probably smallest bison in North America. The three extinct species include the long-horned bison, the giant bison, and *Bison antiquus* (Geist 1996).

There's one question that almost always comes up before any other. How many bison were there? Many early descriptions left people with images of solid masses of bison.

> You may see them for whole days on each side of you as far as your sight will extend, apparently so thick, that one might easily walk for miles upon their backs. (Pike 1832)

> This plain was literally covered with buffaloes as far as we could see. (Bradbury 1810)

Reports from the 1870s state that the size of herds, or bands or family groups, rarely exceeded sixty, were never greater than two hundred, and that bands of fifteen were the most common (Haines 1970). These small herds were scattered over wide areas with hundreds of yards between bands. There may have been fifteen to twenty bison per acre to twenty-six bison per square mile (Shaw 1995). At a larger scale, the Lewis and Clark Expedition saw bison only on 15 percent of the days they were in the grasslands (Botkin 1995). That's hardly bison standing shoulder to shoulder across the plains and prairies.

Sixty million bison is a commonly cited number and probably dates to Seton (1929). These estimates "contain serious shortcomings" (Shaw 1995), but this number is "as close to religious dogma as a secular society's belief can be" (Lott 2002). Thirty million bison may be a more realistic estimate (McHugh 1972; Flores 1991).

Coming up with any number, no matter how carefully it's done, almost implies there is some right or correct number of bison, or any wildlife, that was supposed to be on the prairie.

> The grass on one hand and the wolves on the other gave the wandering herds of herbivores a social organization and put a premium on proper numbers. (Milne and Milne 1960)

The term "proper numbers" gets back to the balance of nature concept and people wanting the natural world to be predictable and at equilibrium. There's a question that may be more interesting than how many there were. How much did populations fluctuate? To build on that idea, we need to understand what factors, singly or working together, caused the population to fluctuate.

Both Charles Elton, who is sometimes referred to as the father of modern animal ecology, and Aldo Leopold try to dispel the notion of the "balance of nature" (their quotes) as it applies to animal populations. Elton (1930) wrote, "The number of wild animals are constantly varying to a greater or less extent, and the variations are usually irregular in period and always irregular in amplitude. Each variation in the numbers of one species causes direct and indirect repercussions on the numbers of the others, and since many of the latter are themselves independently varying in numbers, the resultant confusion is remarkable." Three years later, Leopold (1933) wrote, "Fluctuation in numbers is nearly universal." These statements provide further evidence that there is no balance in the natural world. Elton also describes how changes in one population can affect many other populations, often in unpredictable ways. His phrase that the "confusion is remarkable" summarizes the prairie pretty well.

Several factors could control the bison population size, or the size of any animal population. We can imagine a period of relatively wet summers and mild winters when the population may have increased significantly. We can also imagine extended droughts or a series of very severe winters that would have reduced the population. Imagine a late winter storm when a herd is probably stressed and fat reserves in their bodies are getting low. First, there is a heavy snowstorm. That is followed by freezing rain, locking everything under a layer of ice. Now, already weakened bison have to plow through deep drifts and break through the ice layer. These winter storms could be a "major check" on bison numbers (Madson 1979). These storms weren't rare. Catastrophic losses of bison to winter weather were "were almost regular events in historic times" (McHugh 1972). Summer droughts would be equally deadly. There are many accounts of early explorers finding areas covered with bison skeletons. It's hard to imagine what, besides the weather, could kill this many animals.

White buffalo skulls and bones glisten everywhere. (Maximilian of Wied 1832)

Here we found the prairie completely black, having been thoroughly burnt over; and soon we came to where the ground was strewed with countless bleached skeletons of buffaloes. (Featherstonhaugh 1847)

Another common observation of early European explorers is bison killed trying to cross rivers, especially in the spring as the ice was starting to break up (Catlin 1844).

> (April 1) It is really astonishing what vast numbers have perished, they formed one continuous line in the current for two days and nights.
>
> (April 18) Rain, downed buffalo still drifting down the river, but not in such vast numbers as before, many having lodged on the banks and along the beach.
>
> (April 30) Drowned buffalo drift as usual.
>
> (May 1) The stench from the vast numbers of drowned buffalo along the river was intolerable. . . . They tell me the number of buffalo lying along the beach and on the banks above passes all imagination; they form one continuous line, and emit a horrid stench.
>
> (Henry and Thompson 1799)

> During the remainder of that day we paddled onward, and passed many of their carcasses floating in the current, or lodged on the heads of islands and sandbars. (Catlin 1844)

If the "horrid stench" was "intolerable," we can only imagine the quality of drinking water along those rivers. If it wasn't ice, fire may have caught and injured entire herds at once.

> Plains burned in every direction and blind buffalo seen every moment wandering about. The poor beasts have all the hair singed off; even the skin in many places is shriveled up and terribly burned, and their eyes are swollen and closed fast. . . . In one spot we found an entire herd lying dead. (Henry and Thompson 1799)

However, not all fires were this intense.

> [T]he fire slowly creeps with a feeble flame, which one can easily step over, where wild animals often rest in their lairs until the

flames almost burn their noses, when they will reluctantly rise, and leap over it, and trot off among the cinders. (Catlin 1844)

These, and similar factors, then have to be weighed against the impact of predation by grizzly bears, wolves, mountain lions, as well as the impact of human hunting on the bison population. Then add disease and parasites.

Next, we can add a spatial component. We can imagine a period of mild climates in the southern prairies and plains when herd size increases. At the same time, a series of severe winters in the north could seriously reduce those herds. Or there could be a mild period in the north while the south suffers a severe drought. Within any region, and between regions, herds were constantly on the move.

Scientists are pretty sure that the vast herds of bison described of the western Plains were not characteristic of the eastern prairies. Given how lush and productive eastern grasslands were compared to the drier and less productive western grasslands, it seems like there was a lot more forage and therefore should have been more foragers: bison, elk, and other grazers. The differences in the amount of grass and the densities of bison "seems an enigma." One possible explanation is that western grasses have higher protein levels than eastern grasses. It was the distribution of protein in the grasses, not the amount of grass, which affected bison distribution (C. W. Johnson 1951).

One major question, both historically and perhaps relevant to modern management, is the prevalence of bison in the tallgrass region, especially the eastern tallgrass region. We know that bison were seen as far east as Maryland in 1612 (Dary 1974). And we know that there were relatively large herds in the southeastern pineries (Belue 1996). How long had they been there, in ecological and evolutionary time? The answer is probably not very long.

Some argue that it probably wasn't until after European diseases started to decimate Native American tribes, and reduce their hunting pressure, that bison moved into the eastern extent of the tallgrass region and beyond (Geist 1996; Flores 2001).

This relates back to the influence of Native Americans on both the land itself as well as wildlife populations. Were there enough people and were they efficient enough hunters to hold wildlife populations at low numbers before European diseases came to North America? Were they efficient enough to exclude an animal like bison from half a continent? What role did human predation play on wildlife numbers relative to predation from four-legged predators, thawing rivers, blizzards, and droughts?

Looked at another way, were Native Americans so effective at habitat manipulation, fire, that they created more grassland habitat in the east, and therefore wildlife, than there would have been without people or with fewer people? Diseases ravaging Native American populations could have had two contrasting effects. The reduced hunting pressure allowed bison to expand eastward. Alternatively, fewer people presumably reduced the amount of fire that could have led to rapid forest expansion and less grassland available to the bison.

Was the wealth of wildlife reported by early European explorers a result of an inherently productive continent? Was it the result of habitat manipulation on a broad scale by Native Americans to favor wildlife? Did introduced diseases create a scenario where "game overran the land" and "the massive, thundering herds were pathological, something that the land had not seen before and was unlikely to see again" (Mann 2005)?

Regardless of the reasons, it appears that bison in the eastern extent of the tallgrass prairie were a relatively recent phenomenon of the last few centuries. This brings up the question of management in the modern day. Was the Mississippi River a barrier to movement (Geist 1996)? If so, is grazing more natural in eastern Iowa, but less natural in western Illinois? Should management of prairies on either side of the river be different because of this?

Had bison been in the eastern tallgrass prairie region for an extended period of time, ecologically speaking? No. Are the plants in this region the same plants in the western tallgrass prairie that are evolutionarily adapted to periodic grazing? Yes. Therefore we might conclude that grazing can be an effective management tool in eastern grasslands, even with a short grazing history, because those prairies are composed of species evolutionarily adapted to grazing.

This doesn't take into account the modern size of the prairies in Wisconsin, Michigan, Illinois, and Indiana. Moving eastward, prairies tend to be smaller and more fragmented. These small fragmented remnants, often dotted with tombstones, are clearly not suited to any type of grazing, no matter how well managed.

For decades, wilderness advocates and conservationists told each other and the general public that livestock are bad. Two of the strongest voices were John Muir in the alpine meadows of California's Sierra Mountains and Edward Abbey in the desert Southwest. Livestock were "hoofed locusts" (Muir 1911) or "a pest and a plague" Abbey (1977). These words are obviously both powerful and inflammatory.

Today, many prairie managers are trying to promote grazing as a management tool. This is leading to some confusion and angst among conservationists. Alpine tundra has a very short growing season and thin soils, while deserts have little rainfall and generally nutrient-poor soils. Neither of these ecosystems has an ecological history of grazing and the plants are not evolutionarily adapted to large animal grazing. As such, it may take years or decades for these ecosystems to recover from even a single grazing event. In this context, Muir and Abbey's comments may be partially or fully justified, even if intended to be provocative.

However, tallgrass prairie isn't tundra or desert. Tallgrass prairie has deep, rich, fertile soils, sufficient rain most years, a long growing season, and is a very productive plant community dominated by species adapted to grazing.

That's not to say that all prairie grazing is good or beneficial to grasslands (Figure 7). It's very easy to graze prairies too much, too often, and for too long and impact their diversity and long-term productivity. Done

FIGURE 7. Overgrazed pasture (top photo) and grazing intended to benefit wild-life habitat at Glacial Ridge National Wildlife Refuge (bottom photo). Photos courtesy of the author.

carefully and thoughtfully, grazing can be beneficial to prairie plants, wildlife, and livestock. Perhaps more than any other management practice, grazing requires close monitoring. Note the contrast in Figures 7a and 7b. One general rule of thumb is that if you can see hooves, especially for too long or too many years in a row, the grass is too short. In the second photo, the bellies of the cattle aren't even visible.

One way to think about sustainable grazing is the old range management adage of "take half, leave half." Take half for this year's grazing, leave half to improve the forage quality for next year. Or put into a conservation perspective, take half for the livestock, leave half for the wildlife.

Taking half can be done in several ways. The grass could be lightly grazed each year, removing about half of the vegetation. An area could be grazed intensively for the first half the summer and completely rested for the second half of the summer. (This does cause some heartburn, especially among ornithologists, since the most intensive grazing is during the nesting season.) An area could be heavily grazed for an entire summer, but then completely rested for a year or more. Each scenario depends on the management objective for the livestock, the vegetation, and the wildlife at a specific location.

Grazers such as bison and domestic cattle prefer to graze on grasses (Plumb and Dodd 1993; Coppedge et al. 1998). When a disturbance decreases one group of dominant plants (grasses) disproportionately, other plants (forbs) increase. Bison select areas with higher densities of big bluestem and lower densities of forbs (Vinton et al. 1993). Reducing the grass in these areas benefits forbs and increases plant species richness (Collins et al. 1998; Towne et al. 2005). Likewise, forb biomass increases with grazing (Vermeire et al. 2004; Elson and Hartnett 2017).

Some have tried to categorize plants as grazing increasers and grazing decreasers (Weaver 1968). Others take this a step further to imply that grazing increasers are weedier species and grazing decreasers are more valuable or higher quality species. This is where cattle and conservation have collided in the past. Supposedly, cattle degrade prairies by eating the "good" plants and leaving the "bad" plants, or the weeds.

That's where management comes in. What is the grazing intensity and stocking rate? How often is the area grazed? How frequent and how long are the rest periods? Are the pastures grazed all season long every year or is there a short pulse of intense grazing? If there's a drought are the cattle pulled off the pasture? A lot of those increaser and decreaser labels were created from pastures that are grazed season-long year after year regardless of the weather.

This gets us back to the Intermediate Disturbance Hypothesis. Too much grazing can be detrimental, but too little grazing could also impact the prairie. The trick for any landowner or manager is to figure out that happy medium between the two that meets the management objective for the site.

> Although overgrazing can severely damage a prairie over time, so can grazing deprivation. . . . The challenge is to determine a pattern and intensity of grazing that reduces dominance by a few species without eliminating the more conservative species. (Davison and Kindscher 1999)

When done carefully, grazing can increase populations of even the most desirable and conservative species. Weaver (1968) listed a number of grazing decreaser species. All the species on his list were legumes. I looked at the average number of plots from 2009–18 in two ungrazed (4A and 4B) and two grazed (N4A and N4D) watersheds on Konza Prairie where each of the species Weaver listed occur. All four watersheds had a four-year burn interval. I didn't do the statistics, but leadplant, ground plum, white prairie clover, purple prairie clover, round-headed bush clover, silver-leafed scurfpea, prairie turnip, and scurfpea were all more common in grazed areas. It's hard to argue that leadplant, prairie turnip, and ground plum are undesirable prairie plants.

There are a few ways in which grazing and fire have similar effects, such as removing the plant canopy. In this way, grazing can be beneficial to some species that emerge early in the spring and don't do well with spring fires. Species such as pasqueflower and prairie smoke emerge early and are low growing. Although they both grow primarily on hilltop or thin-soiled prairies, they can have trouble emerging though even the thin thatch layer of these prairies and grazing may be especially beneficial for these species. In my own adventures, I can find a few prairie smoke scattered around ungrazed sites, but grazed sites often have dense blankets of prairie smoke that sometimes cover several acres.

It's difficult to talk about fire effects, because there can be so many different effects depending on the timing of the fire. The same applies to grazing and grazing effects, as well as the interactions between grazing and fire. One study concluded that relying solely on fire as the "only restoration tool was not effective at achieving a species-diverse prairie community" (Heslinga and Grese 2010). Similarly, a study comparing grazing and fire separately and when used in combination concluded that "to maintain maximum diversity across the landscape, however, both approaches are necessary" (D. L. Larson et al. 2020). Managers can't simply say that burning has this effect and grazing has that effect. It depends on how each tool is used and how many tools the manager is using.

An issue that grazing cannot address is replacing fire. Too often managers use phrases such as "I can't burn it, so I'll graze it instead." Grazing is an ecological disturbance. Fire is an ecological disturbance. They are not synonymous, nor are they interchangeable. Probably the easiest example of this is with red cedar invasion into grasslands. Fire kills cedars. Grazing will cause cedars to invade even faster.

One question people have when it comes to management is whether bison are better than cattle (Noss 1994; Kohl et al. 2013). First, for those who do want to graze their natural area, park, or wildlife area, there is obviously a strong visual and psychological appeal to using bison. Bison may just feel or seem better because they look more natural than a herd of Angus or Hereford cattle.

There are some anecdotal and observational differences to these two species. Bison move around more than cattle and will not concentrate around water as much as cattle. On hot days, bison often head to the hilltops to catch a breeze, while cattle often crowd into the shade along streams where they can do some damage. The grazing preferences of the two vary a little when it comes to favorite plants to graze and they may graze in different patterns. However, it's the management of the beast, not the beast itself, which matters the most (Plumb and Dodd 1994; Hartnett et al. 1997; Towne et al. 2005).

Grazing can give managers flexibility in wildlife habitat management. It's an oversimplification, but with prescribed fire we can have burned or unburned prairie. In some cases, we can burn only parts of larger tracts of prairie. Managers can burn in early spring, late spring, late summer, or fall. But that's still not a lot of variability.

With grazing, there is far more flexibility. Managers can adjust exactly where to graze by using temporary fencing. They can control the stocking rate, timing, and duration to meet very specific management objectives. They can graze season-long or they could flash-graze an area for a few days. They can also remove the livestock early if something isn't going right or the objective was met ahead of schedule. With a fire, once the head fire is lit, it's difficult to bring things to a halt.

Haying is another alternative to grazing. Haying removes nutrients from the area while grazing recycles them back into the soil. Haying is also more homogeneous than grazing. However, haying doesn't require writing a complex grazing plan, installing fencing, or providing water. Managers can work with local cooperators to be very specific about where and when to cut the hay to meet a specific management objective.

Perhaps most importantly, livestock and grazing can be a new, or newer, model for grassland conservation. Done properly, properly sometimes being hard to define, grazing can increase the diversity and productivity of prairies as well as manage and manipulate habitat for a range of wildlife species. As importantly, grazing integrates conservation lands into local agricultural economies, benefitting both wildlife and the ranching community.

An Acceptable Substitute

A FEW WEEKS AGO, dawn echoed with the booming of prairie-chickens. Today we watch marbled godwits circle overhead while upland sandpipers and western meadowlarks serenade us from the tops of fenceposts. I think of Aldo Leopold. "Whoever invented the word 'grace' must have seen the wing-folding of the plover." We see more meadowlarks here than anywhere else.

After a couple of hours surveying plants, my four-legged field assistant and I sit on the tail gate; he snoozes in the mid-morning sun while I snack on an apple. We think about the steak thawing on the kitchen counter, dinner for me and the last couple bites are treats for him.

This is one of my favorite prairies. There are a couple of birds and plants we find only on this prairie. Other plants that are rare or scattered at other sites are abundant here.

As the morning warms, we continue our surveys, my partner close at heel due to the nesting season. There's a new sound now. Under the birdsong, beneath the ever-present prairie wind, there is a buzzing and droning of hundreds of bees. Once I'm aware of it, the hum becomes louder and louder. Looking down, there seems to be a bee on every other flower. If my entomologist friends were here, they might identify as many as a score of different native bee species and who knows how many butterflies.

To our south there are stacks of commercial beehives literally humming with activity. To our northeast a herd of cattle stand knee deep in lush grass and a kaleidoscope of wildflowers. As conservationists, our first instincts are often to think about the birds. Where will the prairie-chickens boom on their spring leks? Where will the sharp-tails raise their broods each summer? That's too narrow of a focus.

Grazing is a working lands approach to habitat conservation. Ruffed grouse and woodcock hunters in the east know the value of careful timber harvests for those birds and their habitat. The same basic principle applies for grassland birds and well-managed grazing.

Beekeepers are another group that work the land. Many honeybees start the year in California's almond groves. From there they may go to the Pacific Northwest to pollinate apple orchards, to New England's cranberry bogs, to the mid-Atlantic states for melons, or Florida for citrus groves.

After the crops are pollinated, many beekeepers return their bees to the plains and prairies for the summer and fall. Prairie wildflowers provide an abundance and diversity of pollen and nectar for the bees. A diverse diet is just as important for bees as a well-balanced diet is for us.

Scientists and writers are always looking for connections, interactions, relationships of one species to another. This morning's apple, tonight's steak, prairie-chicken, godwit, sandpiper, meadowlark, cattle, monarch, honeybee, and thousands of insect species all have one connection: prairie.

Prairie conservationists have natural partners in ranchers and beekeepers. Together, we can be a stronger voice for grassland conservation. Just as importantly, the conservation community can and should listen to them. While most conservationists visit prairies only on the weekend or a few times a year, these people are out every day in all weathers. They know a lot and conservationists have a lot to learn from them.

And it's a two-way street. I was talking to a rancher several years ago who rotated his cattle onto public land for the summer. He saw such a good response in both his pasture and his cattle that he decided to shift the way he manages his own pastures quite dramatically. He learned a lot about his herd when he worked with conservationists to enhance bird habitat.

Aldo Leopold stated that the upland plover, now sandpiper, find cattle an "acceptable substitute" for the bison.

The prairie-chickens, meadowlarks, pollinators, and diversity of plants demonstrate that livestock can benefit the habitat and the wildlife. I would like to think that this diversity and productivity are because of, not in spite of, the cattle and the thoughtful rancher who cares for cattle, land, and wildlife.

CHAPTER 11

Prairie Feathers

The left bank of the river here was literally alive with *Tetrao* [prairie-chickens] coming to feed and drink from the burnt prairie. — *Featherstonhaugh 1847*

Spring came to us that year with such a sudden beauty, such sweet significance after the long and depressing winter, that it seemed a release from prison, and when that close of a warm day in March we heard, pulsing through the golden haze of a sunset, the mellow *boom, boom, boom* of the prairie cock our hearts quickened, for this, we were told, was the certain sign of spring. — *Garland 1917*

The next day, over this waste would pass little whirlwinds which would lift columns of ashes in inverted cones to a height far out of sight, at the base of which the ground squirrels, prairie chickens, the plovers, and the other denizens of the prairie were eagerly running about to find whatever there was of interest in the swept and garnished landscape. — *Quick 1925*

Clearly, speciation around the Central Plains has been much more extensive than in them, so that the most important role of the grasslands has been that of an isolating agent. — *Mengel 1970*

In this rich confusion of life there were few distinct "prairie species." Many of the creatures that inhabited tall prairie either extended farther out into the plains or back into the great forests, and sometimes both; few species were confined to the precise limits of the prairie itself. — *Madson 1982*

Do not venture into the prairie if you are attracted only to colorful and conspicuous forest birds, such as orioles, tanagers, and warblers. And you must not only look down into the grass but also search high above, for the prairie birds are as likely to be singing their fine melodies when nearly out of sight above as from the earth below.
—*Johnsgard 2001*

BIRDS ARE ONE OF THE first and best ways people become engaged in the natural world. Like many people, my original field guide contains notations where and when I saw each species. A flip through that book is a trip down memory lane. I've led a number of prairie birding trips. While many people on the bus trips were hard-core birders with extensive life lists of forest birds they had seen, many of them had seen few to almost no grassland birds. They are always eager to add "rare" birds to their life lists. Many of their rare birds are common in my life.

Many others are rare even for those of us who spend quite a bit of time in the prairies. The 2019 *State of the Birds Report* concluded that grassland birds had declined 53 percent since 1970 and that "grassland birds have suffered the steepest losses" among all groups of birds. Although that's as far back as some of the data go, 1970 isn't exactly a high point for any group of birds.

Much like discussions of plants and bison in previous chapters, when it comes to declining or small populations of birds, we have to look at variability. Figure 8 shows the population fluctuations of eastern meadowlarks per Breeding Bird Survey route across Iowa. There's little predictability in this line. The line looks relatively flat over this time period, but with lots of annual fluctuations. In fact, the population appears to either double or halve from one year to the next in some cases.

When large populations bounce around and fluctuate from year to year, there isn't much of a problem. If there's a catastrophic year or event with a large number of individuals die, there are still plenty of individuals left. After a couple good breeding years, the populations will probably increase to pre-disaster levels. However, if populations get really small, even endangered, things change.

When we start at a small population size and there's a large reduction in the size, often from a random, unforeseen, and unpredictable event, that small population could go from small to very small. In extreme cases, the population would go from small or very small to zero. This would be extinction, either locally or globally. This is where the randomness in the

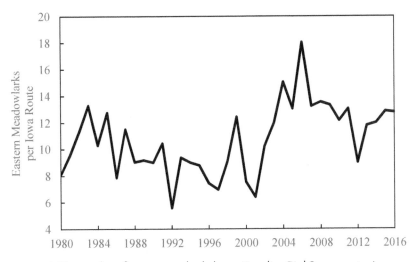

FIGURE 8. The number of eastern meadowlarks per Breeding Bird Survey route since 1980. Public data from USGS Breeding Bird Survey.

natural world affects conservationists trying to save a species. Given the best plans and intentions, a purely unforeseen event can be catastrophic for the population, or the species.

Birds follow the similar patterns to vegetation when it comes to finding species unique to the tallgrass prairie. The tallgrass prairie simply wasn't different enough from the open woodlands and savannas to the east or the shorter grasses of the Central Plains to the west to develop unique tallgrass prairie wildlife. To an ornithologist, the prairies are a "great faunal crossroads" (Madson 1982) or "melting pot" (Johnsgard 2003). It can be just as much of a challenge to define a prairie bird as it is to define the prairie itself.

If hard to define, they are also hard to count. There are nine species of tallgrass prairie birds that are "quite familiar to everyone" (Shelford 1913). Or, there are six "major bird species" (Risser et al. 1981), nine "core grass-dependent species" (Zimmerman 1993), six birds in the "tall grassland association" (Knopf 1996), or four "most characteristic species" of the prairie (Johnsgard 2001).

Collectively, all of these lists include eighteen tallgrass prairie species. The eastern meadowlark is the only species on all five of these lists as tallgrass prairie birds. The dickcissels had four votes, while Henslow's sparrow, upland sandpiper, grasshopper sparrow, and greater prairie-chicken each received three votes. Bobolinks were on two of these lists while eleven species were only listed as a prairie bird by one of these researchers. Clearly, it's difficult to define precisely what a prairie bird is.

If some think of the prairies as a melting pot or meeting spot, others refer to the plains and prairies as a hybrid zone (Rising 1983) or isolating agent (Mengel 1970) between eastern and western bird species. The prairie has many faces.

There are about 130 bird species that reach their limits in the Great Plains. Of those, about twenty-eight are replaced by closely related species on the other side of the Great Plains. For instance, to the east and west respectively we have indigo buntings and lazuli buntings, rose-breasted grosbeaks and black-headed grosbeaks, Baltimore orioles and Bullock's orioles, eastern bluebirds and mountain bluebirds, blue jay and Steller's jay, and yellow-shafted flickers and red-shafted flickers (Rising 1983).

Most of these birds are tree nesters. When the prairies and plains were largely treeless, the grasslands served as an isolating mechanism keeping these paired species separated from each other. Over the last two centuries as more and more trees have been planted across the central grasslands and reduced fires allowed trees to creep farther up streams and creeks, eastern birds moved west, and western birds moved east, allowing species to hybridize and colonize new areas.

Some of the most pitched environmental battles of the late 1980s and early 1990s were over the spotted owl in the Pacific Northwest. The battle was portrayed as being between loggers who supposedly wanted to cut down every tree and environmentalists who supposedly wanted to hug every tree. In more recent decades that story has become more nuanced and complicated.

Barred owls from the eastern forests crossed the central grasslands by using these expanded woodlands in the central grasslands. In the past "it appears the historical lack of trees in the Great Plains acted as a barrier to the range expansion and recent increases in forests broke down this barrier" (Livezey 2009a). In western forests, barred owls compete aggressively with spotted owls. This creates a new and additional risk to spotted owl populations, such that "land managers and regulatory agencies should regard Barred Owls as a threat to Spotted Owls" (Livezey 2009b).

By breaking down that barrier or wall, that is by planting trees, we allowed barred owls to move westward. We created a situation where a species native to one region of the continent is acting like an invasive species in another region and impacting an endangered species. Who would have thought planting some trees in the central grasslands would impact a species in the old-growth forests of the Pacific Northwest? Ignore the irony of a flat horizontal expanse acting as a vertical wall.

It's surprising how large of a tract of grassland some relatively small birds need before they will consider nesting there (Johnson and Igl 2001; Herkert et al. 2003; Weidman and Litvaitis 2011). Habitat size can affect species in different ways, such as the density of individuals of a particular species or the nest success of a species (Winter and Faaborg 1999). In Illinois the minimum area requirements for grasshopper sparrows is 30 acres, 136 acres for northern harriers, 160 acres for prairie-chickens and upland sandpipers, and 185 acres for Henslow's and savannah sparrows (Walk and Warner 1999). In another Illinois study, individual area requirements for eastern meadowlarks are 12 acres, grasshopper sparrows are 74 acres, savannah sparrows are 99 acres, bobolinks are 124 acres, and Henslow's sparrow are 163 acres (Herkert 1994). Maximizing bird species diversity means that the grassland needed to be at least 124 acres in size (Helzer and Jelinski 1999). So much grass for such small birds.

When it comes to habitat, there are a couple of ways, or scales, to consider. The smallest is the level of the individual patch or parcel. The largest is the region. Figure 9 shows the pheasant harvest in Minnesota, an index of pheasant populations, relative to acres enrolled in the Conservation

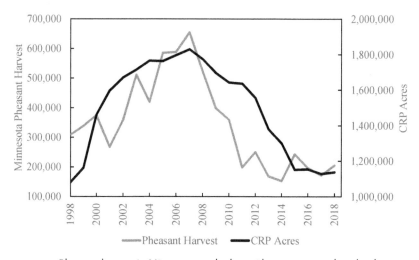

FIGURE 9. Pheasant harvest in Minnesota, and other midwestern states, has closely tracked acres enrolled in the Conservation Reserve Program (CRP). Public data from Farm Service Agency and Minnesota Department of Natural Resources.

Reserve Program (CRP). There are two takeaways from this graph. First, it's easy to see that generally pheasant populations track CRP acres. The more acres in CRP, the more pheasants. When CRP declines, so do pheasant numbers. However, even given these larger trends over the decades, there's still a lot of year-to-year ups and downs in the pheasant harvest. It would be difficult to predict any year's harvest based on the previous years. So, pheasant populations are generally predictable in the long-term as they relate to large-scale habitat trends but still fairly unpredictable in the short-term due to weather and other factors.

In recent years, researchers have stepped away from the idea of looking narrowly at a grassland patch. The surrounding landscape may be just as important as the patch itself (Cunningham and Johnson 2006; Winter et al. 2006a, 2006b; Ribic et al. 2009; Walk et al. 2010; S. J. Thompson et al. 2014). Wildlife will respond very differently to an isolated twenty-acre patch of grass with no other grass within several miles compared to a twenty-acre field with other pastures, hayfields, wildlife areas, and other grasslands in the immediate or near vicinity.

This gets back to the acquisition and restoration aspects of grassland conservation. All acres are not the same. Restoring an isolated forty-acre grassland will not be nearly as beneficial as restoring forty acres next to an eighty-acre grassland. That won't be as beneficial as a forty-acre parcel that connects two eighty-acre grasslands to make a single two-hundred-acre grassland.

One of the most studied aspects of grassland birds is nest destruction. There are several ways eggs, nestlings, or females are destroyed or harmed. The first is the weather. One rainstorm or hailstorm, and resulting flooding, could destroy a large percentage of nests over a large area. Nesting hens also must deal with nest predation and nest parasitism.

Nest parasitism occurs when another female of the same or a different species lays their eggs in a nest. The most famous, or infamous, songbird nest parasite is the brown-headed cowbird. The parasitized female ends up incubating, hatching, and caring for another bird's young. Pheasants will parasitize each other's nest as well as the nests of prairie-chickens. Pheasant eggs need one or two less days to incubate than prairie-chickens. When a pheasant parasitizes a prairie-chicken nest, the pheasant eggs will hatch a couple days before the prairie-chicken eggs. The prairie-chicken hen assumes they are her chicks and leaves the nest as soon as the pheasant chicks' downy feathers have dried. She inadvertently abandons her own eggs to care for the pheasant chicks.

When it comes to nest predation and parasitism, researchers frequently focus on the size of grassland, the shape of a grassland, and surrounding landscape. The edge-to-interior ratio is important for at least six species of grassland songbirds (Helzer and Jelinski 1999). Edge-to-interior ratios depend on both the size and shape of the grassland.

Edge is important as predators often prefer these areas to the centers of large grasslands. Edges can have different effects on different species.

Henslow's sparrows had lower densities near edges while dickcissels have lower nest success near edges (Winter et al. 2000). In Iowa, nesting success of songbirds was lower in areas with high amounts of edge habitat (Fletcher and Koford 2002). Similarly, pheasant hens in Iowa had a higher mortality rate in landscapes with high edge-density (Schmitz and Clark 1999).

One of the issues with grassland edges is that they are often up against hostile habitats, from a nesting grassland bird's perspective. Trees provide perches for hawks, owls, crows, ravens, and magpies. The base of trees or hollow trunks of trees provide dens for skunks, raccoons, and foxes. Additionally, rock piles, foundations of old houses and other buildings create ideal den sites. Grasshopper and Henslow's sparrows simply avoid grasslands near trees while dickcissels, red-winged blackbirds, and eastern meadowlarks had two to five times the nest parasitism rates in these edges (Patten et al. 2006). Similarly, nest predation of five songbirds was higher within fifty yards of woody vegetation and parasitism was also higher near woody vegetation (Johnson and Temple 1990).

Compare a small square, five acres, of habitat to a prairie that is 640 acres in size. Let's assume the outer fifty yards of each prairie have high nest predation and parasitism rates. That leaves only 0.64 acres of prairie in the center of the five-acre prairie with higher nest success rates. In the 640-acre prairie, a square mile, there are still 569 acres on the interior of the prairie that should have high nest success rates. Put another way, 87 percent of the small prairie has low nest success due to the proximity to the edge, while only 11 percent of the larger prairie counts as edge habitat.

If the prairie is a narrow strip of grass along a roadway or railroad, virtually all of the grass will be within fifty yards of the edge. Nest parasitism and predation will be high, and nest success low, everywhere.

One attitude is that "bad" predators kill "good" wildlife. If we just kill off the predators, then grouse, pheasants, quail, ducks, and songbirds will thrive. Paul Errington was an accomplished and well-known wildlife biologist who spent his career in Iowa prairie country. He was especially well known for studying predator-prey interactions. In his 1987 book *A Question of Values* he writes that some of the highest populations of pheasants and quail "were maintained *despite large numbers of foxes and other wild predators.*" Errington went on to point out that the reason those wildlife populations thrived in the presence of predators is that the rabbits, pheasants, and quail "all had in common the tremendous advantage of suitable environment." If there's good, productive habitat, there's room for predator and prey species alike. Errington dedicated that book to Frederick and Frances Hamerstrom, famous prairie-chicken researchers from Wisconsin. They had similar views.

> Frederick pointed out that there had been foxes and prairie chickens since time immemorial and what was needed was good brood cover. "Look," he said, finally raising his voice, "It doesn't matter how many foxes there are if the chickens have good habitat! What prairie chickens need is *land*, not fox trappers." (Hamerstrom 1980)

When it comes to bird nesting success, the amount of habitat and the weather are probably the dominant factors. Each year hunting magazines provide reviews of grassland gamebird populations. The following quotes were published in the October/November 2019 issue of *The Retriever Journal* (D. Smith 2019). "The question of the day: How favorable was Mother Nature to upland game birds over the last year? . . . Winter was hard across the Upper Midwest . . . heavy rains during the nesting season may have negatively impacted nest success . . . brood habitat was almost uniformly good this summer." The section on pheasants began, "The dramatic decline in CRP enrollment from 36.8 million acres at its peak in 2007 to 22.4 million acre today is well-recognized as the primary driver of declines in pheasant populations."

The article goes on to cover individual states. South Dakota reported that "extreme weather extended into the important nesting months. . . . On the bright side, the abundant moisture resulted in great habitat conditions for nesting and brood rearing." North Dakota reported that hunting "is a great bet this season due to a series of favorable weather-related outcomes." Kansas "received its best precipitation in a decade, and the habitat conditions were outstanding." Minnesota reported that "populations will vary locally based on the impacts of adverse weather and the availability of high-quality upland habitat." Note how prominently weather, amount of habitat, and quality of habitat were mentioned. Predators were never mentioned.

Everyone is interested in renewable and clean energy. And, indeed, climate change ranks next to habitat loss as the greatest threat to most ecosystems and wildlife species. However, not all green energy is always beneficial to wildlife. Specifically, wind turbines in grassland habitat can be detrimental to many species. First, and probably the smallest impact is wildlife, especially birds, directly colliding with turbines (G. D. Johnson et al. 2002). The larger issue is the roads, infrastructure, and human activity that follows energy development. These collectively reduce the quality of the habitat more than the towers themselves (Pitman et al. 2005). For instance, prairie-chickens will generally avoid areas near turbines (Winder et al. 2014) and powerlines (Pruett et al. 2009a, 2009b).

"Bigger is better" is easy to say, but why? First, there's the edge effect described. Second, there's only so much habitat variability in a ten-acre patch of grassland. However, if the patch of grassland is 640, 1,000, or 2,000 acres in size, there is a greater probability that it will contain some hilltop prairie, wet sedge meadow, brushy areas, small temporary wetlands, and larger permanent wetlands.

Larger blocks of habitat also allow for a greater range of management. One area is burned in the spring, another burned in the summer. One area is flash grazed in late spring while another is grazed season long at a low stocking rate. Another area is hayed. In a large grassland, managers can conduct all these management practices and still have plenty of tall, undisturbed grass.

Why is a range of habitats important? It's important because there's no such thing as "grassland bird habitat." What does ideal grassland bird habitat look like? What grassland? Which bird? Below are some descriptions of habitat preferences from Paul Johnsgard's 2001 book *Prairie Birds: Fragile Splendor in the Great Plains*.

> [Henslow's sparrow] . . . grasslands with well-developed litter, a considerable amount of residual dead vegetation, and a high percentage of grass cover but with scattered forbs. . . .
>
> [bobolink] . . . hayfields and grassy meadows, typically those having a mixture of grasses and forbs and preferably with moderate to high overall vegetation height. . . .
>
> [clay-colored sparrow] It is perhaps more accurately described as a low-shrub species than a true grassland bird . . .
>
> [marbled godwit] . . . the birds seek out relatively short and sparsely vegetated habitats. . . . Grazed habitats are preferred. . . . They [nests] are also in quite short grassy cover.
>
> [upland sandpiper] Hay meadows, large pastures, agricultural lands that include stubble, moderately grazed pastures, and similar habitats are used during the breeding season.

Descriptions of nesting habitats for different waterfowl species would show a similar range of preferred grass height and structure. There are multiple descriptions of grasshopper sparrow habitat relative to other birds.

> When they are found together, grasshopper, Baird's, and savannah sparrows can be found in the same field, at the same times apparently in the same habitat. However, grasshopper sparrows tend to favor more xeric habitats, and Baird's in more mesic ones, than the others. (Rising 1996)

> [T]he birds are likely to use areas of sparser vegetation than do the Henslow's and Savannah sparrows, but denser than that of the vesper sparrow, and with fewer shrubs present than on sites favored by clay-colored sparrows. (Johnsgard 2001)

And then there are the dickcissels, who seem to be happy almost any-where. Dickcissels are "extremely tolerant of habitat variation," living in "most every other vegetational combination that is mostly herbaceous" (Johnsgard 2001).

Just leaving habitat alone, preserving it, won't create the habitats all these species need. If we want a lot of different species of birds in any one grassland, then we need a lot of different grasslands. Birds need un-grazed and unburned grassland with some thatch. But they also need some burned grassland, lightly grazed grass, and heavily grazed grass.

Different species, or the same species at different times of year, need short, mid, and tall grasses. That's not to say they necessarily need differ-ent grass species, but they may need different grass structures. Prairie-chickens need hayed or heavily grazed areas for their booming grounds in the spring, denser cover for nesting, and lightly grazed areas for brood rearing. It's hard to fit all that in a few acres. In addition to protection and restoration of grassland, we need management of grassland to get that structural variability and diversity within a single grassland patch.

Birds like prairie-chickens can serve as "umbrella species" for all grass-land birds (Poiani et al. 2001). It can be almost impossible to develop conservation plans for many species. However, because prairie-chickens need large and diverse grasslands, by managing for this species we are almost by default managing for all species.

So what's the best prairie for grassland birds? The best prairie is large and has a little bit of everything in it; tall, short, low and wet, high and dry, dense, sparse, burned, grazed, hayed, rested. Put another way, there is no one way to manage or one habitat type that will make every bird species happy. Every management action will benefit one set of species and be, at least temporarily, detrimental to other species.

Grassland conservation and habitat management requires the long view. Some think spring prescribed fires destroy nests, and that does sometimes happen. Yes, they are temporarily destroying nesting habitat for some species for one year. But other species respond positively to the post-fire environment (Quick 1925).

These plovers (settlers called them "prairie pigeons") hunted
burned hillsides for grubs and insect eggs, and the dark slopes were
spangled with moving gold and silver as the great flocks of plover
fed. (Madson 1979)

The post-fire habitat won't be the best nesting habitat for most species,
but it will be very good brood-rearing habitat. That area will provide good
nesting habitat over the next few years. Without periodic fires that temporarily remove nesting habitat, trees would encroach and permanently
remove grassland wildlife habitat.

Management, such as grazing, may work in unexpected ways. In Iowa,
there were more skunk dens in ungrazed pasture compared to either grazing treatment. Skunks and other nest predators such as foxes and raccoons also like thick cover because it hides them from their predators
(Bennett 1938). Thus the goal could be using cattle to remove just enough
cover to expose the nest predators but keep enough cover to conceal
nesting birds. This goes back to the take half, leave half idea for grazing
management.

As a general rule, cattle and ducks can live together reasonably
well on the same sites when grazing is sufficient to remove half the
average amount of the primary forage plants produced annually.
(Bossenmaier 1964)

Find a prairie that hasn't burned in a couple years. Lie down on your
belly, fold your hands in front of you, and rest your chin on your hands.
What do you see? You probably see a nearly impenetrable wall of this
year's green grass and last year's brown thatch. Think of how tired your
legs can get after walking through the prairie, kicking through all that
vegetation with each step. Now imagine life as a week-old prairie-chicken,
pheasant, or quail chick.

The shorter, sparser grass and paths through the grass created by grazing can also make travel easier for prairie-chickens (Baker 1953), blue-
winged teal (Bennett 1938), and presumably most other birds.

The amount of bare ground or short vegetation was important for pheasant and quail chicks to move easily through the habitat when foraging for insects (Doxon and Carroll 2010). Likewise, ideal brood habitat for prairie-chickens is vegetation between one and a half and four inches. This height is "significantly less than the range . . . suggested for management of tallgrass prairies" (L. C. Anderson et al. 2015). Similarly, total bird abundance and the abundance of dickcissels, grasshopper sparrows, meadowlarks, cowbirds, and upland sandpipers were greater in grazed pasture than ungrazed CRP fields (Klute et al. 1997).

That thick grass you saw while lying on your belly is still important at certain times of the year. There needs to be some of that structure in the grassland. That thick thatch makes ideal nesting cover and probably good winter cover for many species. Managing for "dense nesting cover" has been a wildlife mantra for decades. If the grass isn't tall, thick, and dense, then it isn't any good. However, especially during the brood-rearing season, it doesn't all have to be that thick. Together, these studies show that our former picture of what good bird habitat looks like, the taller, thicker, and denser the better, may not be completely accurate.

Prairie management is often about doing something, but not too much of anything. Management is essentially a form of ecological disturbance and is needed to keep grasslands diverse and productive. Habitat management is using tools to control "the plant succession in the right direction at the right time and place" (Leopold 1933). Birds may not be the best botanists, and probably care more about the structural diversity of their habitat than the actual species diversity of the habitat. Fire and grazing are two of the best ways to diversify that structure. The key is determining how much, where, and when. Not too much fire, not too much grazing or haying, but not too little either.

All this information tells us that we may need to reevaluate our numbers when we total up grassland acres. In any particular county or region in the Midwest, there may be some remnants of native prairie, some CRP fields, pasture, hayfields, and maybe a few public Wildlife Management

Areas or Waterfowl Production Areas. However, if we want to add up acres of good nesting habitat, we may need to subtract some edge acres, subtract acres near woody vegetation or abandoned structures, subtract acres near roads, powerlines, and other infrastructure, and ignore some of the smallest patches. If there's little grass out there in many areas, the acres of nonhostile habitat may be much smaller.

Counting Chickens

THE SKIES OF a Minnesota March are usually gray, cloudy, overcast. Rural roads are a mix of mud and ice. And there's that prairie wind. But now it's April, with the sun just below the eastern horizon. My big brown furry constant companion and I arrived fifteen minutes before we had to. For now, we just enjoy the sound of silence. The prairie-chickens are just fifty yards out in that field. They are there every day of every spring.

We hear the first *whoop!*, but it's still too dark to see anything. A couple minutes pass and a couple more *whoops!* echo from the dark. There are several birds out there now, judging by the noise. I scan the binoculars across the area, looking for a mottled brown bird against a mottled brown background in the dark. On the third pass, there is a flash of white feathers on the birds' backside. Then another appears. A few seconds later there are two dozen birds at this booming ground, cooing, cackling, dancing, jumping, fighting, and fluttering. All this is raucous ruckus, a stark and joyous contrast to the silence of minutes ago. They seemed to appear instantly, as if the dead stubble suddenly became animated and starting dancing around.

The third booming ground of the morning is just west of a small country cemetery, set back from the road a quarter mile. Fifteen males are booming in some chisel-plowed corn stubble. Immediately behind the birds is a herd of dehorned bison standing amid sixty years of rusted and abandoned farm equipment. A person could call this a pasture, but it's hard to find even a standing thistle from last year. Two miles behind the herd, traffic roars along the interstate. Prairie-chickens, plowed up soil, dehorned bison in a feedlot, and an interstate. There's a metaphor or allegory or something here about modern life in the rural Midwest, but I can't quite put my finger on it.

By the fourth booming ground things are really hopping. I'd like to just sit and watch the prairie-chickens at one booming ground all morning. But the goal is to count eight to ten booming grounds before the sun gets too high and the birds settle down for the morning. In fact, the last couple of counts are usually pretty hurried.

One thing I dislike about these surveys is that I rarely leave the truck. The binoculars are in my lap, the spotting scope is clamped to the window. If it's a distant booming ground well off the road, I may get out to better locate the sound. But even then, I usually only get a few feet away from the truck.

My field assistant much prefers the booming grounds far off the road, on the backside of some USFWS Waterfowl Production Area. This gives us a good excuse for a long hike to get a good count. After a winter of inactivity, nothing beats walking through prairie grass to get the blood flowing. Ducks and sparrows flush in front of us by the dozen. We usually spot at least one moose each spring.

As with everything, there are trade-offs. Although I couldn't just sit and watch as we'd like, we made a good survey of all the wildlife in this part of the county. Perhaps the biggest problem in wildlife research is staying focused on the species you're supposed to be counting without getting distracted by all the other wildlife out there. What we missed in the detail of one area, we made up for in the breadth of a much larger area. As soon as we get all our booming grounds counted at least three times this spring, we will drive out here and sit in one spot for the whole morning. The pup and I will just sit, watch, and listen. And maybe we'll learn something.

CHAPTER 12

Prairie Insects

Insects not only inspired this floral riot, but complemented it with life and color of their own. — *Madson 1982*

Thus while fire itself imparts relatively little predictability to grasshopper community dynamics in periodically burned prairie, such dynamics are nevertheless to a limited degree predictable. — *Evans 1988a*

The composition of the grasshopper community at a given location depends on the species composition of the plant community. — *Kaufman et al. 1998a*

All of these arthropod variables were significantly positively correlated to plant species richness in the fields. — *Siemann et al. 1999*

It appears that the main question of whether to burn or not burn tallgrass prairie out of concern for prairie-insects does not have a simple answer. — *Larsen and Work 2003*

[D]ifferences in insect communities between native and restored prairie may best be explained by the presence of insect host plant rather than by whether a site is native or restored. — *Nemec and Bragg 2008*

IN MY DAY JOB, I'm supposed to be focused on grassland birds, especially pheasants. However, 90 percent or more of the calls I've received from the public in the last few years have been about pollinators. That's fine, because good pollinator habitat is also very good pheasant and songbird habitat. All of them are dependent on a diverse and productive plant community.

A chapter on prairie insects can start where the chapter on prairie birds left off. Insects play many roles in grasslands, but one of those roles is to provide food for birds and other wildlife. Insects have a high protein content, important for egg-laying hens and fast-growing chicks.

Larger grassland birds such as pheasant and prairie-chicken hens need to eat tens of thousands of insects to gain enough protein to lay a clutch of eggs. Newly hatched pheasants and prairie-chickens weigh about six tenths of an ounce. Just a few weeks later they are adults weighing up to two pounds. That's a large amount of growth in a small amount of time, requiring a lot of protein-rich invertebrates.

Pheasant chicks consume invertebrates from seventeen different families of insects (Doxon and Carroll 2010). Each family may have scores of species. The most common insects were bees and beetles. In the shortgrass prairie of southwest Kansas, lesser prairie-chicken broods spend most of their time in areas with high densities of invertebrates. These also happen to be areas with high densities of forbs (Jamison et al. 2002; Hagen et al. 2005). In Nebraska, pheasant broods selected sites with greater forb diversity (Matthews et al. 2012). Birds are able to find where the insects are and stay there. Presumably grassland birds in the tallgrass prairie are able to do the same. Therefore, because of the vital role insects play in their diet, gamebird and songbird management may actually be more about insect management. That said, insects do far, far more in the prairie than feed birds.

Pollinators get a lot of attention these days due to: colony collapse in the economically important honeybee, concern over the shrinking monarch populations, and a focus on overall native pollinator diversity. Invertebrates play many roles on the prairie. Insects, such as bees and butterflies, are pollinators. Some insects, such as grasshoppers and leaf hoppers, are herbivores. Other invertebrates, such as spiders, are predators. Still others are parasites.

Getting back to one of the themes of this book, pollination is often held up as a prime example of cooperation or mutualism in nature. Plants give insects nectar, insects pollinate plants, and everyone is happy.

It's not that simple. Plants give insects nectar as a reward for visiting them, picking up pollen, and then going to another flower of the same species to deposit the pollen. If the plant gives the insect too much nectar, the insect won't be hungry anymore, will quit, and won't deliver pollen to the next plant. If the plant doesn't produce enough nectar, the insect won't get enough of a reward and will stop visiting that flower. Plants also need to keep the insect from visiting other species. Picking up pollen from a blazingstar and delivering it to a goldenrod won't benefit either plant. This is another form of plant-plant competition. Other plants have flowers that look like female insects. Males visit these flowers, try to mate, inadvertently collect pollen, and then fly off to try and mate with the next flower.

Insects don't purposefully collect pollen in many cases. They accidentally pick it up while drinking nectar. Some insects find it easier to chew into the base of the flower, sipping the nectar but never picking up any pollen. Ideally, a plant would want its pollen spread as far as possible. The insect wants to expend the least amount of energy and visit the next closest flower. Pollination looks like a cooperative venture, but only if it's given a quick glance. A closer inspection shows that, if not a battle of weapons, pollination is definitely a battle of wits. As Gary Larson (1998) writes in his ecological classic *There's a Hair in My Dirt*, "In a field of flowers, all is fair in bugs and war."

The previous chapter highlighted the idea that there were few prairie birds, but that each prairie bird had a specific habitat type. There are nine common and three uncommon grassland dependent birds at Konza Prairie (Kaufman et al. 1998a). There are 307 insect species that have been identified on Konza Prairie, but only about 10 percent of the species have probably been documented (Kaufman et al. 1998b). This means that there are probably at least three hundred insect species for every bird species.

Even that is almost surely an underestimate, maybe by an order of magnitude or more. In *Hidden Prairie*, Chris Helzer (2020) spends a summer photographing one square meter of restored prairie in Nebraska. Over the summer he recorded ninety-seven species of invertebrates, including twenty-two flies, eighteen beetles, fourteen bees, seven true bugs, seven spiders, four wasps, five ants, and five hoppers (C. Helzer, pers. comm.).

Even those numbers need to be put in context. Helzer was very clear in his book that this was a photographic effort, not a comprehensive scientific effort. A thorough scientific study would surely reveal many more species in that square meter. Imagine what a survey of even a one-acre remnant prairie might reveal when it comes to invertebrate diversity.

On the western edge of the tallgrass region, there are at least forty families of beetles, including sixteen plant eating, nine predator, seven fungus eating, six scavenger, and one gatherer family. There are six families of grasshoppers, and within the short-horned grasshopper family, there are at least twenty-six species (Jonas et al. 2002). There are a lot of invertebrates out there. However, like plants, a simple count of species doesn't really tell us much about the ecology or conservation of prairies.

Studies of several groups of insects generally show that there are common species and rare species (Bomar 2001; Kwaiser and Hendrix 2007; Moranz et al. 2012). Perhaps because so many insects are so closely tied to specific plants, it's not surprising that they follow a pattern similar to the Core-Satellite Hypothesis (Kaufman et al. 1998b). Each prairie remnant is a unique community of plants and the same applies to insects. Tonietto et al. (2017) titled their study "Bee communities along a prairie restoration chronosequence: similar abundance and diversity, distinct composition."

Several studies show that insect communities are closely tied to the plant community in general (Evans 1988b; Siemann et al. 1998; Nemec and Bragg 2008; Tonietto et al. 2017). There is also a strong relationship between the abundance or density of flowers and insects (Kwaiser and Hendrix 2007; Harmon-Threatt and Hendrix 2015), as well as complex relationships among the invertebrates within the prairie and even within a single plant.

[L]ocal arthropod herbivore diversity may also be maintained by and, in turn, maintain a diversity of parasites and predators that prevent competitive exclusion, allowing a high diversity of herbivore to coexist on even a single plant species. (Siemann et al. 1998)

Stepping down from the plant community, and building on the idea that a single plant species can host a high number of invertebrates, we can look at individual plant and insect species. Most schoolkids know that monarch butterflies are closely tied to milkweeds. However, many insect taxonomists have taken this a step further and incorporated a plant's name into the insect's name. In one survey, twenty of forty-nine insect species had a prairie plant in the insect's common name (Panzer 1988). A survey of Wisconsin prairies revealed Amorpha borer, alumroot flea beetle, iris weevil, leadplant gall-midge, Silphium aphid, sage leafhopper, cordgrass bug, leadplant plantlice, scurf-pea argid sawfly, Amorpha stem gall moth, and Liatris borer moth, to name a few. To get even more specific, some insects take the names of specific parts of a specific plant: bushclover stemborer beetle, phlox stem borer, bluestem leaf-mining beetle, Silphium leafminer, spiderwort leaf beetle, Baptisia seed weevil, sunflower seed bug, Silphium internal stem gall wasp, and false boneset flower moth, among many others (names provided courtesy R. Henderson, WI DNR retired). At the end of Chapter 11, I stated that birds weren't good botanists. Insects are very good botanists.

Other insects are closely tied to one species of plant, even if they don't take the plant's name. The karner blue butterfly is tied to lupine. The regal fritillary butterfly is tied to prairie violets. This may sound counterintuitive. It makes sense for a grazer like bison to focus on grasses like big bluestem because bluestem is large, abundant, and common almost everywhere. Lupines and violets are small plants scattered across the prairie. However, that's a modern viewpoint. In previous times, violets may have provided an abundant food resource for regal fritillaries (Wilder 1935; Madson 1982).

On southern-sloping hillsides one could surprisingly note some bright morning that the birds-foot violets had turned the slope to a patch of blue like sky. (Quick 1925)

It winked with blue-eyed grass and yellow grassflower, there were acres and miles of bird-foot violet. (Peattie 1938)

If managing for a dozen species of birds is a challenge, managing for hundreds to thousands of invertebrates is far more complex. The most common management tool in prairie, fire, is especially controversial among invertebrate ecologists. Much like many suburbanites prefer a nice homogeneous green lawn, fire managers like solid homogeneous black when they are done. Many of us, myself included, have gone back after a fire and held a drip torch over every last little patch that didn't burn. It's always nice to have a good clean complete burn.

What that does is destroy any last little refugium for insect eggs or larvae in the thatch. It's fine to leave a few "skips" in the middle of the burn (Panzer 1988). This may be where grazing can play another role in invertebrate conservation. Burning areas that were grazed creates a complex patchwork of burned and unburned.

Unfortunately, we can't simply make general statements like "burning is bad for butterflies" or "grazing is good for grasshoppers." With insects, it's especially important to know what the questions are. Are we interested in the effects of management on insect diversity? Are we interested in overall insect abundance or abundance of a particular species or group of insects? Is the management targeted at a population of one specific insect species? Are we interested in the immediate response of the species to the management? Or are we looking for a response two or three years later? The science is quite mixed relative to fire and insects.

Greatest species diversities [grasshoppers] occurred on sites subjected to intermediate frequency of fire. (Evans 1984)

[S]ome species were more abundant the year immediately following the burn, while others were found in greater abundance in
areas with increased time since fire. (Larsen and Work 2003)

[B]utterfly abundance was lowest in the burned only restoration
practice. However, we found that butterfly diversity was highest on
these burned only sites. (Vogel et al. 2007)

In one study, 40 percent of insects were fire-negative and 54 percent
were fire-positive or fire-neutral (Panzer 2002). The next question is what
fire-negative means. If there's an immediate drop in a population but the
population recovers within a year or two, then the negative effects are
short-lived. If the fire drives a local population to extinction and there's
little opportunity for recolonization, that becomes more of a problem.

This fire/no fire may be a false debate. Fire will kill individuals, but lack
of fire will kill the prairie they depend on. Panzer (2002) points to some
entomologists who would like to see burning reduced or eliminated. At
the same time botanists are calling for the same level or increased burning
to maintain natural processes, combat invasive plants, or remove woody
vegetation. This controversy around fire creates what some researchers
call the prairie butterfly paradox (Moranz et al. 2014).

Absent frequent disturbance, remnant tallgrass prairie rapidly
converts to a dominant cover of woody plants. This creates unique
challenges for conservation of prairie-specialist insects. . . . Regal
fritillary butterflies (*Speyeria idalia*) exemplify this problem, with
sharp population declines in recent decades and considerable
disagreement on management practices, particularly the use of prescribed burning to maintain habitat. (R. A. Henderson et al. 2018)

Inconsistencies among findings have only heightened the confusion behind what is commonly referred to as the "prairie butterfly
paradox," where butterflies like the regal [fritillary] appear to be

sensitive to the very processes considered necessary to maintain their grassland habitat. (McCollough et al. 2019)

Insects need a place to lay eggs, grow into adults, and then they need abundant pollen and nectar sources once they are adults. At some sites "regal fritillaries deemed recently burned units more suitable" than unburned prairie (Moranz et al. 2014). This is undoubtedly because burning stimulates flowering of many species of prairie forbs. Adult foraging habitat may be more critical than host plants for prairie butterflies (Panzer 1988). Eggs don't do well in burned areas, but burning dramatically stimulates blooming of most prairie wildflowers. Within each grassland, pollinators need a mix of unburned prairie for the juvenile stages of their lives and prefer burned prairie full of flowers for the adult stage of their lives.

In Pennsylvania, frequently burned grasslands had a higher probability of supporting the violets that regal fritillaries depend on (Adamidis et al. 2019). The researchers also point to direct effects of fire, such as mortality of immature butterflies, and indirect effects, such as host plant and nectar plant abundance, vegetation structure and composition, as largely unknown in telling the full conservation story for many species. Often the most useful management tool is "creating and maintaining high quality habitat with abundant violets (*Viola* spp) and varied nectar sources" (R. A. Henderson et al. 2018). They also determined that quality habitat is more important than reducing fire, a goal that can be met with burning every three to five years.

It's always been accepted as common wisdom that insects that are in the plant canopy during a fire during a stage in their life when they can't move, such as eggs or larvae, will face nearly 100 percent mortality in a fire. Therefore fire is a negative because it kills individual insect eggs, larvae, and pupae. However, regal fritillary larvae can survive at least some fires (McCullough et al. 2017). Perhaps some larvae or eggs are low enough in the leaf litter that the fire goes right over the top of them. By contrast, insects that overwinter as eggs in the soil may be stimulated by the sun-warmed soils in the days after a fire.

Along with fire, grazing also affects invertebrates. Grasshopper densities for seven of nine of the most common grasshoppers in Kansas responded positively to grazing (Joern 2004) and there were 45 percent more grasshopper species in grazed areas than ungrazed prairie (Joern 2005). Grazing increases forb diversity, which benefits the forb-feeding species. Grazing can also keep grasses short, tender, and succulent, which may benefit the grass-feeding insects.

We can relate modern conservation back to historic landscape patterns with regal fritillaries and other invertebrates. If there are other unburned prairies within a reasonable dispersal distance from the burn, then invertebrates should readily recolonize the area after the fire (Moranz et al. 2014; R. A. Henderson et al. 2018). Unfortunately, in today's world many of our small remnants are so isolated that there aren't other grasslands, native or restored, within a reasonable dispersal distance.

Today, managers are encouraged to break up burns into many small units so that there's always some unburned vegetation nearby. In some of the historical descriptions of fire in Chapter 4, observers describe fires running for mile after mile after mile. Where were the refugia for insect eggs and larvae during these fires? How did invertebrates recolonize the center of these large burns?

Similar to burning, another factor is mowing. Some will argue that haying or mowing is a good alternative to fire that is less detrimental to insects. However, especially in the northern states, there can be conflict between the ornithologists and entomologists when it comes to mowing.

In Minnesota, several of my colleagues and I have noticed that monarchs prefer to lay eggs on younger common milkweeds that regrew after landowners mowed or hayed the field in mid-summer. Older milkweeds, in areas that were not mowed, can be tough and leathery by the time monarchs make it to the northern end of their range. There are similar patterns of monarchs using the succulent milkweeds that regrew after a summer fire in Oklahoma (Baum and Sharber 2012).

Some monarch advocates, especially in northern states, would like to see mowing of roadsides and hayfields in early summer so there's sufficient time for the milkweeds to regrow by the time the monarchs arrive. However, that would be at the peak of the nesting season for birds. Bird advocates would like to see mowing and haying done in mid- to late summer after bird nests have hatched and the young are old enough to escape the mower. That is the peak of the monarch egg-laying season in northern latitudes. As is often the case with prairies, there are no easy answers.

Fire and grazing, two factors managers can exert some control over, clearly affect invertebrate diversity and abundance. The third factor cited when discussing the prairie is of course the weather. Daily, weekly, and seasonal vagaries of local weather patterns obviously affect insect populations. However, events practically on the other side of the globe can affect prairie insects. The North Atlantic Oscillation correlate to annual changes in grasshopper populations in Kansas (Jonas and Joern 2007). Weather literally on the other side of the world can affect insects in the prairie.

Hundreds to thousands of invertebrates may be affected, directly or indirectly, to a greater or lesser extent, and independent of other species by fire, grazing, and climate. We know generally what will happen if we burn a prairie. We know generally what will happen if we don't burn a prairie. But those generalities and the unknown variability within those generalities become problematic especially when discussing rare, threatened, or endangered species on small prairie remnants.

Pollinators and other invertebrates will probably be a focus for grassland restoration in the future. Diversity in general is important. However, there may be key species that are especially important to pollinators, such as leadplant, purple prairie clover, yellow coneflower, and golden alexanders (Harmon-Threatt and Hendrix 2015). These four species in restorations seem to be disproportionately important to pollinating insects. Also, when thinking about restorations and invertebrates, the surrounding landscape may be just as important as the actual restoration site (Hines and Hendrix 2005; Kwaiser and Hendrix 2007; Nemec and Bragg 2008; Griffin et al. 2017).

As with everything in prairie management, the simple answer is to not do too much burning or haying or grazing at any one time in any one place, but don't do too little either. How do we manage for prairie insects? Do a little bit of everything, but not too much of any one thing.

Two Worlds

I HAVE TWO FEARS about both myself and the conservation community, and time to think about those fears as I sit in the back of a legislative hearing room this morning. I swore it would never happen to me. I'd spend my life in the field with a clipboard, binoculars, and a good dog by my side collecting data and later analyzing data with the pup asleep under my desk. Yet here I am, working in a cubicle in a big building in a large city in a job that revolves around policy, economics, meetings, hearings, budgets, paperwork, forms, politics, plans, and more meetings. And I'm wearing a tie!

Every passing month I feel more and more disconnected from the grasses, wildflowers, and prairie wildlife I'm supposed to be focused on. I used to be a pretty good botanist. Anymore, I really struggle with a lot of common and Latin names when I do get out. "Looks familiar . . . used to know that one . . ." I'm afraid I've lost touch, and that's not good.

My other fear is that people out in, what I like to call, the real world don't understand all the policies, politics, economics, and associated administrivia it takes to make conservation happen. We head to the natural world as a refuge from the vagaries and doldrums of daily life, whether that refuge be a camping tent, canoe seat, duck blind, deer stand, or a path through prairie flowers and grasses. However, to continue to engage with the natural world, we also have to engage with the politics and economics of conservation. Too often, people don't want to get involved.

So here I sit, waiting to present my proposal for funding my program. It's an odd situation. I think of all the other presenters in the room as colleagues and friends. Today we are competitors for the same funds, but in a collegial and friendly way.

Biodiversity, or diversity, is a commonly used word. There's another type of diversity that gets much less attention: people. We need people to join conservation organizations and pay their annual membership. We need hunters to buy hunting licenses and stamps that go to habitat management. We need people to call local, state, and federal legislators and have their voices heard. We need researchers at federal and state agencies, at universities, and working for conservation groups. We need people with specialized training and skills to safely conduct prescribed fires, restore wetlands with bulldozers, and all the other habitat management that needs to get done. We need lobbyists and policy specialists. We need lawyers who can, when needed, file suits against those who wish to destroy habitat. Most importantly, we all need to support one another.

Perhaps we need the conservation population to look like the American population. Diversity or biodiversity is mentioned at almost every meeting. However, the ethnic and cultural diversity of all the meetings I go to and people I work with, is, well, not very diverse. If conservation is going to be relevant to America's future, then conservationists need to look more like the United States, in all of its glorious diversity.

It would be great to just live out on the prairie, listening to the wind, collecting and planting seed. Unfortunately, the decisions, the economics, the policies, and the politics that affect wildlife and habitat are rarely made out here. Those decisions are made in marble halls and hearing rooms, around conference tables, usually in large cities. For many of us, those places are as stressful as time alone with a good dog is relaxing.

It's not enough to live in the insulated world of bluestem and just hope things are going well other places, or that others will take care of those issues for us. Just as importantly, those who do work in those places need frequent contact with the natural world to remind themselves why they do what they do. It's pretty easy to get so absorbed in the politics and policies that we forget the ultimate goals of our efforts.

Therein lies the challenge of living in two worlds.

CHAPTER 13

Patches, Mosaics, and Management

Indeed, it is the interaction of ungulate grazing activities and fire, operating in a shifting mosaic across the landscape, that is the key to conserving and restoring the biotic integrity of the remaining tracts of tallgrass prairie. — *Knapp et al. 1999*

The heterogeneity-based approach to rangeland management that we propose is an attempt to mimic historical grazing-fire interactions on mesic North American prairies, which have a long evolutionary history of ungulate grazing.
— *Fuhlendorf and Engle 2001*

Fire-grazing interaction may provide a management alternative that enables sustainable livestock production, through increased carrying capacity in focally disturbed patches, concomitant with biological diversity in tallgrass prairie.
— *R. H. Anderson et al. 2006*

The shifting mosaic created by the Patch Burn treatment provides habitat that meets requirements for a broad range of invertebrate species. — *Engle et al. 2008*

So, in contrast to rotational grazing, patch-burn grazing subjects a prairie to extended periods of intensive grazing followed by multiyear rest periods, creating a very heterogeneous array of vegetation structure across the pasture. — *Helzer 2010*

Management strategies such as patch-burn grazing offer opportunities to restore landscape heterogeneity to benefit bird communities while maintaining livestock production goals. — *Davis et al. 2016*

IN 1832, GEORGE CATLIN painted *Prairie Bluffs Burning.* In this painting fire moves across a hilly, grass-covered landscape. There are two deer in the foreground. One is at rest before the flames. The other is jumping over the flames into the black, not fleeing in front of the flames. Catlin knew that wildlife were attracted to recent burns almost two centuries ago, as

Native Americans knew before that. We've finally been able to put some science and numbers behind those historic observations over the last two decades.

Earlier chapters made the argument that prairie is largely defined by fire, grazing, and climate. Fire and grazing are the two factors managers have control over. Fire and grazing also strongly interact at landscape scales. Bison and other grazers are strongly attracted to the flush of succulent new growth after a fire.

> These results indicate that grazing distribution can be controlled with some precision using prescribed fire. (Vermeire et al. 2004)

Fire can control where bison graze. At the same time, grazing removes biomass, fuel for fires. Grazing can control where fires go. Fire can attract grazers, but grazing can prevent fire.

Areas that are heavily grazed won't have enough fuel to carry a fire. In other cases, where the grazing is patchy and heterogeneous, the resulting fire will also be patchy and heterogeneous. The fire will burn the ungrazed patches and be stopped at the grazed patches. In this way, a fire can percolate across an area. Instead of ten- or twenty-foot tall flames racing through an area leaving solid black in its path, the fire may creep slowly through a grazed area with flames only inches high and leave a complex mosaic of ungrazed and burned, grazed and unburned, and ungrazed areas surrounded by grazed areas that serve as a firebreak. This mosaic leaves refugia for insects and other wildlife.

Traditionally, the goal of livestock operators is to graze an entire pasture or set of pastures as evenly as possible. Ranchers rotate cattle from paddock to paddock, put up fencing and cross-fencing, and space water and mineral blocks across the pasture to evenly distribute grazing pressure by the livestock. The more homogeneous the pasture looks at the end of the growing season the better (reviewed in Fuhlendorf and Engle 2001). From a wildlife perspective, this means that there's only one habitat structure across all that grass.

Almost by definition, a fence is designed to keep an animal within an area or out of an area. A fence is designed to block movement, to keep animals from going where they want to be or keep them in an area where they don't want to be. This works against the natural behaviors of the livestock, trying to get them to go where we want them instead of where they want to be. This of course creates a lot of work for the people managing the livestock.

Native Americans frequently burned the prairie to attract wildlife. Today, we are able to apply science to those historic anecdotal observations and explain those patterns. At the same time, we can use natural grassland processes and the behaviors of livestock to our benefit. We can get the livestock to work with us instead of against us, creating less work for people, presumably happier and healthier livestock, and better habitat for wildlife. And we can do all that at the same time. Just as important for this book, the process called patch-burn grazing shows how multiple aspects of prairie ecology interact.

Patch-burn grazing is simply burning part of a larger pasture each year. Livestock are attracted to the fresh green-up of grass in this area, spending more time in the recently burned grassland than unburned grassland. The next year managers burn a different area within the pasture and the livestock move to this area. In this way, managers can rotate livestock around the pasture without any cross-fencing or other infrastructure.

There are at least two explanations for livestock being attracted to recently burned areas. All the vegetation in these burned areas is lush and green. In unburned prairie, livestock have to dig through the old, brown, dead vegetation from previous years to get to the good green vegetation.

The grass isn't just greener, it may be more nutritious. Compared to annual burned prairie, infrequently burned prairie produces more biomass of grass (J. M. Blair 1997; Knapp et al. 1998) as described in the Transient Maxima Hypothesis in Chapter 9. Another important fact from the grazing perspective, grasses in a four-year burn rotation have higher nitrogen levels than annually or biennially burned prairie (J. M. Blair 1997). Therefore, with periodic burning there is large quantity of high-quality grasses for livestock. Grazers will readily respond to these differences in forage (Raynor et al. 2015).

The reason nitrogen is so important for livestock producers, as well as wildlife, is that nitrogen is the key component of protein. Protein is one of the key components of muscle, and muscle to a livestock producer is meat. Meat is what they ultimately sell and make a living from.

With grazing, we can add another level of complexity to the nitrogen story. Grazing can increase plant nitrogen levels because the grazers urinate and defecate on the prairie. In the following days and weeks the plants are able to absorb the nitrogen from the soil and thus become more nutritious. These nutritious plants influence grazing behavior (Steinauer and Collins 1995, 2001) and can become a source of nitrogen in a grazer's diet (Day and Detling 1990).

As livestock keep the plants grazed low, the plants are constantly re-growing and therefore remain succulent and nutritious. If fire initially attracts the animals to an area, the repeated grazing can keep them there (R. H. Anderson et al. 2006), even to the point that "bison use recent burns even after they are virtually devoid of vegetation" (Schuler et al. 2006). Grazing the same acres year after year will use up root reserves of the plant, making them slower to regrow and less nutritious. However, in the case of patch-burn grazing, this intense grazing occurs for only a summer and the plants then have three or more years to recover their root reserves.

So how can ranchers and wildlife managers use this information? Imagine a section, or square mile, of grassland, 640 acres, divided into four even-sized units of 160 acres. Traditionally, each of these areas would be fenced and cattle would be rotated from one area to another. At the end of the year the entire 640 acres will look similar and homogeneous.

With patch-burn grazing there is no cross-fencing, just one perimeter fence. In the first spring, ranchers burn the northeast quarter and livestock spend most of the summer here. The following spring, ranchers burn the northwest quarter. Now the cattle graze this area and the northeast quarter starts to recover. The southwest and southeast quarters haven't been burned or grazed and are accumulating a fair amount of thatch. That's a lot of structural diversity and heterogeneity across those 640 acres.

The high quantity of high-quality forage should lead to increased weight gain in cattle, and that should be more money in the rancher's bank account. Cattle performance, weight gain, and body condition were equal to and sometimes better under patch-burn grazing compared to more traditional pasture management (Limb et al. 2011). Because cattle are grazing "new" pasture each summer, this pattern of movement could potentially help break parasite cycles in the livestock, improving health and decreasing the cost of the rancher for deworming chemicals.

This management method can maintain sustainable livestock production and biological diversity at the same time (R. H. Anderson et al. 2006; Fuhlendorf et al. 2006). Wildlife benefit primarily because there are so many different types of vegetation structure in different stages of recovery from fire and grazing (Fuhlendorf and Engle 2001). Patch-burn grazing shows that ranchers can meet production goals and conservationists can meet wildlife objectives at the same time on the same piece of land.

Conservationists can now conserve *ecological patterns* and *evolutionary processes* using patch-burn grazing (Fuhlendorf et al. 2012). This may be more important than just "preserving" the prairie as described in earlier chapters. This method of grazing management can help merge the utilitarian and preservationist schools of conservation, which date all the way back to the time of John Muir and Gifford Pinchot in the early 1900s. Most importantly, wildlife managers and ranchers can conserve land, biodiversity, patterns, processes, and local livestock economies. These ideas can also help unite the conservation and agricultural community to show how each can be mutually reinforcing and beneficial (Limb et al. 2011). What's good for beef is good for birds, bees, and butterflies. Ranchers, bird hunters, and bird watchers have a good reason to talk together and work together.

We can return to the bird and invertebrate data to show the wildlife benefits of this system. Some species of grassland birds respond positively to grazing, "even at moderately high stocking rates" (Ahlering and Merkord 2016) or grazing so intense that the cattle create distinct grazing lawns (Hovick et al. 2012) but still leave some patches with sufficient nesting cover nearby. Grazing can be the best tool for getting the structural diversity in the prairie that the range of grassland birds require (Fuhlendorf et al. 2006) and can even work in fragmented landscapes (Pillsbury et al. 2011).

Among the invertebrates, some species are associated with taller, denser vegetation (Moranz et al. 2012), while others respond well to shorter grasses or the variability in grass height (Joern 2004). There isn't a uniform invertebrate response to burning and grazing. Grasshoppers reached peak biomass in the second spring after the fire, twelve to twenty-four months since the fire. True bugs did well in both the fall and spring for the same period. Leafhoppers and aphids did best in unburned and in the twelve to twenty-four–month post-burn period. Spiders and ticks showed mixed results (Engle et al. 2008). Most interesting, from a bird's perspective, is that peak invertebrate biomass was highest in the spring following the fire. Spring is when grassland birds are most in need of the high-protein diet invertebrates provide. Patch-burn grazing, "is a viable and perhaps even ideal management strategy" for regal fritillaries (McCullough et al. 2019) and presumably other prairie butterflies and insects.

We can imagine traveling back in time to what the prairies looked like from the perspective of a bird flying overhead. First, we can think of migratory sandhill and whooping cranes at high altitudes. When they looked down, they saw some areas of the prairie that hadn't been burned or grazed in several years and had significant fuel build-up. Other areas would have recently blackened with fire. The cranes would also see heavily grazed areas that couldn't burn.

We can imagine a similar scenario for a grassland sparrow flying from perch to perch in a lightly grazed area that a recent fire percolated through. A sparrow flying from spot to spot around a territory might have seen the same pattern of grazed areas, standing vegetation protected from fire by grazed areas around it, and recently burned areas. It would be a similar pattern as the cranes saw, but at a much smaller scale.

Last, we can imagine how spatially and temporally dynamic this was. An area that hadn't been grazed and had heavy fuel build-up burned. The green, succulent regrowth attracted herds of bison and elk that moved into this area, thereby abandoning areas that grazed last year. The area heavily grazed this year is effectively "fire-proofed" for at least a year because the grazing removed the fuel. The area that was grazed last year now has a recovery period of one to several years before it burns again. Every year this pattern would have shifted around on the landscape and probably occurred at different scales.

The noted examples illustrate at least three principles. First, the different patterns each year are what ecologists refer to as the shifting mosaic of habitat across a landscape. Second, in many cases the patterns that occur at one scale, cranes high overhead, are very similar to the patterns at another scale, a sparrow foraging on the ground. Last, prairies can be working landscapes, on both public and private lands. Working lands both preserve and manage prairies as well as keep those acres in the local agricultural economy.

Although there are many benefits to grazing, patch-burn or otherwise, it isn't always appropriate everywhere and it takes a lot of work. With a prescribed burn, once the fire is out and the perimeter secured, managers can essentially walk away from the site for the rest of the year. To graze "properly" to meet wildlife or habitat objectives, as well as herd health and safety, someone needs to be checking the livestock at least weekly, and probably more frequently. This can be a significant time investment for a public grassland manager with many other responsibilities. Are the livestock congregating in an area and having too much of an impact? Is it a dry summer and the cattle need to come off a little earlier than planned? Grazing is a lot of work, and unless public lands managers have the time to invest in monitoring the site, cattle can do more harm than good. Burning is a one-day commitment at most sites. Grazing is a season-long commitment at every site.

That said, ranchers and livestock are key to maintaining grasslands and grassland wildlife. Burning is expensive, but doesn't have much of an economic return. There is an economic return for well-managed grazing. Government agencies and conservation organizations will never own enough acres to sustain and support the wildlife populations that the conservation community would like to see across the Midwest. The best, and in some places only way, conservationists will meet their goals is by working closely with private landowners, especially those who work the land and own cattle. Often what's good for ranchers and livestock is also good for conservationists and wildlife. This creates a natural and mutually beneficial partnership.

By looking at the interactions of fire and grazing, instead of studying each separately (Fuhlendorf et al. 2006), scientists have been able to replicate the patterns and processes that probably occurred on the early prairie landscape, create habitat for a wide range of prairie wildlife, and do it in a way that is economically viable to the ranching community. Indeed, for many prairies, bison and other grazers play a "keystone role" in the tallgrass prairie's ecology (Knapp et al. 1999)

Through a Lens

W HEN I WAS AN UNDERGRADUATE, many of my prairie visits
were in the company of my professor, Dave. Dave introduced me not only to the prairie but also to photography.
We always brought full bags of camera equipment with us. Most of
my memories of those Indiana prairies are of me on my knees, getting
close-ups of flowers with a macro lens.

Especially in the late summer when the bluestem and Indian grass
were at their peak height, this was the only time I really felt like I was in
the prairie. There were only wildflowers and grass beside me, only sky
and clouds above. Even in a small remnant cemetery prairie it was easy
to imagine it was just me and the prairie, and nothing else. One issue
I've always wondered about with photography, especially close-up work,
is whether I become too focused on one small area to the exclusion of
the surroundings. Close-up photography is often about focusing on a
single flower, or insect, to the exclusion of its landscape context.

For graduate school, I moved to the Flint Hills of Kansas. Here I
could stand on a hilltop and look to the prairie horizon. I exchanged
my macro lens for a wide-angle lens. The Kansas Flint Hills taught me
to see the big picture. Indeed I spent most of my years there staring
at satellite images of the Flint Hills studying landscape patterns at the
regional scale. However, seeing the big picture makes all the details in
the photo disappear.

Combined, these two experiences influenced the way I've learned to
look at the world. Indiana's prairies taught me to get on my knees and
look down. Kansas's prairies taught me to stand up and look out. These

experiences, and all the experience since then, make me wonder about lenses in general.

The lens of history is a commonly used metaphor. How do we view the prairie, or how will we view the prairie at some future date? Asked in reverse, is there a lens of the future, and what does that tell us about the tallgrass prairie?

Is the story of the tallgrass prairie one of Native Americans having fundamental and dramatic effects on the landscape, as well as direct and indirect effects on the wildlife? What is the story of the human and nature dichotomy during those times? Is the prairie natural, and why or why not? Can natural areas and natural processes be the work of Mother Nature only, or can people play an active role in natural process, then, now, and into the future?

Is the story of the tallgrass prairie a story of technological challenge with the land being tamed and conquered? Is it about the tragedy of an earlier group of people or the triumph of a later group of people?

If nothing else, working on this book gave me an identity crisis. I like to think of myself as a prairie ecologist or prairie conservationist. But I'm not sure what the prairie is anymore. It's very hard to define. Is a tallgrass prairie any area dominated by big bluestem or Indian grass? Is a tallgrass prairie any grassland roughly in that triangle from Indiana to Kansas to Minnesota? Or do we just default to "I can't define a prairie, but I know it when I see it?" I'm joking of course, but defining the prairie isn't as easy as some may think.

Then we can think about a lens into the prairie future. What if we restored grasslands on all the unproductive cropland? What if we carefully grazed and rested those acres? Would that diversify the rural economy and bring jobs back to rural areas? Would that increase eco-tourism and hunting around small midwestern towns and be a welcome injection of outside dollars into local economies?

Let's get back to that camera lens. What do we see when we look through the lens at the prairie? Is the image closely focused on a small, individual species, or is it focused on the big landscape? Is it a static image or a dynamic moving video?

What is the prairie? If there is no prairie, then what am I? Or is the prairie a metaphor for modern America? The prairie is a melting pot of plants and animals that came to the Midwest from all different directions. The United States is a melting pot of people and cultures from all different directions. That's not a weakness, it's a strength.

CHAPTER 14

Prairie Trees

Every body loves trees, and every one feels a thrill of gratitude toward the man whom they see planting one. A tree is unlike any other ornament. Though set on private property, it is a public blessing. — *Farnham 1846*

Few phenomena have attracted as much attention from layman, amateur and scientific observer alike as the absence of trees from the prairies of the Mississippi valley. — *Shimek 1911*

To the dweller of forests, the prairie pioneer, the landscape of the treeless grassland seemed extremely monotonous. There was an innate longing for the companionship of trees. — *Albertson and Weaver 1945*

Even the sky was shrinking, for the settlers were eager to close it out and have shade trees as quickly as possible. . . . A shade tree in the dooryard of a prairie homestead was a delicious luxury. — *Madson 1982*

Americans love trees. We hug them, we decorate them at holidays, and chain ourselves to them to prevent their destruction. We plant them for shade, for windbreaks, for their fruit, to memorialize loved ones and important events. But mostly, we just like to have them around. Many trees are nurtured and cared for as if they are members of our families. Every child in every school in the nation learns about the importance of trees to our culture, our industry, and our lives. — *Helzer 1999*

Thus, the loss of native grassland bird communities is the currency in which we pay the ecological costs of planting trees in prairie landscapes. — *Kelsey et al. 2006*

IF YOU ARE OF CERTAIN AGE and hear the phrase "Plant a tree for tomorrow" you instantly hear John Denver's voice. Planting trees is a good thing. Good people plant trees. If you want to protect a tree, you can embrace it in a hug, chain yourself and a few friends to the trunk, or sit in the leafy branches high overhead. You can't hug leadplant. Neither can you sit in a compass plant or chain yourself to big bluestem.

In an earlier career, a friend stopped by my office. He had some questions about some land he just purchased that he wanted to manage for prairie-chickens. He is one of the most educated, well-read, thoughtful, intelligent people I've ever met. I asked him what he had been doing since he purchased the land. He and his family had been planting several hundred Russian olive trees each year. He was a conservationist and good conservationists plant trees. His quick question turned into a lengthy conversation.

The Homestead Act of 1862 motivated a lot of people to move into the western parts of the tallgrass region and the Great Plains. Eleven years later Congress passed the Timber Culture Act. Planting a grove of trees became part of improving a land claim.

Historically, and still sometimes today, two commonly planted trees were Russian olive and Siberian elm. From the names it's not hard to tell that these trees are not native to the Midwest, or even North America. These, and a few other trees, are clearly non-native species. Almost every conservationist will agree that they are invasive species and should be eliminated wherever possible.

However, many of the most problematic trees in the prairie are native to the Midwest: cottonwood, boxelder, green ash, red cedar, aspen, and a few others. These species fundamentally change the structure and function of grasslands and habitat for grassland wildlife. By changing these functions and structures, they act as many true invasive species act in other habitats. Yet they are native to the prairie region.

There's a visceral satisfaction in planting a tree or a row of trees. Planting can involve a large hole and heavy, burlap-covered root ball. In other cases, we make a simple slit in the soil, stick in the roots of a twelve-inch-tall sapling, and tamp the slit closed with the heel of our boot. Either way, you'll have dirt under your fingernails, maybe a blister on your thumb, and dirt-stains on the knees of your jeans. Your back and arms will be sore, but it's a good sore. It's an honest sore.

We can even move into the realm of cultural views where those who cut down trees are often labeled with less than flattering names. For many, those with a chainsaw in their hands have a black hat on their heads. And indeed, some forestry practices have historically been devastating to certain parts of this country. However, that has somehow morphed into the idea that every tree is sacred and every tree is good. Helzer (1999) describes the "seriousness of the tree hugger mentality as a threat to prairie conservation efforts."

It's okay. You can not like trees and still be a good person. Actually, there's nothing wrong with liking trees. They have their place; their place just doesn't happen to be in an area where the focus is prairies and grassland wildlife. The conservation question thus becomes, where are grasslands most appropriate and where are forests most appropriate?

Then we can get into the psychology of those earliest pioneers, huddling at the edge of the forest, afraid to move out into the prairie. Trees cover our heads from sun and heat as well as from rain and hail. There were several ways we tried, and we eventually did conquer the prairie. First, we removed the original inhabitants of these lands. We hunted much of the wildlife nearly to the point of extinction. We plowed under the grass. Even after that, the prairie region still didn't feel like home, whether home was New England, Virginia, Norway, or Germany. To make it feel like home, we needed to plant trees.

During the 1930s and 1940s, there was much handwringing among conservationists because the Dust Bowl droughts of the 1930s were killing off planted tree rows and woodlots. Even some natural forests along streams and creeks were dying (Weaver 1968). In the wet period that has settled in over the Midwest since the early 1990s, managers are doing the same handwringing, but this time about not being able to keep trees under control. In many areas today, trees are encroaching into grasslands at a far greater rate than managers can control with fire.

One of the more interesting conservation programs of the 1930s was planting a massive hundred-mile-wide shelterbelt stretching from Canada down to Texas. Actually, it was a hundred-mile-wide zone where shelter-belts would be clustered. The idea was to break up the drying effects of the winds on both crops and soils.

In the book *Trees, Prairies, and People* (1977), Wilmon Droze covers the biology, economics, and politics of this program. He also places the Shelterbelt Project into cultural context. He refers to one newspaper editorial describing the "gospel of tree planting." Droze goes on to describe "a crusade of tree planting," the "morality of tree planting," and a crusade "clothed in all the virtues of a mid-west Protestantism." He quotes an 1872 report stating that orchards were "missionaries of culture and refinement." It's hard to be against trees when put into that context.

Once trees become established in prairies, fire often isn't enough to keep them under control. Managers must bring in bulldozers, backhoes, and other heavy equipment to get rid of the trees. It takes a lot more than a couple of people with chainsaws to keep ahead of the trees these days. It also takes repeated treatments, which can get expensive. Trees need to be cut and then hauled away. Stumps need to be chemically treated or grubbed out. Burning alone just isn't enough in many situations.

While tree management creates a workload issue for managers, it also creates a public perception issue. The conservation community has promoted tree planting for decades. Now, similar to changing views of grazing covered earlier, conservationists are telling the general public that not all trees are always good everywhere. In fact, we should be cutting many of those trees down.

Almost any manager with state or federal agencies or organizations like The Nature Conservancy who has done tree removal projects has had concerned citizens question their actions, often quite emotionally. How can an environmentalist or conservationist or anyone who claims to love wildlife cut down a tree?! Often passions can run high and it takes a significant effort to explain what managers are doing and why they are doing it. Even then, many aren't convinced. Every tree is sacred, and people become emotionally attached to them.

When leading trips at a local birding festival, we always tour some high-quality prairie sites first to get the few grassland specialist birds that people want to add to their life lists. We then visit the local woodlot or riparian area where we rack up the number of mostly generalist species. One year the big attraction for the festival was a magpie nest on some public land. Everyone wanted to see the magpies. No one had the heart to tell those on the field trip that this coming winter managers would cut down all those trees and shrubs.

These are the decisions managers have to make every day. Managers need to focus on the rarer species or species of concern that have limited amounts of habitat, prairie, on the landscape. If any habitat, forest or brush, for generalist species is destroyed, those species will find other habitats nearby. These actions don't *destroy* trees or brush, they *create* prairie. However, that's not always how people see it.

There are several types of tree invasion in the prairie. In some cases, gallery or riparian forests along streams and rivers become wider or extend farther up toward the headwaters of the stream (Knight et al. 1994). In other cases, trees and shrubs colonize out into the prairie itself well away from riparian areas.

Once established and able to rain seeds into the surrounding prairie, trees can take over an area very quickly. Native prairie can turn into closed canopy red cedar forest in as little as thirty years without fire (Hoch et al. 2002). The shifts in the prairie-forest border described in earlier chapters didn't occur over geologic time. They often happened over the course of a few years, a period of time when a single person could recognize those changes. In historic times, when there were few trees, there weren't any trees to rain seed into the prairie. A prairie probably could have gone for a significant period of time without fire and without tree encroachment with no tree seeds around.

[A] distance of forty or fifty miles, there was not a tree or bush to be seen in any direction. (Catlin 1844)

Trees can in a way fireproof their immediate surroundings. Even isolated trees can create enough shade to reduce grass growth next to the tree trunk. This leads to reduced fuel loads and less intense fire next to the trunk when the prairie does burn.

In theory, fire was one of the chief factors that kept the prairie a prairie by controlling woody vegetation. However, it's not quite that easy. There isn't a direct relationship between more fires and fewer trees and shrubs. A lot of the recent research on woody vegetation comes from the Flint Hills of Kansas. This is the westernmost and driest part of the tallgrass prairie region. Any changes in woody cover in Kansas would surely be much stronger and more rapid in the wetter parts of the tallgrass prairie to the east.

At Konza Prairie, shrubs expanded by 24 percent in unburned prairie and 4 percent in annually burned prairie over a nearly two-decade period (Heisler et al. 2003). Even annual fires are not enough to completely eliminate shrubs once established. What is perhaps most interesting is that in prairie burned every four years, shrubs expanded by 28.6 percent. In other words, four-year burn frequencies can cause shrubs to expand more than unburned prairie. Post-fire there was a 600 percent increase in stem density in some shrubs (Heisler et al. 2004). I have seen the same pattern in many parts of Minnesota. There are similar patterns across entire watersheds when comparing the same three fire treatments (Briggs et al. 2005).

How can we explain this? Fire top kills the shrubs, which is different than killing the entire shrub, roots and all. Fire prunes the shrubs. Then fertilizer in the form of ash is added. Last, fire removes all the thatch at the base of the shrub. Instead of the base of the plant being in darkness from the thatch, there is full sunlight at the soil surface. Pruning, fertilizing, and more sunlight all lead to increased growth. The plants are then left alone for three years. In this context it makes perfect sense that periodic fires can stimulate shrub growth. This is analogous to the Transient Maxima Hypothesis for grass productivity (McCarron and Knapp 2003).

Modern fires are conducted under moderate winds and high humidity. Drought periods and high wind days are generally red flag days when burning is banned. The conditions in which fires might do the most to set back trees are the same conditions when we can't and don't burn, for obvious reasons. Legally, and in most cases ethically, managers can't light fires if there is a reasonable risk of those fires escaping and causing property damage or personal injury.

Seasonality might also be an issue. Most prescribed fires today are conducted in the spring months. The spring season has cool temperatures, snowmelt, and spring rains. It's a wet time of the year. A person can simply grab a twig in their bare hand to feel how moist and cool it is. Historically, most fires were in October. Fall is often a much drier season. Are fall fires more damaging to woody vegetation? Some have started experimenting with summer fires for habitat management. These prescribed fires are set in late summer once the grasses have started to dry out and young birds are able to fly.

One area where woody management practices interact in the prairie is fire and grazing. Grazing increases plant diversity because the grazers remove the dominant plants, providing resources, especially light, for other species. Grazing also alters the pattern and intensity of fire. For the same reasons grazing increases plant diversity, grazing can and almost always does, increase woody encroachment if there is some woody vegetation established in the area.

There can be a forty-fold increase in woody vegetation in annually burned and grazed prairie compared to annually burned and ungrazed (Briggs et al. 2002). There is nearly 100 percent fire mortality in red cedars up to five feet tall in the ungrazed prairie. In the grazed prairie, fire killed only 50 percent of the shorter trees and killed only 20 percent of the trees over six feet tall (Hoch et al. 2002). Fires in grazed prairies have less fuel, are less intense, and incomplete so that not every tree would be exposed to flames.

As noted in Chapter 10, people still use phrases such as "we can't burn

FIGURE 10. The large trunk testifies to the age of the tree. The large horizontal limbs tell us this was once an open prairie. Today, the tree is surrounded by a dense stand of young trees, primarily basswood. The basswood have shaded out all the grass and essentially fire-proofed this area. Photo courtesy of the author.

it, so we'll graze it instead" or "we'll graze to control woody vegetation." Cattle are grazers, grasses, not browsers, twigs. Except in a few specific circumstances, cattle grazing will almost always increase woody vegetation because it reduces competition for seeds and seedlings and reduces fire intensity. In some cases, cattle can control young woody vegetation, but this is usually when the stocking rate is very high and it's often more hoof action than grazing that damages the plants. Those high stocking rates are often well past what most conservationists are trying to do with grazing.

There were trees, especially oaks, on the prairie, as described in Chapter 3. These old oaks are characterized by their wide-spreading horizontal limbs. Even as a prairie lover, a lone bur oak with its massive limbs on a hilltop is an impressive sight. However, with fewer fires today, these former open savannas or single trees are now engulfed in a thick forest (Figure 10). Once the tree canopy closes, almost no grasses or other fine fuels will grow. These areas are effectively fire-proofed until the trees are cut down and there's enough light to encourage the grasses and forbs to grow.

What's the best tree in the prairie? A stump. Just remember the immortal words of Smokey the Bore: Only you can prevent forests.

Lawns of God

J OHN MUIR famously called forests "god's first temples." Temples are sacred and are not to be touched. In his classic *Where the Sky Began*, John Madson titled his third chapter "The Lawns of God." This brings up another issue in the prairies related to the previous chapter on trees. Midwesterners do like grass, just as long as it's short, shorn, and monotypic. We will spend large sums of money on fertilizers to make it grow tall, equipment to cut it short, gas to run that equipment, and chemicals to reduce the diversity to a single species. We will invest countless hours on weekends and evenings generating air and noise pollution.

Some rural midwestern home lawns are enormous. And they are small in comparison to the lawns around some office buildings, churches, and in industrial parks. Some rural residents mow wide ditches past their lawn along the front of corn and soybean fields. Municipalities mow roadsides all summer long.

I remember asking a neighbor when I lived in Kansas why he spent so much time mowing ditches. I pointed out the time, fuel, and wear and tear on his tractor. His response was that he could either spend the afternoon with his tractor or his wife. That was twenty-five years ago, and I still haven't figured out a response.

Another homeowner told me last year that he tries to spend two hours on his mower every evening after work. He finds it relaxing and it is how he decompresses at the end of the day. He was very proud of how his property looked, and rightly so. It would have been hard to say I'd like him to stop mowing and have his anxiety level increase.

To others, native or restored prairies just look weedy, untidy, and unkempt. Anything that isn't carefully manicured bluegrass, not blue-stem, is a weed. Prairies make the news every couple years when a suburban homeowner converts their chemically soaked, maintenance-intensive, monoculture to prairie grasses and wildflowers. Neighbors complain and local politicians invoke ordinances. It often doesn't end well for the homeowner. That said, with the recent focus on pollinators, people are taking a greater interest in native plants.

It's always frustrating to go to garden centers and see what they advertise as "native plants." Most are monstrous cultivars while others are plants such as Korean so-and-so grass. Nothing against the country, the people who call it home, or who came from there, but doesn't the name imply the species may not be native to the American Midwest?

One of the prairies I used to visit frequently as a college student has for the last two decades or more been mown to putting green height once a week. Families of the people buried in that cemetery didn't like the "weeds" growing on their ancestors. While I want to cry every time I think about how beautiful this remnant prairie once was, I can't say that these are terrible people for wanting this cemetery to look like every other well-kept and nearly shorn cemetery.

These situations take conservation out of the realm of ecology into psychology and sociology. People just like a golf course–looking landscape because that's what they are used to. No one can fault anyone else for that. It's part of our cultural esthetic. There's an entire industry and advertising campaign to convince people they've done a good thing and need to keep doing it. And of course buy more chemicals and equipment to achieve that look.

People who mow grass aren't bad or wrong. I wish they'd leave it alone and plant native grasses and forbs, but then I'd be forcing my cultural values on them. They probably wish I'd mow more and keep the weeds under control. This is where the conservation message gets tricky and where bad feelings develop if words aren't chosen carefully. These are hard conversations to have.

However, the prairie lover in me thinks about the hundreds of thousands of acres of mown grass across the Midwest. What if we wanted all those lawns and ditches and other places to look like meadows of native wild flowers? How much pollinator habitat could we create in a very short time? How much time, fuel, and money could homeowners and businesses save? How much carbon could we sequester and erosion could we prevent? Then again, perhaps some questions are better left unasked.

CHAPTER 15

Prairie Restoration

All the charm and mystery of that prairie world comes back to me, and I ache with an illogical desire to recover it and hold it, and preserve it in some form for my children. It seems an injustice that they should miss it. — *Garland 1917*

[A] memory of what was gone before I came. — *Peattie 1938*

To those who wish to bring together the multitude of species represented in a prairie — or any other natural community for that matter — would seem to have a task exceeding that allotted to Noah. — *Kline 1997*

Consideration of evolutionary history rather than anecdotes from European travelers presents a dilemma for nostalgists fixated on a particular image of pre-contact nature.... [T]he best course is probably to define restoration objectives in terms of ecological or biocultural processes, rather than as arbitrarily chosen or illusory static communities. One may wish to preserve diversity as a key to the past and an offering to the future, but the particular composition of plant communities in any single place or time, as far as anyone can determine, is ephemeral. — *Howe 1999b*

However, our efforts at prairie restoration are usually limited to establishing prairie plants with little attention given to other prairie organisms. — *R. C. Anderson 2006*

MOTHER NATURE IS PRETTY SMART. Surely if we just leave things alone, take a hands-off approach, nature will heal itself? In the words of Paul McCartney, just "Let It Be." One of the themes of this book is the role people played in maintaining and expanding, and possibly creating, the tallgrass prairie. Researchers at Cedar Creek in Minnesota studied fields that had been plowed but abandoned for more than nine decades. Even after all that time, plant diversity and productivity were only 73 and 53 percent, respectively, of adjacent native prairie (Isbell et al. 2019). They state that bringing back the prairie will require "active restoration efforts."

This chapter will not provide a how-to for reconstructing prairie from the ground up or restoring the health of an existing prairie. There are a number of books that cover this topic well. The goal of this chapter is to take a step back and provide food for thought before the restoration begins. Restoration can be as philosophical as practical. Restoration requires that the practitioner be up on the latest science. However, that isn't enough. Restoration is both an art and a science, and it needs to be viewed from both perspectives.

Prairie restoration may be one of the best places for an individual or group to leave a legacy on the land. My own research and the research of others clearly shows that each native prairie is a unique assemblage of plant species. After the pup and I had surveyed numerous restorations over a couple summers, I could almost tell who was in charge of the restoration just by looking at the results. That's an exaggeration, but not by much. My fear was that people were using a standard seed mix and all the restorations would be essentially the same. I was pleasantly surprised to find that, while not nearly as diverse and distinct as each individual native prairie, each restoration was somewhat distinct from every other one.

One reason for this is the role weather may play, especially in the summer after the site is seeded. Imagine using the same seed mix on two restorations two years apart. In the first restoration, the summer is cool and rainy, ideal for germination and seedling survival. In the second restoration, there are some timely spring rains promoting good seed germination. The rest of the summer is hot, windy, and dry, shriveling up and killing all those seedlings. Three years later, those two restorations will look very different, even with the same starting point (Middleton and Bever 2012; Stuble et al. 2017; Groves et al. 2020). This again shows the role that weather can play as a major factor in prairies.

Much of the restoration activities today are about trying to capture something that we, individually and as a society, have lost.

The stranger ignorant of the history of the country is struck with
the sense of some difference; but there is nothing to admonish
him that here was once a land of unbroken sky-line with no object
in sight taller than the yellow blossoms of the compass plant
or rosinweed. A thing of great beauty has passed away forever.
(Quick 1925)

Today, I think of my great-grandad's quarter-section of old Iowa. He
saw prairie as something to be broken for his children; I see it as
something to be saved for mine. (Madson 1993)

Some who participated in the death of the prairie lived to regret their
actions.

I felt for the first time the poetry of unplowed spaces.
(Garland 1917)

The seed is in, fateful and indomitable; we have populated where
we have slain. Still sometimes when in fall or spring the wind
turns, coming from a fresh place, we smell wilderness on it, and
this is heartbreak and delight. (Peattie 1938)

Many people like to restore old houses or old cars. Someone restoring
a car can look at old photos and blueprints and restore the car to what it
looked like when it rolled off the assembly line. A person can look at ar-
chitectural styles, paint colors, wallpaper patterns, and restore a house to
exactly what it looked like when it was first built. If a famous individual
was born in that house, the goal may be to restore the house to that date
as opposed to what the house looked like when it was first built.

We can say that there is a time we can call age zero, when construction
is done on the house or the car rolls out of the factory. What is the starting
point for the prairie, or any other ecosystem someone is trying to restore?

The following quotes were taken from Leopold's dedication of the University of Wisconsin's Arboretum.

> This Arboretum may be regarded as a place where, in the course of time, we will build up an exhibit of what was, as well as an exhibit of what ought to be.

> The first step is to reconstruct a sample of what we had to start with. (Leopold 1934)

These quotes bring up some interesting points. The words "start with" imply that there was some point in time that we can say things started, a time zero. The phrase "what ought to be" implies a judgment call and perhaps that judgment is open to interpretation. There are many who think natural areas ought to be fields of corn or subdivisions of trophy homes.

The "re-" part of re-storing implies that we are going backward in time, re-turning to an earlier period. So that invites the question of what time are we going back to? Are we going back to the year the first European explorer entered the area? The year the General Land Office Survey mapped the area? The year the site was plowed under? Are we going back to 1492? (Notice how all of these arbitrary dates have a Euro-American or European perspective?) Are there specific times before this we should aim for? Or should we try to return the area to what it looked like right after the last glacier retreated?

> Should managers maintain or re-create a particular image of presettlement prairie climax determined by soil, hydrology, and climate? Or should their goals include several historically plausible images of grassland communities? Or should the objective be to maximize grassland species diversity for its own sake? (Howe 1994b)

These discussions can get silly, but they are serious. I don't know if anyone could really argue that we should restore the landscape to the years immediately following the glacier's retreat. That's ridiculous. However, we can get serious about this topic also. Let's go back to the end of Chapter 3 and the descriptions of the Driftless Area of southwestern Wisconsin. Should the aim be to restore the open grassy landscape that

Jonathon Carver and George Catlin described or the Big Woods Laura Ingalls Wilder described? Which landscape is "correct" and what is the justification for that answer?

Pick any spot or plot of land in the eastern tallgrass region, especially east of the Mississippi River. At some point in time over the last several thousand years that acre has probably been a forest, savanna, and prairie as the prairie-forest boundary shifted east and west. In fact, the acre may have been several forest or grassland types over that time.

Right now, the land is currently an agricultural field. What condition or plant community should we restore it to? In some cases, there may be a landscape context. If there is an oak-hickory forest on two sides of the land, maybe we should restore it to this forest type. If there is native prairie on either side of the land, then planting trees would obviously be detrimental to grassland nesting birds in these areas.

There are also some practical considerations to restoration. Imagine an eighty-acre parcel in a floodplain along a river. We want to restore this to prairie, which at one time it was. Every few years those acres will be inundated by floodwaters and most falls the acres will be carpeted with seeds from cottonwood, silver maple, boxelder, and green ash trees.

It may require almost annual burning to keep these acres a grassland, and even then, the area would probably need some mechanical tree re-moval every few years. Does the agency or private landowner have the time, resources, equipment, and staff to devote to keeping those acres an open grassland? If the answer is no, then it may be best to restore those acres to floodplain forest even if the General Land Office Survey said those acres were in prairie at the time of the survey.

What are we trying to restore? Are we simply trying to replicate the plant community in the nearby pioneer cemetery? Have those plant communities changed in the last 100, 200, 500 years and how have they changed? When it comes to plant diversity is more always better? Why? Although there are scores of prairie plants, no one prairie has them all.

Restoration can invite as much philosophy as it does pragmatism. What is the purpose of the restoration? Why does someone want to restore these specific acres? Is it possible to restore something that is constantly changing? Are we trying to restore a plant or animal community, an elaborate garden or zoo, or are we trying to grow some quail to hunt in the fall? Or are we trying to restore or replicate large-scale ecological patterns and processes?

> Patterns and assemblages of taxa are clearly transitory. Perhaps conservation would be more constructive if efforts focused on preserving the processes and opportunities of change. (Brown 1993)

Should restorations only look backward in time or should they also consider the future? Does it make sense to restore a particular plant community to an area if we know we can't maintain it or if it may not match existing or future climates? What role does future climate change play in restorations?

> Because restoration often seeks to undo the last several centuries of human influence, restoration ecologists often focus on the past. However, this focus obscures a goal that is more important than simply recreating past conditions: the restoration of ecosystems that will be self-sustaining and resilient. (White and Walker 1997)

One theme of this book is the large role people played historically in maintaining and possibly expanding the prairie, primarily by the use of fire. People are also responsible for the destruction of the prairie. Today people need to play a strong role in bringing the prairie back. Prairie is not a hands-off ecosystem. In most deserts and forests, people can largely leave the land alone, or apply management actions only periodically. Prairie needs a human touch, if not annually, then fairly frequently. A hands-off prairie is a forest.

> Well-meaning conservationists continue today to argue against ill-conceived assaults on ecosystems as interfering with the balance of nature. Arguments are occasionally heard in which it is said that

"nature knows best," and should be left to its own devices. Such a view is obviously based on the presumption of a natural balance. (Kricher 1998)

As late as the early 1960s, prairie managers thought that the best way to preserve the remaining fragments was to put fences around them and keep people out. People had done enough harm, and nature would know how to heal itself. The fatal flaw in this approach is that one key species is missing, but is critical to the survival of even small prairies and savanna remnants. That species is us. Show me a black-soil prairie remnant in good condition, and I'll show you an attentive prairie steward. (Drobney 1999)

Restoration has undergone a number of positive changes over the years and decades. Many early grassland restorations were done with brome and sweetclover. The seed was cheap. Farmers knew they would get good germination and a quick establishment. Today, these and similar species are some of the worst invasives we battle in the name of grassland conservation and biodiversity.

Next, we moved to native species, but often with little regard for where the seed came from. These restorations were frequently heavy on grasses and light on forbs. Often, we planted grasses from western areas into eastern restorations. Given more rainfall than they were used to, the grasses grew so well they crowded out all the forbs, creating almost a monoculture (Figure 11). Not surprisingly, plant richness is often negatively correlated to the amount of the dominant grasses in restorations (McCain et al. 2010).

Today's restorations often use much more diverse mixes of locally harvested seeds. Instead of using one seed mix over an entire area, managers may be able to customize seed mixes to different soil types and topographies within the restoration.

One of the key features of native prairie is that there is always something in bloom, and each week or two there is a different set of species in full bloom.

FIGURE 11. In this image, there's a ninety-pound Labrador retriever fifteen feet in front of me hidden in the tall dense grass. Photo courtesy of the author.

> This [late spring] was the surface of the prairie, a soft fragrant cheek turned to the sun; this was the most passing and innocent vernal aspect, before the coming to full stature, to the war paint colors of final bloom. (Peattie 1938)

> One glories in its beauty, its diversity, and the ever changing patterns of its floral arrangements. (Weaver 1954)

> From the first pasqueflowers of March to the towering sunflowers of October, the tallgrass prairie will never be without flowers. (Madson 1993)

However, still today most restorations are often missing most or all of the spring and early summer flowering species. This is usually related to seed availability and price. Aster and sunflower seed is easy to produce and harvest. There's a lot of seed commercially available and it's relatively inexpensive. Pasqueflower, prairie smoke, blue-eyed grass, birds-foot and prairie violet, and other spring blooming species are more difficult to harvest, not as available in the commercial trade, and often much more expensive. For instance, one commercial seed dealer sells a quarter ounce of early blooming prairie violet for twenty-five dollars. Late blooming long-headed coneflower sells for five dollars an ounce.

When it comes to diversity in seed mixes for restorations, all species aren't necessarily equal. Diversity of blooming times, plant families, sizes, shapes, and colors of flowers are just as important as species diversity. If there are already five species of fall asters in a seed mix, adding one more fall aster may not add that much. If there aren't any penstemons in the mix, adding a penstemon may be far more beneficial to pollinators than one more aster. It makes the process of developing the seed mix longer and more complicated, but, picking what seed to use in a restoration is usually a pretty fun part of the job. And this is often where the art comes into the restoration.

It makes sense that if someone is restoring a prairie in Illinois, they should use seed from Illinois instead of from Kansas. Local seed, or local ecotype seed, will be better adapted to local soils and climate. However, that can be easier said than done.

The titles of some of the research published on the topic of local eco-type seed in restorations is revealing. Edmands (2007) titled her paper "Between a rock and a hard place," while Millar and Libby (1989) use "Restoration: Disneyland or a native ecosystem?" McKay et al. (2005) used "How local is local?" Schaal and Leverich (2005) title their paper "Conservation Genetics: Theory and Practice." "Ecological genetics and the restoration of plant communities: Mix or match?" is the title Lesica and Allendorf (1999) chose. Mortlock (2000) titled his study "Local seed for revegetation: where will all that seed come from?" Finally, Miller and Hobbs (2007) used the title "Habitat restoration—do we know what we're doing?" It is interesting to see how many studies in this area have question marks in the title of the research paper. It's also clear that resto-ration ecologists don't operate in a perfect world.

In a perfect world, there would be a large native prairie of the same soil types near the restoration where managers could harvest seed. Obviously, that doesn't characterize most of the Midwest today. Without the option of a nearby native prairie to harvest, the manager has to determine where they are going to get their seed. How far away is too far away for me to get seed? A manager may be able to get thirty species nearby but really wants ten more species. Is it better to have a lower diversity planting of local seeds or a higher diversity planting using seeds from farther away? There may be a nearby native wet prairie. If you're trying to restore a dry hilltop, you'll want to look farther away than the closest prairie.

And then there is climate change. The Midwest is expected to get warmer and drier. Species may shift from the southwest to the northeast. Should managers try to get seed from southwest of the restoration and move it northeast to the restoration? We can look at this in two ways. Instead of using "local" big bluestem seed in our mix, should we look for seed from southwest of the restoration to better match future climates? The next question is whether we should select entirely new species from southwest of our restoration and use them even though the restoration site is technically outside of the "currently" designated range for that species but may be in the "future" range. This is sometimes called assisted migration. These are hard questions, and few of them have absolute right or wrong answers.

So how far should you go? Seed should come from a "reasonable distance" (Millar and Libby 1989). However, reasonable may be in the eye of the beholder and it's difficult to come up with "unambiguous recommendations" for seed collection relative to distance between local and restoration sites (Moncada et al. 2007).

What does local even mean to a plant? Big bluestem is almost everywhere and wind-pollinated. We can imagine that through pollen the genes of big bluestem moved around quite a bit. Another species may be limited primarily to small hilltops and pollinated by an insect that doesn't travel very far. Other plants may naturally self-pollinate and be genetically adapted to this reproductive strategy.

There's one area of research that so far has had little attention. We bring plant seeds to an area to restore grasses and forbs. We assume the birds will find the site, as will the most mobile insects. But what about soil bacteria, fungi, and other microorganisms? What about the insects that can't disperse or travel over long distances? Do we need to cultivate and then "seed" these organisms into the site? How do we do that? For the most part, we just don't know. But it's interesting to think about and researchers are starting to investigate these questions (Fierer et al. 2013; Klopf et al. 2017).

For most restorations, managers are literally starting with a blank slate. They plant seed into or onto bare soil, often soybean stubble. In other cases, managers want to either: 1) convert a (near) monotypic field of brome or similar non-native grass to a diverse stand of native grasses and forbs, or 2) convert a low diversity native planting dominated by native grasses to a more forb-rich plant community.

When seeding into bare dirt, managers are putting seed into what is at least initially a relatively competition free environment. Interseeding into an established plant community is a very competitive environment.

Clipping or mowing can remove enough of the canopy of the dominant grasses to aid seedling establishment (Williams et al. 2007; Dickson and Foster 2008). Grazing can also help seedlings become established when seeds are added to established grasslands (Martin and Wilsey 2006; Doll et al. 2011; Wilsey and Martin 2015). Put another way, interseeding probably only works when followed by a significant amount of disturbance to remove or weaken the existing vegetation and reduce competition. Throwing seed out and just hoping for the best will rarely if ever increase species richness. It will waste seed, effort, and money.

One method that can cause significant heartburn in some people is seeding into native prairie, even highly degraded native prairie. There are several reasons for this. First, if some of the seed does germinate and plants get established, they could introduce new genes into an existing population of a species that could be detrimental to future generations. Second, it may damage the site for future research into plant community composition. Future researchers would have to ask whether that species was part of the original or historic plant community or a species someone planted recently.

Everyone who has been around prairie for a reasonable period of time has a story of burning a prairie that is in poor condition and being amazed at what pops up the following summer. A little more tender loving care may reveal an incredibly diverse plant community that just needed a little help to be "released."

I look for several species when investigating a new site, and if I find them, I'm pretty sure I'm standing on prairie that has never been plowed. If I'm on a hilltop, and I find some combination of pasqueflower, prairie smoke, ground plum, violets, puccoons, and similar species, I'm pretty sure I'm on unplowed soil. These are species that rarely show up in restorations. If I find them, they've probably been there for a long time. The site may have been heavily grazed in the past and dominated by brome. However, if there are some high-quality plants poking through, there are almost always more hiding in the soil. It's probably best to do a few years of management. If there are still very few native species at very low densities, then some sort of additional seeding may be in order.

In a way, restoration implies a fair amount of hubris and arrogance. It took Mother Nature, with a lot of help from human hands, thousands of years to put together the prairie. Do we really think we can recreate the prairie in her image in a few years?

> Of course, prairie restorations are not the genuine article. For a long time they can be only reasonable facsimiles at best. If we knew everything we needed to know, and had exactly the right equipment and seed sources, we might be able to re-create a fairly authentic prairie in as little as a century—although it may take from 300 to 500 years. (Madson 1982)

Restoration is an "acid test" for ecologists (Bradshaw 1987) and the "ultimate test of ecological theory" (Ewel 1987). If we really know all the pieces and parts of a prairie and how they all fit together, it shouldn't be any problem to put them together. Watchmakers with a fully stocked workshop should be able to build a functioning watch that accurately keeps time. Prairie restorationists can't say the same thing.

> Ecosystem restoration is an activity at which everyone wins: when successful, we are rewarded with having returned a fragment of the earth's surface to its former state; when we fail, we learn an immense amount about how ecosystems work, provided we are able to determine why the failure occurred. (Ewel 1987)

> Prairie restoration is an exciting and rewarding enterprise. It is full of surprises, fantastic successes, and abysmal failures. You learn a lot— usually more about what not to do than what to do. Success is seldom high, but prairie plants are resilient, and even a poor beginning will in time result in a beautiful prairie.
> Prairie restoration is also a humbling experience. You find out how little you really know and how intricately interrelated the species and their physical environments really are. (Cottam 1987)

However, none of that is a reason to slow down or stop our conservation efforts. If we don't know certain answers, like how to restore soil microorganisms, we shouldn't stop. That's a good reason to accelerate our restorations, monitoring, and research so that we learn from what we're doing today so that tomorrow's restorations are better. No time like the present to get started.

In a letter to his friend Bill Vogt on January 25, 1946, Aldo Leopold wrote that "the situation is hopeless should not prevent us from doing our best." First, the prairies aren't hopeless, even if it sometimes seems that way. Yes, we've lost a lot of prairie. Yes, our restorations aren't quite as diverse as native prairie. We just always need to do our best, even if that best isn't perfect, with every management action and every restoration. The important thing is to learn from every restoration, every burn, every grazing event. If something didn't work, study it, understand it, learn from it, and try again.

Keeping the Cogs and Wheels

I
T'S EARLY SUMMER. The prairie-chickens and sharp-tails are done displaying. Roosters no longer crow from the ditches. Bobolinks don't circle overhead and meadowlarks don't sing. It's quiet . . . as it should be in this season when hens sit silently and cryptically on nests.

Today we carry only paper bags as my best friend and I walk slowly across the prairie. He is close at heel so as not to disturb any nests. I am stooped over, looking closely at the ground in front of me. We are here to hand-harvest wildflower seeds from a native prairie.

Formally and informally, we've been surveying plant diversity in native prairie and restored grasslands on public lands near home. Although restorations are more diverse than they were just a few years ago, they still have only a fraction of the plants in a native prairie. As importantly, there are a number of species that almost never show up in restorations. These are usually species that are short, or bloom early, or grow on hilltops or wetland margins where the big harvest equipment can't go. Our efforts focus on these species, one handful of seed at a time.

With full bags, we get in the truck and start to drive away. A prairie-chicken hen and her brood sneak out of the grass, dart across the sandy two-track, and just as quickly disappear. Those young chicks are the reason we're out here.

After we get home, we pour the seeds into cardboard boxes and spread them out to dry. The seed pile starts to squirm and wiggle with all the insects we inadvertently collected. This may be the most important reason to consider plant diversity when restoring grassland bird habitat.

At this time of year I keep each species of seed separate, everything dried and in carefully labeled paper bags. But there's always that one bag I forget to label. Then I get the fun of trying to identify seed and chaff at the end of the summer.

Late summer finds massive gleaners noisily marching back and forth across the prairie, harvesting wide swaths of grass and wildflower seed. This time of year we harvest the sunflowers, asters, blazingstars, legumes, mints, and warm-season grasses in bulk. The gleaners will harvest tens of thousands of pounds of seed in a few days. We'll add our seed to this mix.

We spread the seed from the gleaners out in long three-foot tall windrows on top of perforated PVC pipes. Once we turn the blowers on, we need ear protection, and any communication is done by yelling or hand signals. After the seed is dry, a large group will come together to bag the seed and store those bags in rodent-proof cages for the winter. We store tens of thousands of pounds of seed, forty-pound bags at a time.

As fall progresses, it's just the two of us again on the quiet prairie. We have plenty of seed for the year. Now it's just an excuse to be outside, alone together.

Next March we will scatter the seed over snow-covered soybean stubble. The snow will melt, and the daily freeze and thaw will pull the seed down into the soil. In another couple years, a former monoculture agricultural field will be turned into habitat with a diversity of native grasses and wildflowers and an abundance of gamebirds, waterfowl, songbirds, and pollinators. There are few rewards in the field of conservation, and most gratification is delayed. Finding wildflowers in a restoration that you know wouldn't be there without your efforts is very gratifying.

Hand-harvesting seed is just one more excuse to be outside, to walk more miles, to explore new habitats, and spend time alone with my best friend. It's about walking slowly, observing closely, and listening carefully.

Aldo Leopold tells us "that the first part of intelligent tinkering is keeping all the cogs and wheels." Hand-harvesting seed is one way to ensure that our habitat restorations, our tinkerings with nature, have as many cogs, wheels, grasses, wildflowers, insects, and birds as possible.

CHAPTER 16

New Advocates for Prairie Conservation

What is the most valuable part of the prairie? The fat black soil, the chernozem. Who built the chernozem? The black prairie was built by the prairie plants, a hundred distinctive species of grasses, herbs, and shrubs. — *Leopold 1949*

Natural areas restoration is a realm of ecology destined to become the single most important environmental effort of the future. — *Schramm 1990*

We conclude that restoration of tallgrass prairie vegetation can restore SOM [soil organic matter] lost through cultivation and has the potential to sequester relatively large amounts of SOC [soil organic carbon] over a sustained period of time. — *Matamala et al. 2008*

Perhaps the current diminished condition of the tallgrass prairie is a blessing, a unique opportunity for our society to come together and begin the healing process with prairie restoration. — *D. Smith 2010*

[L]and-use change in a region experiencing rapid and extensive grassland loss is likely to significantly increase the number of contaminated private drinking water wells. — *Keeler and Polasky 2014*

Our results suggest that restoration of high plant diversity may greatly increase carbon capture and storage rates on degraded and abandoned agricultural lands. — *Yang et al. 2019*

A FEW YEARS AGO when the pup and I lived in south-central Minnesota, we had a seven-inch rain. The creek that ran through our small property jumped about eight or nine feet overnight and the water in the creek was the color and consistency of a chocolate milkshake. Living at the top of our watershed, the only damage was a foot of water over the driveway for a few days. Cities to the north and east of us did have some flood damage when all the water in all the creeks flowed downstream.

The afternoon following that overnight rainstorm, the pup and I visited a Waterfowl Production Area just a mile to the east of our house. There were no signs of run-off around the edges of the area and the wetlands simply filled up with crystal-clear, clean water. That water just sat there. Some of it percolated down into the soil, recharging groundwater supplies. Over the following weeks, some of it evaporated up into the air. The rest provided habitat for ducks. What that water didn't do was run horizontally, cause any erosion, or add to any potential flooding issues downstream.

In *The Land Ethic*, Aldo Leopold writes that "one basic weakness in a conservation system based wholly on economic motives is that most members of the land community have no economic value." While Leopold may be correct that individually each species has little economic value, collectively the prairie can have significant economic value to everyone, not just those who most love the prairie. And in that, we have a new audience and new advocates for prairie conservation.

Acre for acre, some of the largest grassland restoration programs have been in the Federal Farm Bills. In 1936, President Franklin Roosevelt signed the Soil Conservation and Domestic Allotment Act. (None of them are actually named "Farm Bill.") This act contained the Agricultural Conservation Program, or ACP, which paid farmers to plant cropland to perennial grasses. In 1956, President Eisenhower signed the Agricultural Act, which included the Soil Bank program. In 1985, the Food Security Act contained the modern Conservation Reserve Program, CRP. Across the Midwest, CRP greatly outnumbered acres of remaining prairie in most states. For instance, Iowa has approximately 29,300 acres of native prairie (Samson and Knopf 1994). Iowa's peak CRP enrollment in the mid-1990s was 2,203,800 acres.

One of the biggest issues with all these programs, from a conservation perspective, is that they are temporary. Millions of acres are planted with perennial grasses. The grasses are plowed under and planted back to row crops when the contracts end. However, the language used in these three Farm Bills points to new conservation opportunities and new messages to new audiences. We can look to the past to plot a new future for grassland conservation.

The conservation section of the 1936 Soil Conservation and Domestic Allotment Act mentioned in the first paragraph "wastage of soil and moisture resources . . . soil erosion, is a menace to the national welfare . . . prevention of soil erosion . . . preserve natural resources . . . control floods." Title I of the 1956 legislation is named the Soil Bank Act. The bill lists "soil erosion, depletion of soil fertility and too rapid release of water from lands where it falls." In 1985, Subtitle D (Conservation Reserve) of Title XII (Conservation) lists "conserving and improving soil and water resources." These programs weren't primarily focused on habitat or wildlife. They were focused on soil and water health as well as a commodity market that was flooded with surplus grain. Those surpluses were driving prices down and driving many farms into bankruptcy.

The descriptions of the benefits of grassland restoration for water and soil in these bills laid the groundwork for the modern concept of ecosystem services. Restoring prairie for prairie's sake, or for pollinators, or for pheasants or meadowlarks is a good thing. However, there are many in our society who just don't care about these things and probably never will. Ecosystem services give the conservation community an opportunity to sell our ideas to a new and much larger audience.

There are some people who are never going to listen to, or understand, Leopold's Land Ethic. Nor are they going to be moved to action by the poetry of any of dozens of outdoor writers and artists. They can only listen to dollars and cents. Today, we have numbers and data that speak to both a conservation ethic and economic self-interest, for the landowner, the neighbor, and society as a whole.

It's hard to assign a dollar value to a mallard or pheasant, and more difficult to assign a dollar value to a grasshopper sparrow or a compass plant.

We can put an economic value on using grassland restoration on a wellhead protection area to safeguard a city's drinking water supply. We can put an economic value on the amount of carbon natural habitats absorb.

In the past, conservation has almost been seen as some sort of societal or personal sacrifice. Conservation is only for the elite who can afford it, according to some. Conservation sacrifices agricultural land, taking the land out of production, according to some. We have to "set aside" land for conservation, land that could be doing something productive and beneficial for society, according to some.

In other cases, conservation land is seen solely as wildlife habitat. This leaves some people who aren't bird hunters, birdwatchers, or botanists asking, "what's in it for me?" That's a perfectly valid question.

We may be entering a new realm of grassland conservation. It may not be enough to restore prairie because native wildflowers are pretty or because some like to hunt pheasants in the fall. There are very good reasons to restore grasslands across the Midwest that benefit everyone. This is exciting because it creates new opportunities and new audiences to discuss grassland conservation.

The soils under prairies and wetlands are often black. They are black from carbon. Unfortunately, when prairies are broken and wetlands drained, and then these acres are plowed and disced by farm equipment each year, the soils release large amounts of the carbon they have stored over the centuries. If plowing under grasslands releases carbon, doesn't it make sense that restoring grasslands and wetlands removes carbon from the atmosphere? It does.

Because each site has a different soil type, moisture level or precipitation pattern, growing-season length, plant community, and different management, it's impossible to make the general statement that every acre of restored prairie removes a certain amount of carbon from the atmosphere. However, a number of studies show that grassland restoration does restore soil carbon and by default removes that carbon from the atmosphere (Knops and Tilman 2000; Baer et al. 2002; McLauchlan et al. 2006; Baer et al. 2010).

And we can even build on this story. For the last couple of decades, we've been using high diversity seed mixes in restorations to enhance bird and pollinator habitat. Turns out, those high diversity restorations store more soil carbon than low diversity mixes (Fornara and Tilman 2008; Ampleman et al. 2014; Yang et al. 2019). What we've been doing for one reason, pollinators and habitat, works perfectly well for other reasons, carbon sequestration. Everything is coming together.

The grass canopy holds large volumes of water during a rainstorm as droplets and a film of water on the leaves and stems. Go out to a prairie after a rain and dig down into the thatch. It's quite often dry. Weaver (1954) cites studies that show big bluestem stems and leaves capture 12,770 gallons per acre or 8,173,500 gallon per square mile. During a two-inch rain in mid-July, big bluestem captured 51 percent of the rainfall on the grass leaves (O. R. Clark 1940). This water will evaporate once the storm passes or slowly percolate into the soil. What the water won't do is rush downstream and cause flooding.

The porous soils beneath grasslands can absorb and store large volumes of water. When soil is annually disced or plowed, the channels and pores in the soil collapse and become compacted. Weaver (1968) reviewed studies that compared run-off and erosion from a prairie and bare area with similar slope and soil type. Run-off from the prairie was "nil" while run-off from the bare area was over 20 percent. Related studies found no soil erosion on prairies, but topsoil loss ranged from five to twelve tons per acre on cropland.

In northwest Minnesota at the Glacial Ridge National Wildlife Refuge, one of the largest prairie restorations in the Midwest, grassland and wetland restoration significantly reduces peak run-off in the flood prone Red River Valley as well as helps recharge groundwater supplies (Gerla 2007; Cowdery et al. 2019). Research at the Neal Smith National Wildlife Refuge in central Iowa, another landscape-level restoration project, showed multiple benefits of the restoration to ground- and surface-water hydrology (Schilling and Drobney 2014a, 2014b). Grassland and wetland restorations across the Midwest presumably have the same effects.

Grasslands not only store and absorb water, they clean it too. Go to an unburned prairie during the summer and lie on the ground on your belly. What you'll see is this incredibly complicated network of living and dead grass and forbs, leaves and stems crisscrossing in a dense and chaotic pattern. Then go home and pull the air filter out of your furnace. It looks very similar.

Across the Midwest many lakes and rivers are polluted with nitrates and phosphates, from several different sources. When nitrates and phosphates reach local lakes, they cause algal blooms. When the algae dies, the bacteria that decompose the algae consume all the oxygen in the water, potentially killing many of the fish and other aquatic life. Over an eight-year period of prairie restoration at Neal Smith National Wildlife Refuge, groundwater nitrates in the uplands declined by 80 percent (Tomer et al. 2010).

When nitrates get into drinking water, they cause a number of human health issues, most infamously, blue-baby syndrome. On page fifteen of the Minnesota Department of Health's *Minnesota Drinking Water 2015 Annual Report for 2014* there is a photo of a group of individuals, several wearing orange hunting shirts, at the dedication of a state Wildlife Management Area. One of the highlighted ways to protect water quality and public health is to restore prairie. If grassland conservation and restoration becomes a human health issue, grasslands have a whole new set of friends. This also creates a potential for new sets of partnerships in the conservation world.

These ideas also give us a new context for planning restoration efforts. If we restore prairie over there, we'll create some wildlife habitat. If we restore prairie here, on a Wellhead Protection Area, then entire communities will support the effort. DWSMA, short for Drinking Water Supply Management Area, is an acronym every prairie advocate needs to understand and start using frequently. DWSMAs and Wellhead Protection Areas are areas where a large percentage of a local community's water comes from. They are often sandy soils that allow water to percolate downward. Sandy soils are often not the best agricultural soils. Do we just want more wildlife habitat from our restorations that will be supported by birdwatchers and bird hunters? Or do we want our restorations to provide wildlife habitat, potentially reduce downstream flooding, reduce nitrates in drinking water, and help the local community protect their drinking water? Now how many local citizens and local politicians are supporting the restoration efforts?

There are social, economic, and political implications to these issues. We now have the knowledge and data to do conservation smarter and more strategically. We know where on the landscape we can restore grasslands to meet "stacked benefits." One action, grassland restoration, can have multiple positive outcomes, if the conservation community has the right conversations with the right people to get them on board and then does the conservation in a strategic way that everyone, or almost everyone, can support.

The most important part is having those conversations early on in the process. Let people know what the plans are, even before they are plans. Get their input and get them involved in the process as early as possible. The conservation world doesn't need anyone thinking that someone is sneaking around, being cryptic, or trying to hide the ultimate goals. Showing everyone how they benefit from the proposed work, and how many different people or groups benefit, makes the process much easier and less contentious.

We can take the conservation message to a much larger audience and build a wider base of support for grassland restoration. The conservation message morphs from those who like to hunt pheasants to those who like to drink water and don't like flood damage, which is most people.

Similar principles about location apply within fields. The Prairie STRIPS (Science-based Trials of Row-crops Integrated with Prairie Strips) project in Iowa demonstrates field-level conservation practices that are beneficial for water quality and agriculture (Schulte et al. 2017). Their research shows that by strategically planting 10 percent of a field with strips of prairie grasses and forbs, run-off decreases by 32 percent, nitrogen loss declines by 82 percent, and phosphorus loss declines by 89 percent. Soil erosion declines by 95 percent. The researchers developed ways to locate the strips in each field in order to maximize the benefits while taking into account the size of a farmer's equipment and to be minimally disruptive to farming practices within each field.

With modern farming equipment, farmers can measure inputs such as fertilizers and yields at harvest almost square yard by square yard. Farmers are losing money on approximately 6.2 million acres of farmlands in Iowa almost every year (Brandes et al. 2016). Several companies have recently developed "precision ag" tools that allow farmers to analyze each field and determine the most and least profitable areas of each field. These tools show that in-field profitability increases dramatically when farms plant only the most productive ground and don't lose money on the least productive acres.

Using these tools, farmers can precisely determine where they frequently lose money. These are acres that are ideal to be put into grassland. In most cases, these may be relatively small areas within any one field. However, if every farm in a township used these tools and strategically planted grass on their least productive acres, that could be a significant amount of grass. Those acres can be planted to grassland for the direct economic benefit of the landowner. A lot of those acres are sandy, allowing for rainwater to percolate into the groundwater, or the acres are low areas that could be restored to wetland and capture water. Restoring these acres might provide a private benefit to the landowner and a public benefit to the community. Decisions for private and personal profit can have larger societal benefits. That's a very different story than the traditional "conservation as sacrifice" storyline.

Prairie Spring

O UR SHADOWS STRETCH almost to the edge of the western landscape as the sun crests the east. It's April in northwest Minnesota. It is tundra cold this morning, but the top layers of clothing will be coming off in an hour or so. Everyone is officially ready to declare the long cold miserable winter over.

Ignoring calendars, day length, and other arbitrary measures, there are two sure signs of prairie spring. The first is the pale lavender bloom of the pasqueflower, inconspicuously hugging the ground, hidden in the grass to avoid the April wind. Pasqueflower is subtle, blooms for a short period of time, and is almost invisible for the rest of the year.

The second sign, a brown, striped bird, remains hidden for most of the year also, a "child of the sullen winter grasses," as William Quayle wrote. But at this time of year, the deep resonant booming of the prairie-chicken echoes across the landscape and can be heard from two miles or more. There is nothing subtle about an April prairie-chicken.

As we walk closer, my four-footed survey partner and I can see them out in the field, the white rump feathers and bright orange sacs on their necks make as stunning of a visual exhibition as the auditory display we've been listening to for the past several minutes.

The pioneer literature is full of somber descriptions of these displays. John Madson, one of the poet laureates of the prairie, stated that "it is a lonely wild sound made by a lonely wild bird. . . . In all of modern America, there is no more lost, plaintive, old-time sound than the booming of the native prairie chicken" (1982). Other writers describe the sound as "dirge-like strains" or "a long, loud, mournful note." Paul Johnsgard (2001), who has written more about prairie birds than anyone else, said the sound reminds him of the "melancholic aspect of some lost soul seeking forgiveness."

These birds look neither sad nor mournful. Those orange sacs on their neck and the combs above their eyes fluoresce as the sun crests the eastern horizon. Hamlin Garland was one of the few members of the pioneer generation that took a different view of the prairie-chicken. To him, "at the mellow boom, boom, boom of the prairie cock our hearts quickened, for this, we were told, was the certain sign of spring."

In recent years, heavy breaking plows have been gouging into the earth, flipping the remaining native prairie and Conservation Reserve Program fields rootside up at nearly unprecedented rates. We have more room for king corn and less room for prairie-chickens, pheasants, quail, mallards, songbirds, and all the other species that call the prairies home. The prairie world is wounded, and some of us take those wounds very personally. Those losses are painful.

That tension between living in Leopold's "world of wounds" but not doing it in Hamerstrom's "sepulchral atmosphere" is never more evident than on these mornings. After all the destruction of habitat we've seen in recent years, the pasqueflowers are still blooming on the hilltops and gravel ridges. There are still prairie-chickens in the field in front of us. There are fewer birds than there could or should be, and every year we lose another booming ground or two in our survey area. But some birds are still hanging on. The birds are still holding out hope, because they don't know what else to do on a spring morning. As Emily Dickinson told us, "hope is the thing with feathers."

If you ever need an uplifting experience or a sense of renewal, ever need something to revitalize the will to continue the fight for these habitats and all of the birds that call these grasslands home, spend a morning watching prairie-chickens, in the words of Leopold, "booming from the mists of nowhere." If they haven't given up, if they still have faith for future generations, then we should have that same faith. I have to keep fighting for these birds and their habitat, because, like them, I don't know what else to do.

As my Grandma's King James says in the thirtieth chapter of Psalms, joy cometh in the morning.

Conclusion

Its sublimity arises from its unbounded extent, its barren monotony and desolation, its still, unmoved, calm, stern, almost self-confident grandeur, its strange power of deception, its want of echo, and, in fine, its power of throwing a man back upon himself and giving him a feeling of lone helplessness, strangely mingled at the same time with a feeling of liberty and freedom from restraint. — *Pike 1832*

May I not be permitted, in this place, to introduce a few reflections on the magical influences of the prairies? It is difficult to express by words the varied impressions which their spectacle produces. Their sight never wearies. — *Nicollet 1838*

I think the prairie will die without finding a voice. Its democracy may be against it. Prairie grass never seems to know anybody. — *Quayle 1905*

My feeling for tallgrass prairie is like that of a modern man who has fallen in love with the face in a faded tintype. Only the frame is still real; the rest is illusion and dream. — *Madson 1979*

Whatever else prairie is — grass, sky, wind — it is most of all a paradigm of infinity, a clearing full of many things except boundaries, and its power comes from its apparent limitlessness. — *Least Heat-Moon 1991*

To understand and enjoy them fully, one must be sensitive to the whispers and expect to encounter neither forbidding mountains nor spectacular shorelines. Instead their long, unencumbered vistas are an invitation to look inward toward the soul as well as outward toward the horizon, to look down on tiny prairie wildflowers and upward toward endless cerulean skies with equal appreciation. — *Johnsgard 2003*

AS I WAS PUTTING the finishing touches on this book, a couple friends with the US Fish and Wildlife Service told me about a new tract of land the Service had just acquired, not too far from the first house I bought when I moved to Minnesota. It was so new they didn't have signs posted around the perimeter yet. I had to debate whether it was worth a four-hour drive to see it, but some of their photos were just too tempting. It was an amazing tract of native prairie. I saw more individuals of blanket flower, locoweed, downy paintbrush, prairie milkvetch, prairie smoke, at this site than I've seen collectively over my career. It was worth the drive. Why was it still prairie? Why wasn't it a cornfield, or a series of trophy homes, or a gravel pit like the adjacent property? It was still prairie because it still had cattle on it in recent decades.

In each of the following quotes, we can probably substitute "prairie" for "prairie-chicken." These quotes have two ideas. First, private landowners play a key role in prairie conservation. Second, as we understand more and more of the science of the prairie, we are starting to see that economic uses and ecological goals can mesh very well with a little conversation and planning.

> The future of the prairie chicken is in the hands of the landowners of America. (Grange 1939)

> The future of the prairie chicken in Missouri is in the hands of all the people in the state, but it depends most of all upon those who use the soil. (Schwartz 1945)

> Fortunately, the practices recommended for the most profitable long-time use of grasslands are beneficial to prairie chickens. (Baker 1953)

We don't always need to build fences, literally or figuratively, and decorate those fences with signs to protect the prairie. Directly or indirectly, those fences and signs can divide people from nature. Here's a line, with people, society, and the economy on one side and wildlife, plant communities, and ecology on the other. If there's one theme for this book it's the role people played historically in the development of the prairie and the role people need to play in the future of the prairie. If there has ever been an ecosystem that shows there's no good divide between people and nature, it's the tallgrass prairie.

I'm a huge advocate for public lands. But I also realize that a lot of conservation can happen on private lands. Prairie conservationists need to work with federal and state wildlife agencies. They also need to work with organizations such as The Nature Conservancy or The Prairie Enthusiasts. Just as importantly, they need to become friends with ranchers, beekeepers, and others who work the land. The examples used throughout this book demonstrate repeatedly that what's often good for ranchers and cattle, bees and beekeepers, is good for conservationists and wildlife. And vice versa. This is the most natural partnership out there.

Yes, some of the smallest remnants in the eastern prairie region do need to be managed very carefully. They almost need to be treated as gardens. No one is advocating grazing or haying in a one-acre cemetery prairie in eastern Illinois or western Indiana.

However, managing prairie landscapes, areas large enough for prairie-chickens, variable fire seasons and frequencies, some grazing and haying, and containing wet, mesic, and dry prairies, can be done in both an ecological and an economic context. In fact, those two words have the same Greek root, *oikos*. In few other areas of conservation can ecology and economics be so well connected for the mutual benefit of both as they can with prairie conservation.

Is every private pasture managed perfectly? No, but a lot of them are managed pretty well. Grazing gives the conservation and agricultural communities a reason to sit down together and discuss how they can help each other. If land isn't growing cows, it's probably going to be growing corn or condos. Of the three, I know which one is the best friend of prairie wildlife.

If we want a vibrant prairie ecology, then we need a robust prairie economy.

In the frequently quoted final sentences of Wallace Stegner's essay "Coda: Wilderness Letter," he writes, "We simply need that wild country available to us, even if we never do more than drive to its edge and look in. For it can be a means of reassuring ourselves of our sanity as creatures, as a part of the geography of hope" (1969). I'm not sure this works for the prairie. It's not enough, you'll miss too much, if you just go to the edge and look in. Prairie requires entry and immersion.

> To know prairie, one must be immersed in it in some way. You don't come to know the prairie by standing at its edge and looking in; you must be *in* the prairie and let it get into you. (Drobney 1999)

> [M]any of this grand landscape's best features, paradoxically, are visible only close at hand. (Gruchow 1999)

> Grasslands are never best appreciated from afar; distance might well lend enchantment to mountains, but prairies require close and personal contacts to deliver their subtle brand of magic. (Johnsgard 2003)

Once you do learn to look out across, at, and into the prairie, to see the prairie at multiple scales of space and imagine multiple scales of time, you will start to understand the mystery of what's out there. Or maybe better understand that none of us can understand all that's out there. Once you get into the prairie, once you fall in love, the grasses and forbs and birds and mammals and clouds and weathers will slowly but surely seep into you.

And here a warning is in order. As Friedrich Nietzsche wrote about staring into the abyss, sometimes the prairie will make you fall under its spell. And if it does, something will happen to you on the prairie that probably can't happen anywhere else. What that something is, is for everyone to find and find out for themselves.

> But raise the eyes to the bare prairie, and they sweep the horizon. Nothing stops them. They stare, stare—and sometimes the prairie gets to staring back. (Humphrey 1931)

> It's a dangerous place, this vast ocean of prairie. Something happens to us here. (Norris 1993)

The prairie is both small and big, near and far, intimate and remote, familiar and unknowable. The prairie may be unique in all these paradoxes and contradictions. Perhaps more than anything the prairie is a mixture of sadness and joy. It's impossible not to feel uplifted standing in the summer prairie with the wind making all the flowers and grasses dance. It's impossible not to feel downhearted knowing this experience is so rare today.

If it is almost gone, is it worth fighting for that last 1 percent? Yes! Why? We can again turn to Stegner's "Coda: Wilderness Letter": "Something will have gone out of us as a people if we let the remaining wilderness be destroyed . . . if we drive the few remaining members of the wild species into zoos or to extinction." We can't let that happen. We need to take national, regional, and cultural pride in this once magnificent ecosystem.

> Then as to scenery (giving my own thought and feeling,) while I know the standard claim is that Yosemite, Niagara falls, the upper Yellowstone and the like, afford the greatest natural shows, I am not so sure but the Prairies and Plains, while less stunning at first sight, last longer, fill the esthetic sense fuller, precede all the rest, and make North America's characteristic landscape. (Whitman 1882)

> The prairie, in all its expressions is a massive subtle place, with a long history of contradictions and misunderstanding. But it is worth the effort at comprehension. It is, after all, the center of our national identity. (Fields 1888 quoted in Least Heat-Moon 1991)

> Every American has the right as part of his cultural heritage to stand in grass as high as his head in order to feel some small measure of history coursing through his veins. (Elder 1961)

The prairie is a land of paradox and contradiction. The tallgrass prairie is both a melting pot and barrier that prevents mixing of species. People largely helped create and shape the tallgrass prairie over millennia. People eliminated the tallgrass prairie in decades. Is the prairie artificial or un-natural, or is it one of the best examples on the planet of how people and the natural world can work together sustainably? People often used the ocean as a metaphor for the early prairie. Today the prairie is a series of tiny islands and atolls in a sea of corn and beans. The landscape that is most alive from a prairie lover's perspective is often on the ground con-secrated to the dead. The prairie is chaotic, confusing, and constantly changing. Over the decades, the science and our understanding of the prairie changes almost as fast as the prairie itself changes. Those changes won't stop. Although I tried to represent the latest science in this book, eventually this book will look a little old-fashioned as science reveals even more and our understanding changes.

None of that should discourage anyone from getting to know, trying to understand, and falling in love with the prairie in general and their special prairie specifically. The prairie is worth the effort at comprehen-sion. Even if we know that we'll never reach our goal of complete under-standing, this is one of those cases where the journey may be even more important than the destination.

Edward Abbey's quote from the end of my disclaimer bears repeating because of its importance. "Any good poet in our age at least, must begin with the scientific view of the world; and any scientist worth listening to must be something of a poet, must possess the ability to communicate to the rest of us his sense of love and wonder at what his work discovers." The prairie needs more science. There's still so much we don't understand. But even more, the prairie needs poets, artists, writers, and photographers who can capture the beauty and emotion of the prairie. And they need to share that beauty with others. The prairie requires full engagement with both the head and the heart.

Aldo Leopold wondered whether it was even worth asking the question of what a thousand acres of Silphiums looked like when they tickled the bellies of the buffalo. Let's ask the question.

Whether you go afield holding a camera, binoculars, shotgun, pen and paper, artist's brush or pencil, or a child's hand, ask the question. Whether you're most worried about gamebirds or songbirds, ask the question. Whether you're worried about honeybees, monarch butterflies, or regal fritillaries, ask the question. If you're interested in carbon sequestration to slow climate change, ask the question. If your town is interested in protecting its drinking water or minimizing downstream flooding, ask the question. If you're interested in the history of the Midwest, ask the question. If you want your children to have the opportunity to hear the lost, plaintive, booming of the prairie chicken, ask the question. If you don't want to deny future generations the opportunity to drown in a field of big bluestem and feel history coursing through their veins, ask the question.

My hope is that this book gives every reader a new understanding of the science, the history, and the story of the tallgrass prairie. Visit new prairies. Revisit familiar prairies again, and again, and again. Enjoy, immerse, appreciate, absorb, engage, learn, and love. Just get out there.

Bibliography

Abbey, E. P. 1977. *The Journey Home*. New York: Plume Book.

———. 1988. *One Life at a Time, Please*. New York: Henry Holt and Company.

Adamidis, G. C., M. T. Swartz, K. Zografou, and B. J. Sewall. 2019. "Prescribed fire maintains host plants of a rare grassland butterfly." *Nature Research Scientific Reports* 9 (1): 16826.

Ahlering, M., D. Carlson, S. Vasek, S. Jacobi, V. Hunt, J. C. Stanton, M. G. Knutson, and E. Lonsdorf. 2020. "Cooperatively improving tallgrass prairie with adaptive management." *Ecosphere* 11 (4): 1–21.

Ahlering, M., and C. L. Merkord. 2016. "Cattle grazing and grassland birds in the northern tallgrass prairie." *Journal of Wildlife Management* 80 (4): 643–654.

Albertson, F. W., and J. E. Weaver. 1945. "Injury and death or recovery of trees in prairie climate." *Ecological Monographs* 15: 393–433.

Aldrich, B. S. 1928. *A Lantern in Her Hand*. N.p.: D. Appleton and Co.

Allen, M. S., and M. W. Palmer. 2011. "Fire history of a prairie/forest boundary: more than 250 years of frequent fire in a North American tallgrass prairie." *Journal of Vegetation Science* 22: 436–444.

Ampleman, M., K. Crawford, and D. Fike. 2014. "Differential soil organic carbon storage at forb- and grass-dominated plant communities, 33 years after tallgrass prairie restoration." *Plant and Soil* 374 (1–2). https://doi.org/10.1007/s11104 -013-1916-5.

Anderson, L. C., L. A. Powell, W. H. Schacht, J. T. Lusk, and W. L. Vodehnal. 2015. "Greater prairie-chicken brood-site selection and survival in the Nebraska Sandhills." *Journal of Wildlife Management* 79 (4): 559–569.

Anderson, R. C. 1983. "The eastern prairie-forest transition-an overview." In *Proceedings of the Eighth North American Prairie Conference*, edited by R. Brewer, 86–92. Kalamazoo: Western Michigan University.

———. 2006. "Evolution and origin of the Central Grasslands of North America: climate, fire, and mammalian grazers." *Journal of the Torrey Botanical Society*. 133: 626–647.

Anderson, R. H., S. D. Fuhlendorf, and D. M. Engle. 2006. "Soil nitrogen availability in tallgrass prairie under the fire-grazing interaction." *Rangeland Ecology and Management* 59: 625–631.

Archer, S., and C. Bunch. 1953. *American Grass Book: A Manual of Pasture and Range Practices.* Norman: University of Oklahoma Press.

Atwater, C. 1818. "On the prairies and barrens of the West." *American Journal of Science* 1: 116–125.

Axelrod, D. I. 1985. "Rise of the grassland biome, Central North America." *The Botanical Review* 51: 163–201.

Baer, S. G., D. J. Kitchen, J. M. Blair, and C. W. Rice. 2002. "Changes in ecosystem structure and function along a chronosequence of restored grasslands." *Ecological Applications* 12: 1688–1701.

Baer, S. G., C. K. Meyer, E. M. Bach, R. P. Klopf, and J. Six. 2010. "Contrasting ecosystem recovery on two soil textures: implications for carbon mitigation and grassland conversion." *Ecosphere* 1 (1): 1–22. https://doi.org/10.1890/ES10 -00004.1.

Baker, M. F. 1953. *Prairie Chickens of Kansas.* Lawrence: State Biological Survey, University of Kansas.

Barbour, M. G. 1995. "Ecological fragmentation in the fifties." In *Uncommon Ground: Toward Reinventing Nature,* edited by W. Cronon, 233–255. New York: W. W. Norton and Company.

Batek, M. J., A. J. Rebertus, W. A. Schroeder, T. L. Haithcoat, E. Compas, and R. P. Guyette. 1999. "Reconstruction of early nineteenth-century vegetation and fire regimes in the Missouri Ozarks." *Journal of Biogeography* 26 (2): 397–412.

Baum, K. A., and W. V. Sharber. 2012. "Fire creates host plant patches for monarch butterflies." *Biology Letters* 8: 968–971.

Beltrami, G. 1828. *A Pilgrimage in Europe and America.* London: Hunt and Clarke.

Belue, T. F. 1996. *The Long Hunt: Death of the Bison East of the Mississippi.* Mechanicsburg: Stackpole Books.

Bennett, L. J. 1938. *The Blue-Winged Teal: Its Ecology and Management.* Ames: Collegiate Press, Inc.

Benson, E. J., and D. C. Hartnett. 2006. "The role of seed and vegetative reproduction in plant recruitment and demography in tallgrass prairie." *Plant Ecology* 187: 163–177.

Benson, E. J., D. C. Hartnett, and K. H. Mann. 2004. "Belowground bud bank and meristem limitation in tallgrass prairie plant populations." *American Journal of Botany* 91: 416–421.

Berry, W. 1981. *The Gift of Good Land*. San Francisco: North Point Press.

Betz, R. F. 1972. "What is a Prairie?" In *The Prairie: Swell and Swale*, edited by T. Korling. Dundee, IL: Korling.

Betz, R. F., and H. F. Lamp. 1989. "Species composition of old settler silt-loam prairies." In *Proceedings of the Eleventh North American Prairie Conference*, edited by T. Bragg and J. Stubbendieck, 33–39. Lincoln: University of Nebraska Press.

———. 1992. "Species composition of old settler savanna and sand prairie cemeteries in northern Illinois and northwestern Indiana." In *Proceedings of the Twelfth North American Prairie Conference,* edited by D. D. Smith and C. A. Jacobs, 79–88. Cedar Falls: University of Northern Iowa Press.

Birkbeck, M. (1817) 1968. *Notes on a Journey in America, from the Coast of Virginia to the Territory of Illinois, with Proposals for the Establishment of a Colony of English*. Ann Arbor: University of Michigan Press.

Blair, J. M. 1997. "Fire, N availability, and plant response in grasslands: a test of the transient maxima hypothesis." *Ecology* 78: 2359–2368.

Blair, W. D. 1989. *Katherine Ordway: The Lady Who Saved the Prairies*. Alexandria, VA: The Nature Conservancy.

Bliss, L. C., and G. W. Cox. 1964. "Plant community and soil variation within a northern Indiana prairie." *American Midland Naturalist* 72: 115–128.

Bomar, C. R. 2001. "Comparison of grasshopper (Orthoptera: Acrididae) communities on remnant and reconstructed prairies in western Wisconsin." *Journal of Orthoptera Research* 10 (1): 105–112.

Borchert, J. R. 1950. "The climate of the central North American grasslands." *Annals of the Association of American Geographers* 40: 1–39.

Bossenmaier, E. F. 1964. "Cows and cutter bars." In *Waterfowl Tomorrow,* edited by J. P. Linduska, 627–634. Washington, DC: US Government Printing Office.

Botkin, D. B. 1995. *Our Natural History: The Lessons of Lewis and Clark*. New York: G. P. Putnam's Sons.

Bourne, A. 1820. "On the prairies and barrens of the west." *The American Journal of Science and Arts* 2: 30–34.

Bradbury, J. 1810. *Travels in the Interior of America in the Years 1809, 1810, and 1811*. London: Sherwood, Neely, and Jones.

Bradshaw, A. D. 1987. "Restoration: an acid test for ecology." In *Restoration Ecology: A Synthetic Approach to Ecological Research*, edited by W. R. Jordan, M. E. Gilpin, and J. D. Aber, 23–30. New York: Cambridge University Press.

Brandes, E., G. S. McNunn, L. A. Schulte, I. J. Bonner, D. J. Muth, B. A. Babcock, B. Sharma, and E. A. Heaton. 2016. "Subfield profitability analysis reveals an economic case for cropland diversification." *Environmental Research Letters* 11 (1). https://doi.org/10.1088/1748-9326/11/1/014009.

Braun, E. L. 1928a. "Glacial and post-glacial plant migration indicated by relic colonies of southern Ohio." *Ecology* 9 (3): 284–302.

———. 1928b. "The vegetation of the Mineral Spring Region of Adams County, Ohio." *Ohio Biological Survey* 3: 375–517.

Braun-Blanquet, J. 1932. *Plant Sociology: The Study of Plant Communities.*

Bray, J. R. 1957. "Climax forest herbs in prairie." *American Midland Naturalist* 58: 434–440.

Briggs, J. M., and A. K. Knapp. 1995. "Interannual variability in primary production in tallgrass prairie: climate, soil moisture, topographic position, and fire as determinants of aboveground biomass." *American Journal of Botany* 82: 1024–1030.

Briggs, J. M., A. K. Knapp, J. M. Blair, J. L. Heisler, G. A. Hoch, M. S. Lett, J. K. McCarron. 2005. "An ecosystem in transition: causes and consequences of the conversion of mesic grassland to shrubland." *Bioscience* 55 (3): 243–254.

Briggs, J. M., A. K. Knapp, and B. L. Brock. 2002. "Expansion of woody plants in tallgrass prairie: a fifteen-year study of fire and fire-grazing interactions." *American Midland Naturalist* 147: 287–294.

Brink, W. 1951. *Big Hugh: The Father of Soil Conservation.* New York: The Macmillan Company.

Brown, D. A. 1993. "Early nineteenth-century grasslands of the midcontinental plains." *Annals of the Association of American Geographers* 83: 589–612.

Brunson, A. (1835) 1968. "A prairie fire and claim association." In *Prairie State*, edited by P. M. Angle, 161–165. Chicago: University of Chicago Press.

Butler, W. F. 1872. *The Great Lone Land: A Narrative of Travel and Adventure in the North-west of America.* London: Sampson Low, Marston, Low, & Searle.

Callicott, J. B. 1994. "The wilderness idea revisited." In *Ecological Prospects: Scientific, Religious, and Aesthetic Perspectives*, edited by C. K. Chapple, 37–63. Albany: State University of New York Press.

Camill, P., C. E. Umbanhower, Jr., R. Teed, C. E. Geiss, J. Aldinger, L. Dvorak, J. Kenning, J. Limmer, and K. Walkup. 2003. "Late-glacial and Holocene climatic effects on fire and vegetation dynamics at the prairie-forest ecotone in south-central Minnesota." *Journal of Ecology* 91: 822–836.

Cather, W. 1918. *My Ántonia.* Boston: Houghton Mifflin.

Catlin, G. 1844. *Letters and Notes on the Manners, Customs, and Conditions of the North American Indians.* London.

Changnon, S. A., K. E. Kunkel, and D. Winstanley. 2003. "Quantification of climate conditions important to the tall grass prairie." *Transactions of the Illinois State Academy of Science* 96: 41–54.

Clark, O. R. 1940. "Interception of rainfall by herbaceous vegetation." *Ecological Monographs* 10: 243–277.

Clark, S. L., S. W. Hallgren, D. M. Engle, and D. W. Stahle. 2007. "The historic fire regime on the edge of the prairie: a case study from the Cross Timbers of Oklahoma." In *Proceedings of the 23rd Tall Timbers Fire Ecology Conference*, edited by R. E. Masters and K. E. M. Galley, 40–49. Tallahassee: Tall Timbers Research Station.

Clements, F. E. 1936. "Nature and structure of the climax." *Journal of Ecology* 24 (1): 252–284.

Collins, S. L. 1990. "Introduction: fire as a natural disturbance in tallgrass prairie ecosystems." In *Fire in North American Tallgrass Prairies*, edited by S. L. Collins and L. L. Wallace, 3–7. Norman: University of Oklahoma Press.

Collins, S. L., and S. M. Glenn. 1991. "Importance of spatial and temporal dynamics in species regional abundance and distribution." *Ecology* 72: 654–664.

———. 1995. "Grassland ecosystems and landscape dynamics." In *The Changing Prairie: North American Grasslands*, edited by A. Joern and K. H. Keeler, 128–156. New York: Oxford University Press.

Collins, S. L., A. K. Knapp, J. M. Briggs, J. M. Blair, and E. M. Steinauer. 1998. "Modulation of diversity by grazing and mowing in native tallgrass prairie." *Science* 280: 745–747.

Connell, J. H. 1978. "Diversity in tropical rain forests and coral reefs." *Science* 199: 1302–1310.

———. 1980. "Diversity and the coevolution of competitors, or the ghost of competition past." *Oikos* 35: 131–138.

Copeland, T. E., W. Sluis, and H. F. Howe. 2002. "Fire season and dominance in an Illinois tallgrass prairie restoration." *Restoration Ecology* 10: 315–323.

Coppedge, B. R., D. M. Leslie, and J. H. Shaw. 1998. "Botanical composition of bison diets on tallgrass prairie in Oklahoma." *Journal of Range Management* 51 (4): 379–382.

Corbett, E. A., and R. C. Anderson. 2001. "Patterns of prairie plant species in Illinois landscape." In *Proceedings of the 17th North American Prairie Conference*, edited by N. Bernstein and L. Ostrander, 177–181. Mason City: North Iowa Area Community College.

———. 2006. "Landscape analysis of Illinois and Wisconsin remnant prairies." *Journal of the Torrey Botanical Society.* 133: 267–279.

Corneli, H. M. 2002. *Mice in the Freezer, Owls on the Porch: The Lives of Naturalists Frederick and Frances Hamerstrom*. Madison: University of Wisconsin Press.

Costello, D. F. 1969. *The Prairie World: Plant and Animals of the Grassland Sea*. New York: Thomas Y. Crowell Company.

Cottam, G. 1987. "Community dynamics on an artificial prairie." In *Restoration Ecology: A Synthetic Approach to Ecological Research*, edited by W. R. Jordan, M. E. Gilpin, and J. D. Aber, 257–270. New York: Cambridge University Press.

Coulter, J., and H. Thompson. 1886. "The origins of the Indiana flora." In *15th Annual Report, Department of Geologic and Natural History*, 253–282. Indianapolis.

Cowdery, T. K., C. A. Christenson, and J. R. Ziegeweid. 2019. "The hydrologic benefits of wetland and prairie restoration in western Minnesota—Lessons learned at the Glacial Ridge National Wildlife Refuge, 2002–15." *US Geological Survey Scientific Investigations Report 2019–5041*. https://doi.org/10.3133/sir20195041.

Cowles, H. C. 1901. "The physiographic ecology of Chicago and vicinity, a study of the origin, development, and classification of plant societies." *Botany Gazette* 31: 170–177.

———. 1928. "Persistence of prairies." *Ecology* 4: 380–382.

Cronon, W. 1983. *Changes in the Land: Indians, Colonists and the Ecology of New England*. New York: Hill and Wang.

Cunningham, M., and D. H. Johnson. 2006. "Proximate and landscape factors influence grassland bird distribution." *Ecological Applications* 16 (3): 1062–1075.

Curtis, J. T. 1955. "A prairie continuum in Wisconsin." *Ecology* 36: 558–566.

———. 1959. *The Vegetation of Wisconsin*. Madison: University of Wisconsin Press.

Curtis, J. T, and H. C. Greene. 1949. "A study of relic Wisconsin prairies by the species-presence method." *Ecology* 30: 83–92.

Cutter, B. E., and R. P. Guyette. 1994. "Fire frequency on an oak-hickory ridgetop in the Missouri Ozarks." *American Midland Naturalist* 132: 393–398.

Dahlman, R. C., and C. L. Kucera. 1965. "Root productivity and turnover in native prairie." *Ecology* 46 (1/2): 84–89.

Dalgleish, H. J., and D. C. Hartnett. 2009. "The effects of fire frequency and grazing on tallgrass prairie productivity and plant composition are mediated through bud bank demography." *Plant Ecology* 201: 411–420.

Dary, D. A. 1974. *The Buffalo Book: The Full Saga of the American Animal*. Chicago: The Swallow Press, Inc.

Davis, C. A., R. T. Churchwell, S. D. Fuhlendorf, D. M. Engle, and T. J. Hovick.

2016. "Effects of pyric herbivory on source-sink dynamics in grassland birds." *Journal of Applied Ecology* 53: 1004–1012.

Davison, C., and K. Kindscher. 1999. "Tools for diversity: fire, grazing and mowing on tallgrass prairie." *Ecological Restoration* 17: 136–143.

Day, T. A., and J. K. Detling. 1990. "Grassland patch dynamics and herbivore grazing preference following urine deposition." *Ecology* 71 (1): 180–188.

DeGannes. 1695(?). "The Chicago portage, Mount Joliet, the Illinois Valley." In *Prairie State,* edited by P. M. Angle, 21–26. Chicago: University of Chicago Press.

DeSantis, R. D., S. W. Hallgren, and D. W. Stahle. 2010. "Historic fire regime of an upland oak forest in south-central North America." *Fire Ecology* 6 (3): 45–61.

Dickson, T. L., and B. L. Foster. 2008. "The relative importance of the species pool, productivity and disturbance in regulating grassland plant species richness: a field experiment." *Journal of Ecology* 96: 937–946.

Dillard, A. 1974. *A Pilgrim at Tinker Creek.* New York: Harper Collins.

Dolan, R. W. 1994. "Patterns of isozyme variation in relation to population size, isolation, and phytogeographic history in royal catchfly (Silene regia: Caryophyllaceae)." *American Journal of Botany* 81 (8): 965–972.

———. 1995. "The Royal Catchfly (Silene Regia; Caryophyllaceae) in Indiana." *Proceedings of the Indiana Academy of Science* 104 (1–2): 1–10. Accessed July 1, 2021, http://digitalcommons.butler.edu/facsch_papers/155.

Doll, J. E., K. A. Haubensak, E. L. Bouressa, and R. D. Jackson. 2011. "Testing disturbance, seeding time, and soil amendments for establishing warm-season grasses in non-native cool-seasons pasture. *Restoration Ecology* 19 (1): 1–8.

Dornbush, M. E. 2004. "Plant community change following fifty-years of management at Kaslow Prairie Preserve, Iowa, U.S.A." *American Midland Naturalist* 151: 241–250.

Dorney, C. H., and J. R. Dorney. 1989. "An unusual oak savanna in northeastern Wisconsin: the effects of Indian-caused fire." *American Midland Naturalist* 1222: 103–113.

Doxon, E. D., and J. P. Carroll. 2010. "Feeding ecology of ring-necked pheasant and northern bobwhite chicks in Conservation Reserve Program fields." *Journal of Wildlife Management* 74 (2): 249–256.

Drobney, P. 1999. "The phoenix people of sod corn country." In *Recovering the Prairie,* edited by R. F. Sayre, 164–177. Madison: University of Wisconsin Press.

Droze, W. H. 1977. *Trees, Prairies, and People: A History of Tree Planting in the Plains States.* Denton: Texas Women's University.

Drury, W. H. 1998. *Chance and Change: Ecology for Conservationists*. Berkeley: University of California Press.

Edgerton, F. N. 1973. "Changing concepts of the balance of nature." *Quarterly Review of Biology* 48 (2): 322–350.

Edmands, S. 2007. "Between a rock and a hard place: evaluating the relative risks of inbreeding and outbreeding for conservation and management." *Molecular Ecology* 16: 463–475.

Ehrenreich, J. H., and J. M. Aikman. 1963. "An ecological study of the effects of certain management practices on native prairie in Iowa." *Ecological Monographs* 33 (2): 113–130.

Elder, W. H. 1961. "The needs and problems of grassland preservation." *The Bluebird* 28 (2): 2–7.

Elson, A., and D. C. Hartnett. 2017. "Bison increase the growth and reproduction of forbs in the tallgrass prairie." *American Midland Naturalist* 178 (2): 245–259.

Elton, C. 1930. *Animal Ecology and Evolution*. New York: Oxford University Press.

Engle, D. M., S. D. Fuhlendorf, A. Roper, and D. M. Leslie, Jr. 2008. "Invertebrate community response to a shifting mosaic of habitat." *Rangeland Ecology and Management* 61: 55–62.

Erdrich, G. 1994. "Big Grass." In *Heart of the Land: Essays on Last Great Places*, edited by J. Barbato and L. Weinerman, 145–150. New York: Pantheon Books.

Ernst, F. (1819) 1903. "Travels in Illinois in 1819." *Transactions of the Illinois State Historical Society* 8: 150–165.

Errington, P. 1987. *A Question of Values*. Ames: Iowa State University Press.

Evans, E. W. 1984. "Fire as a natural disturbance to grasshopper assemblages of tallgrass prairie." *Oikos* 43: 9–16.

———. 1988a. "Community dynamics of prairie grasshoppers subjected to periodic fire: predictable trajectories or random walks in time." *Oikos* 52: 283–292.

———. 1988b. "Grasshopper (Insecta: Orthoptera: Acrididae) assemblages of tallgrass prairie: influences of fire frequency, topography, and vegetation." *Canadian Journal of Zoology* 66: 1495–1501.

Evans, E. W., J. M. Briggs, E. J. Fink, D. J. Gibson, S. W. James, D. W. Kaufman, and T. R. Seastedt. 1989. "Is fire a disturbance in grasslands?" In *Proceedings of the Eleventh North American Prairie Conference, University of Nebraska*, edited by T. B. Bragg and J. Stubbendieck, 159–161. Lincoln: University of Nebraska Press.

Ewel, J. J. 1987. "Restoration is the ultimate test of ecological theory." In *Restoration Ecology: A Synthetic Approach to Ecological Research*, edited by W. R. Jordan, M. E. Gilpin, and J. D. Aber, 31–34. New York: Cambridge University Press.

Faragher, J. M. 1986. *Sugar Creek: Life on the Illinois Prairie*. New Haven: Yale University Press.

Farnham, E. W. 1846. *Life in Prairie Land*. New York: Harper.

Featherstonhaugh, G. W. 1847. *A Canoe Voyage up the Minnay Sotor*. London: Richard Bentley.

Fierer, N., J. Ladau, J. C. Clemente, J. W. Leff, S. M. Owens, K. S. Pollard, R. Knight, J. A. Gilbert, and R. L. McCulley. 2013. "Reconstructing the microbial diversity and function of pre-agricultural tallgrass prairie soils in the United States." *Science* 342: 621–624.

Fletcher, R. J., and R. R. Koford. 2002. "Habitat and landscape associations of breeding birds in native and restored grasslands." *Journal of Wildlife Management* 66: 1011–1022.

Flores, D. 1991. "Bison ecology and bison diplomacy: the southern plains from 1800 to 1850." *Journal of American History* 78: 465–485.

———. 2001. *The Natural West: Environmental History in the Great Plains and Rocky Mountains*. Norman: University of Oklahoma Press.

Fornara, D. A., and D. Tilman. 2008. "Plant functional composition influences rates of soil carbon and nitrogen accumulation." *Journal of Ecology* 96 (2): 314–322.

Freeman, T., and P. Custis. (1806) 1984. *Southern Counterparts to Lewis and Clark: The Freeman and Custis Expedition of 1806*. Edited by D. L. Flores. Norman: University of Oklahoma Press.

Fuhlendorf, S. D., and D. M. Engle. 2001. "Restoring heterogeneity on rangelands: ecosystem management based on evolutionary grazing patterns." *Bioscience* 51: 625–632.

Fuhlendorf, S. D., D. M. Engle, R. D. Elmore, R. F. Limb, and T. G. Bidwell. 2012. "Conservation of pattern and process: developing an alternative paradigm of rangeland management." *Rangeland Ecology and Management* 65: 579–589.

Fuhlendorf, S. D., W. C. Harrell, D. M. Engle, R. G. Hamilton, C. A. Davis, and D. M. Leslie. 2006. "Should heterogeneity be the basis for conservation? Grassland bird response to fire and grazing." *Ecological Applications* 16: 1706–1716.

Fuller, G. D. 1923. "An edaphic limit of forests in the prairie region of Illinois." *Ecology* 4: 135–140.

Garland, H. 1917. *A Son of the Middle Border*. B. F. Collier and Son.

Geist, V. 1996. *Buffalo Nation: History and Legend of the North American Bison*. Stillwater: Voyageur Press.

Gerla, P. J. 2007. "Estimating the effects of cropland to prairie conversion on peak storm run-off." *Restoration Ecology* 15 (4): 720–730.

Gibson, D. J. 1988. "Regeneration and fluctuation of tallgrass prairie vegetation in response to burning frequency." *Bulletin of the Torrey Botanical Club* 115: 1–12.

Gleason, H. A. 1909. "Some unsolved problems of the prairie." *Bulletin of the Torrey Botanical Club* 36: 265–271.

———. 1912. "An isolated prairie grove and its phytogeographical significance." *Botanical Gazette* 53: 38–49.

———. 1913. "The relation of forest distribution and prairie fires in the Middle West." *Torreya* 13: 173–181.

———. 1922. "The vegetational history of the Middle West." *Annals of the Association of American Geographers* 12: 39–85.

———. 1926. "The individualistic concept of the plant association." *Bulletin of the Torrey Botanical Club* 53: 7–26.

———. 1939. "The individualistic concept of the plant association." *American Midland Naturalist* 21: 92–110.

Gleason, H. A., and A. Cronquist. 1964. *The Natural Geography of Plants.* New York: Columbia University.

Glenn-Lewin, D. C., L. A. Johnson, T. W. Jurik, A. Akey, M. Loeschke, and T. Rosburg. 1990. "Fire in Central North American grasslands: vegetative reproduction, seed germination, and seedling establishment." In *Fire in North American Tallgrass Prairie*, edited by S. L. Collins and L. L. Wallace, 28–45. Norman: University of Oklahoma Press.

Gotelli, N. J., and D. Simberloff. 1987. "The distribution and abundance of tallgrass prairie plants: a test of the core-satellite hypothesis." *American Naturalist* 130: 18–35.

Grange, W. B. 1939. "Can we save the prairie chicken?" *Game Breeder and Sportsman* April: 58–59, 62–63.

Grant, M. C. 1993. "The trembling giant." *Discover* (October): 83–88.

Griffin, S. R., B. Bruninga-Socolar, M. A. Kerr, J. Gibbs, and R. Winfree. 2017. "Wild bee community change over a 26-year chronosequence of restored tallgrass prairie." *Restoration Ecology.* https://doi.org/10.1111/rec.12481.

Grimm, E. 1984. "Fire and other factors controlling the Big Woods vegetation in Minnesota in the mid-nineteenth century." *Ecological Monographs* 54: 291–311.

Groves, A. M., J. T. Bauer, and L. A. Brudvig. 2020. "Lasting signature of plant year weather on restored grasslands." *Nature Research Scientific Reports.* 10: 5953.

Gruchow, P. 1985. *Journal of a Prairie Year.* Minneapolis: University of Minnesota Press.

———. 1988. *The Necessity of Empty Places.* New York: St. Martin's Press.

———. 1999. *Worlds Within a World.* St. Paul: Minnesota Department of Natural Resources.

Gunderson, D. 2012. "Pioneer cemeteries fall under plow's threat." *Minnesota Public Radio News,* December 27, 2012.

Guyette, R. P., D. C. Dey, and M. C. Stambaugh. 2003. "Fire and human history of a barren-forest mosaic in southern Indiana." *American Midland Naturalist* 149: 21–34.

Hagen, C. A., G. C. Salter, J. C. Pitman, R. J. Robel, and R. D. Applegate. 2005. "Lesser prairie-chicken brood habitat in sand sagebrush: invertebrate biomass and vegetation." *Wildlife Society Bulletin* 33 (3): 1080–1091.

Haines, F. 1970. *The Buffalo: The Story of the American Bison and Their Hunters from Prehistoric Times to the Present.* New York: Thomas Y. Crowell Company.

Hamerstrom, F. 1980. *Strictly for the Chickens.* Ames: Iowa State University Press.

Hamilton, K. G. A. 2012. "Unraveling the enigma of an Atlantic prairie." *Northeastern Naturalist* 19 (Special Issue 6): 13–42.

Hanski, I. 1982. "Dynamics of regional distribution: the core and satellite species hypothesis." *Oikos* 38: 210–221.

Harmon-Threatt, A. N., and S. D. Hendrix. 2015. "Prairie restorations and bees: the potential ability of seed mixes to foster native bee communities." *Basic and Applied Ecology* 16: 64–72.

Harper, R. M. 1911. "The Hempstead Plains: A natural prairie on Long Island." *Bulletin of the American Geographical Society* 43 (5): 351–360.

———. 1918. "The vegetation of the Hempstead Plains." *Memoirs of the Torrey Botanical Society* 17: 262–286.

Hartnett, D. C., A. A. Steuter, and K. R. Hickman. 1997. "Comparative ecology of native and introduced ungulates." In *Ecology and Conservation of Great Plains Vertebrates,* edited by F. L. Knopf and F. B. Samson, 72–104. New York: Springer.

Hartnett, D. C., and G. W. T. Wilson. 1999. "Mycorrhizae influence plant community structure and diversity in tallgrass prairie." *Ecology* 80 (4): 1187–1195.

Hayden, A. 1945. "The selection of prairie areas in Iowa which should be preserved." *Iowa Academy of Science* 52: 127–148.

Hedberg, A. M., V. A. Borowicz, and J. E. Armstrong. 2005. "Interactions between a hemiparasitic plant, Pedicularis Canadensis L. (Orobanchaceae), and members of a tallgrass prairie plant community." *Journal of the Torrey Botanical Society* 132: 401–410.

Heisler, J. L., J. M. Briggs, and A. K. Knapp. 2003. "Long-term patterns of shrub expansion in a C4-dominated grassland: fire frequency and the dynamics of shrub cover and abundance." *American Journal of Botany* 90: 423–428.

Heisler, J. L., J. M. Briggs, A. K. Knapp, J. M. Blair, and A. Seery. 2004. "Direct and indirect effects of fire on shrub density and aboveground productivity in a mesic grassland." *Ecology* 85: 2245–2257.

Helzer, C. 1999. "Changing the public's perception of trees and prairies." *Proceedings of the 16th North American Prairie Conference*, edited by J. T. Springer, 24–27. Kearney: University of Nebraska Press.

———. 2010. *The Ecology and Management of Prairies in the Central United States.* Iowa City: University of Iowa Press.

———. 2020. *Hidden Prairie: Photographing Life in One Square Meter.* Iowa City: University of Iowa Press.

Helzer, C., and D. E. Jelinski. 1999. "The relative importance of patch area and perimeter-area ratio to grassland breeding birds." *Ecological Applications* 9 (4): 1448–1458.

Henderson, R. A. 1990a. "Effects of fire timing on pasque-flower (*Anemone patens*) flower-bud survival." In *Proceedings of the Twelfth North American Prairie Conference*, edited by D. Smith and C. Jacobs, 117–120. Cedar Falls: University of Northern Iowa.

———. 1990b. "Ten-year response of a Wisconsin prairie remnant to seasonal timing of fire." In *Proceedings of the Twelfth North American Prairie Conference*, edited by D. Smith and C. Jacobs, 121–126. Cedar Falls: University of Northern Iowa.

———. 2003. "Are there keystone plant species driving diversity in Midwest prairies?" In *Proceedings of the 18th North American Prairie Conference*, edited by S. Fore, 63–66. Kirksville: Truman State University.

Henderson, R. A., D. L. Lovell, and A. Evelyn. 1983. "The flowering responses of 7 grasses to seasonal timing of prescribed burns in remnant Wisconsin prairie." In *Proceedings of the Eighth North American Prairie Conference*, edited by R. Brewer, 7–10. Kalamazoo: Western Michigan University.

Henderson, R. A., J. Meunier, and N. S. Holoubek. 2018. "Disentangling effects of fire, habitat, and climate on an endangered prairie-specialist butterfly." *Biological Conservation* 218: 41–48.

Henry, A., and D. Thompson. (1799) 1897. *New Light on the Early History of the Greater Northwest.* Minneapolis: Ross and Haines, Inc.

Herkert, J. R. 1994. "The effects of habitat fragmentation on midwestern grassland bird communities." *Ecological Applications* 4 (3): 461–471.

Herkert, J. R., D. L. Reinking, D. A. Wiedenfeld et al. 2003. "Effects of prairie frag-
mentation on the nest success of breeding birds in the midcontinental United
States." *Conservation Biology* 17 (2): 587–594.
Heslinga, J. L., and R. E. Grese. 2010. "Assessing plant community changes over
sixteen years of restoration in a remnant Michigan tallgrass prairie." *American
Midland Naturalist* 164: 322–336.
Hickerson, H. 1965. "Deer and intertribal buffer zones in the upper Mississippi
Valley." In *Man, Culture, and Animals: The Role of Animals in Human Ecologi-
cal Adjustments*, edited by A. Leeds and A. P. Vayda, 43–66. Washington, DC:
American Association for the Advancement of Science.
Hines, H. M., and D. D. Hendrix. 2005. "Bumble bee (Hymenoptera: Apidae) diversity and abundance in tallgrass prairie patches: effects of local and landscape
floral resources." *Environmental Entomology* 34 (6): 1477–1484.
Hobbs, N. T., D. S. Schimel, C. E. Owensby, and D. S. Ojima. 1991. "Fire and grazing in the tallgrass prairie: contingent effects on nitrogen budgets." *Ecology* 72:
1374–1382.
Hoch, G. A., J. M. Briggs, and L. C. Johnson. 2002. "Assessing the rates, mechanism and consequences of conversion of tallgrass prairie to Juniperus virginiana
forest." *Ecosystems* 5 (6): 578–586.
Hoover, I. E., and T. B. Bragg. 1981. "Effects of seasonal burning and mowing on
an eastern Nebraska Stipa-Andropogon prairie." *Journal of Range Management*
42: 248–251.
Hovick, T. J., J. R. Miller, S. J. Dinsmore, D. M. Engle, D. M. Debinski, and S. D.
Fuhlendorf. 2012. "Effects of fire and grazing on grasshopper sparrow nest
survival." *Journal of Wildlife Management* 76 (1): 19–27.
Howe, H. F. 1994a. "Managing species diversity in tallgrass prairie: assumptions
and implications." *Conservation Biology* 8: 691–704.
———. 1994b. "Response of early- and late-flowering plants to fire season in experimental prairies." *Ecological Applications* 4: 121–133.
———. 1995. "Succession and fire season in experimental prairie plantings." *Ecology* 76 (6): 1917–1925.
———. 1999a. "Response of Zizia aurea to seasonal mowing and fire in restored
prairie." *American Midland Naturalist* 141: 373–380.
———. 1999b. "Dominance, diversity and grazing in tallgrass restoration." *Ecological Restoration* 17: 59–66.
———. 2000. "Grass response to seasonal burns in experimental plantings." *Journal of Range Management* 53: 437–441.

Hulbert, L. C. 1969. "Fire and litter effects in undisturbed bluestem prairie in Kansas." *Ecology* 50: 874–877.

———. 1988. "Causes of fire effects in tallgrass prairie." *Ecology* 69: 46–58.

Humphrey, S. K. 1931. *Following the Prairie Frontier.* Minneapolis: University of Minnesota Press.

Ingalls, J. J. 1905. *A Collection of the Writings of John James Ingalls.* Kansas City, MO: Hudson-Kimberly Publishing Co.

Ingham, R. E., and J. K. Detling. 1984. "Plant-herbivore interactions in a North American mixed-grass prairie. III. Soil nematode populations and root biomass on Cynomys ludovicianus colonies and adjacent uncolonized areas." *Oecologia* 63: 307–313.

Irving, W. 1835. *A Tour on the Prairies.*

Isbell, F., D. Tilman, P. B. Rech, and A. T. Clark. 2019. "Deficits of biodiversity and productivity linger a century after agricultural abandonment." *Nature Ecology and Evolution* 3: 1533–1538.

Jacobson, G. L., and E. C. Grimm. 1986. "A numerical analysis of the Holocene forest and prairie vegetation in Central Minnesota." *Ecology* 67 (4): 958–966.

James, S. W. 1991. "Soil, nitrogen, phosphorus and organic matter processing by earthworms in tallgrass prairie." *Ecology* 72 (6): 2101–2109.

Jamison, B. E., R. J. Robel, J. S. Pontius, and R. D. Applegate. 2002. "Invertebrate biomass: association with lesser prairie-chicken habitat use and sand sagebrush density in southwestern Kansas." *Wildlife Society Bulletin* 30 (2): 517–526.

Joern, A. 2004. "Variation in grasshopper (Acrididae) densities in response to fire frequency and bison grazing in tallgrass prairie." *Environmental Entomology* 33: 1617–1625.

———. 2005. "Disturbance by fire frequency and bison grazing modulate grass-hopper assemblages in tallgrass prairie." *Ecology* 86: 861–873.

Johnsgard, P. A. 2001. *Prairie Birds: Fragile Splendor in the Great Plains.* Lawrence: University Press of Kansas.

———. 2003. *Great Wildlife of the Great Plains.* Lawrence: University Press of Kansas.

Johnson, C. W. 1951. "Protein as a factor in the distribution of the American bison." *Geographical Review* 41: 330–331.

Johnson, D. H., and L. D. Igl. 2001. "Area requirements of grassland birds: a regional perspective." *Auk* 118: 24–34.

Johnson, G. D., W. P. Erickson, M. D. Strickland, M. F. Shepherd, D. A. Shepherd, and S. A. Sarappo. 2002. "Collision mortality of local and migrant birds at a large-scale wind-power development on Buffalo Ridge, Minnesota." *Wildlife Society Bulletin* 30 (3): 879–887.

Johnson, L. B., and C. B. Lees. 1998. *Wildflowers across America*. New York: Abbeville Press.

Johnson, R. G., and R. C. Anderson. 1986. "The seed bank of a tallgrass prairie in Illinois." *American Midland Naturalist* 115 (1): 123–130.

Johnson, R. G., and S. A. Temple. 1990. "Nest predation and brood parasitism of tallgrass prairie birds." *Journal of Wildlife Management* 54: 106–111.

Jolliet, L. (1673) 1968. "The Illinois country." In *Prairie State*, edited by P. M. Angle, 11–12. Chicago: University of Chicago Press.

Jonas, J. L., and A. Joern. 2007. "Grasshopper (Orthoptera: Acrididae) communities respond to fire, bison grazing and weather in North American tallgrass prairie: a long-term study." *Oecologia* 153: 699–711.

Jonas, J. L., M. R. Whiles, and R. E. Charlton. 2002. "Aboveground invertebrate response to land management differences in central Kansas grasslands." *Environmental Entomology* 31 (6): 1142–1152.

Kaufman, D. W., G. A. Kaufman, P. A. Fay, J. L. Zimmerman, and E. W. Evans. 1998a. "Animal populations and communities." In *Grassland Dynamics: Long-term Ecological Research in Tallgrass Prairie*, edited by A. K. Knapp, J. M. Briggs, D. C. Hartnett, and S. L. Collins, 113–139. New York: Oxford University Press.

Kaufman, D. W., P. A. Fay, G. A. Kaufman, and J. L. Zimmerman. 1998b. "Diversity of terrestrial macrofauna." In *Grassland Dynamics: Long-term Ecological Research in Tallgrass Prairie*, edited by A. K. Knapp, J. M. Briggs, D. C. Hartnett, and S. L. Collins, 101–112. New York: Oxford University Press.

Keating, W. H. (1823) 1959. *Narrative of an Expedition to the Source of the St. Peter's River, Lake Winnepeek, Lake of the Woods, &c. Performed in the Year 1823*. Minneapolis: Ross and Haines, Inc.

Keeler, B. L., and S. Polasky. 2014. "Land-use change and costs to rural households: a case study in groundwater nitrate contamination." *Environmental Research Letters*. http://dx.doi.org/10.1088/1748-9326/9/7/074002.

Keeler, K. H., C. F. Williams, and L. S. Vescio. 2002. "Clone size of Andropogon Gerardii Vitman (Big Bluestem) at Konza Prairie, Kansas." *American Midland Naturalist* 147 (2): 295–304.

Kelsey, K. W., D. E. Naugle, K. F. Higgins, and K. K. Bakker. 2006. "Planting trees in prairie landscapes: do the ecological costs outweigh the benefits?" *Natural Areas Journal* 26: 254–260.

Kline, V. M. 1997. "Orchards of oaks and a sea of grass." In *The Tallgrass Restora-*

tion Handbook, edited by S. Packard and C. F. Mutel, 3–22. Washington, DC: Island Press.

Klopf, R. P., S. G. Baer, E. M. Bach, and J. Six. 2017. "Restoration and management for plant diversity enhances rate of belowground ecosystem recovery." *Ecological Applications* 27 (2): 355–362.

Klute, D. S., R. J. Robel, and K. E. Kemp. 1997. "Will conversion of Conservation Reserve Program (CRP) lands to pasture be detrimental for grassland birds in Kansas?" *American Midland Naturalist* 137 (2): 206–212.

Knapp, A. K. 1984. "Post-burn differences in solar radiation, leaf temperature and water stress influencing production in a lowland tallgrass prairie." *American Journal of Botany* 71 (2): 220–227.

Knapp, A. K., J. M. Blair, and J. M. Briggs. 1998. "Long-term ecological consequences of varying fire frequency in a humid grassland." In *Fire in Ecosystem Management: Shifting the Paradigm from Suppression to Prescription*, edited by T. L. Pruden and L. A. Brennan, 173–178. Tall Timbers Fire Ecology Conference Proceedings, No. 20.

Knapp, A. K., J. M. Blair, J. M. Briggs, S. L. Collins, D. C. Hartnett, L. C. Johnson, and E. G. Towne. 1999. "The keystone role of bison in North American tallgrass prairie." *Bioscience* 49: 39–50.

Knapp, A. K., and T. R. Seastedt. 1998. "Introduction." In *Grassland Dynamics: Long-term Ecological Research in the Tallgrass Prairie,* edited by A. K. Knapp, J. M. Briggs, D. C. Hartnett, and S. L. Collins, 3–15. New York: Oxford University Press.

Knapp, A. K., and M. D. Smith. 2001. "Variation among biomes in temporal dynamics of aboveground primary productivity." *Science* 291: 481–484.

Knight, C. L., J. M. Briggs, and M. D. Nellis. 1994. "Expansion of gallery forest on Konza Prairie Research Natural Area, Kansas, USA." *Landscape Ecology* 9: 117–125.

Knopf, F. L. 1996. "Prairie legacies—birds." In *Prairie Conservation: Preserving North America's Most Endangered Ecosystem*, edited by F. B. Samson and F. L. Knopf, 135–148. Washington, DC: Island Press.

Knops, J. M. H., and D. Tilman. 2000. "Dynamics of soil nitrogen and carbon accumulation for 61 years after agricultural abandonment." *Ecology* 81 (1): 88–98.

Kohl, M. T., P. R. Krausman, K. Kunkel, and D. M. Williams. 2013. "Bison versus cattle: are they ecologically synonymous?" *Rangeland Ecology and Management* 66: 721–731.

Kratz, T. K., L. A. Deegan, M. E. Harmon, and W. K. Lauenroth. 2003. "Ecologi-

cal variability in space and time: insights gained from the US LTER Program."
Bioscience 53 (1): 57–67.

Krech, S., III. 1999. *The Ecological Indian*. New York: W. W. Norton and Co.

Kricher, J. 1998. "Nothing endures but change: ecology's newly emerging paradigm." *Northeastern Naturalist* 5 (2): 165–174.

Kuchler, A. W. 1951. "The relation between classifying and mapping vegetation." *Ecology* 32 (2): 275–283.

———. 1954. "Some considerations concerning the mapping of herbaceous vegetation." *Transactions of the Kansas Academy of Science* 57 (4): 449–452.

———. 1964. "Potential natural vegetation of the conterminous United States." Special Publication No. 36. N.p.: American Geographical Society.

Kumlein, T. 1876. "On the rapid disappearance of Wisconsin wildflowers: A contrast of the present time with thirty years ago." In *Transactions of the Wisconsin Academy of Sciences, Arts, and Letters*. Vol III, 56–57. Madison: Wisconsin State Printer.

Kwaiser, K. S., and S. D. Hendrix. 2007. "Diversity and abundance of bees (Hymenoptera: Apiformes) in native and ruderal grasslands of agriculturally dominated landscapes." *Agriculture, Ecosystems, and Environment* 124: 200–204.

Lark T. J., B. Larson, I. Schelly, S. Batish, and H. K. Gibbs. 2018. "Accelerated conversion of native prairie to cropland in Minnesota." *Environmental Conservation*. https://doi.org/10.1017/S0376892918000437.

Lark, T. J., S. A. Spawn, M. Bougie, and H. K. Gibbs. 2020. "Cropland expansion in the United States produces marginal yields at high cost to wildlife." *Nature Communications*. https://doi.org/10.1038/s41467-020-18045-z.

Larsen, K. J., and T. W. Work. 2003. "Differences in ground beetles (Coleoptera: Carabidae) of original and reconstructed tallgrass prairie in northeastern Iowa, USA, and impact of 3-year spring burn cycles." *Journal of Insect Conservation* 7: 153–166.

Larson, D. L., D. L. Hernandez, J. L. Larons, J. B. Leone, and N. Pennarola. 2020. "Management of remnant tallgrass prairie by grazing or fire: effects on plant communities and soil properties." *Ecosphere* 11 (8): e03213.

Larson, G. 1998. *There's a Hair in my Dirt: A Worm's Story*. New York: Harper Collins.

Least Heat-Moon, W. 1991. *PrairyErth*. Boston: Houghton Mifflin Company.

Leopold, A. 1933. *Game Management*. New York: Charles Scribner's Sons.

———. (1934) 2013. "The Arboretum and the university." In *Leopold: A Sand County Almanac and Other Writings on Ecology and Conservation*, edited by C. Meine, 352–354. New York: The Library of America.

———. (1939) 1991. "A biotic view of land." In *The River of the Mother of God*, edited by S. L. Flader and J. B. Callicott, 266–273. Madison: University of Wisconsin Press.

———. (1942a) 2013. "The prairie: the forgotten flora." In *Leopold: A Sand County Almanac and Other Writings on Ecology and Conservation*, edited by C. Meine, 483–486. New York: The Library of America.

———. (1942b) 2013. "The role of wildlife in a liberal education" In *Leopold: A Sand County Almanac and Other Writings on Ecology and Conservation*, edited by C. Meine, 466–470. New York: The Library of America.

———. 1949. *A Sand County Almanac*. New York: Oxford University Press.

———. 1991. *Round River: From the Journals of Aldo Leopold*. Minoqua: Northword Press, Inc.

———. 1999. *For the Health of the Land*. Edited by J. B. Callicott and E. T. Freyfogle. Washington, DC: Island Press.

Lesica, P., and F. W. Allendorf. 1999. "Ecological genetics and the restoration of plant communities: mix or match?" *Restoration Ecology* 7 (1): 42–50.

Limb, R. F., S. D. Fuhlendorf, D. M. Engle, J. R. Weir, R. D. Elmore, and T. G. Bidwell. 2011. "Pyric-herbivory and cattle performance in grassland ecosystems." *Rangeland Ecology and Management* 64: 659–663.

Livezey, K. B. 2009a. "Range expansion of barred owls, Part I: chronology and distribution." *American Midland Naturalist* 161 (1): 49–56.

———. 2009b. "Range expansion of barred owls, Part II: facilitating ecological change." *American Midland Naturalist* 161 (2): 323–349.

Livingston, R. B. 1952. "Relict true prairie communities in central Colorado." *Ecology* 33 (1): 72–86.

Lott, D. F. 2002. *American Bison: A Natural History*. Berkeley: University of California Press.

Lovell, L. D., R. A. Henderson, and A. Evelyn. 1983. "The response of forb species to seasonal timing of prescribed burns in remnant Wisconsin prairie." In *Proceedings of the Eighth North American Prairie Conference*, edited by R. Brewer, 11–15. Kalamazoo: Western Michigan University.

MacDonald, D. H. 2018. *Before Yellowstone: Native American Archeology in the National Park*. Seattle: University of Washington Press.

Madson, J. 1979. *Out Home*. New York: Winchester Press.

———. 1982. *Where the Sky Began: Land of the Tallgrass Prairie*. New York: Houghton Mifflin Co.

———. 1993. *Tallgrass Prairie*. Helena: Falcon Press.

Malin, J. C. 1967. *The Grassland of North America: Prolegomena to Its History with Addenda and Postscript.* Gloucester, MA: Peter Smith.

Mann, C. C. 2005. *1491: New Revelations of the Americas before Columbus.* New York: Vintage Books.

Marsh, G. P. 1864. *Man and Nature, or Physical Geography as Modified by Human Action.* London: Sampson Low, Son and Marston.

Martin, L. M., and B. J. Wilsey. 2006. "Assessing grassland restoration success: relative roles of seed additions and native ungulate activities." *Journal of Applied Ecology* 43: 1098–1109.

Matamala, R., J. D. Jastrow, R. M. Miller, and C. T. Garten. 2008. "Temporal changes in C and N stocks of restored prairie: implications for C sequestration strategies." *Ecological Applications* 18 (6): 1470–1488.

Matthews, T. W., J. S. Taylor, and L. A. Powell. 2012. "Ring-necked pheasant hens select managed Conservation Reserve Program grasslands for nesting and brood-rearing." *Journal of Wildlife Management* 76 (8): 1653–1660.

Maximilian of Wied. (1832) 2017. *Travels in North America, 1832–1834: A Concise Edition of the Journals of Prince Maximilian of Wied.* Edited by M. Gallagher. Norman: University of Oklahoma Press.

McCain, K. N. S., S. G. Baer, J. M. Blair, and G. W. T. Wilson. 2010. "Dominant grasses suppress local diversity in restored tallgrass prairie." *Restoration Ecology* 18 (1): 40–49.

McCarron, J. K., and A. K. Knapp. 2003. "C3 shrub expansion in a C4 grassland: positive post-fire responses in resources and shoot growth." *American Journal of Botany* 90 (10): 1496–1501.

McClain, W. E., and S. E. Elzinga. 1994. "The occurrence of prairie and forest fires in Illinois and other midwestern states, 1679 to 1854." *Erigenia* 13: 79–90.

McComb, A., and W. Loomis. 1944. "Subclimax prairie." *Bulletin of the Torrey Botanical Club* 71: 46–76.

McCullough, K., G. Albenese, and D. A. Haukos. 2017. "Novel observations of larval fire survival, feeding behavior, and host plant use in the regal fritillary, Speyeria idalia (Drury) (Nymphalidae)." *Journal of the Lepidopterists' Society* 71 (3): 146–152.

McCullough, K., G. Albanese, D. A. Haukos, A. M. Ricketss, and S. Stratton. 2019. "Management regime and habitat response influence abundance of regal fritillary (Speyeria idalia) in tallgrass prairie." *Ecosphere* 10 (8):e08845.

McFarland, J. E. 1969. *The Pioneer Era on the Iowa Prairies.* Lake Mill: Graphics Publishing Co.

McHugh, T. 1972. *The Time of the Buffalo*. New York: Alfred Knopf.

McIntosh, R. P. 1975. "H. A. Gleason—'Individualistic Ecologist,' 1882–1975: His contributions to ecological theory." *Bulletin of the Torrey Botanical Society* 102 (5): 253–273.

McKay, J. K., C. E. Christian, S. Harrison, and K. J. Rice. 2005. "'How local is local?'—A review of practical and conceptual issues in the genetics of restoration." *Restoration Ecology* 13 (3): 432–440.

McLauchlan, K. K., S. E. Hobbie, and W. M. Post. 2006. "Conversion from agriculture to grassland builds soil organic matter on decadal timescales." *Ecological Applications* 16 (1): 143–153.

Mengel, R. M. 1970. "The North American Central Plains as an isolating agent in bird speciation." In *Pleistocene and Recent Environments of the Central Great Plains*. Special publication 3, edited by W. Dort and J. Jones, 279–340. Lawrence: University Press of Kansas.

Menges, E. S. 1991. "Seed germination percentage increases with population size in a fragmented prairie species." *Conservation Biology* 5 (2): 158–164.

———. 1995. "Factors limiting fecundity and germination in small populations of Silene regia (Caryophyllaceae), a rare hummingbird-pollinated prairie forb." *American Midland Naturalist* 133 (2): 242–255.

Middleton, E. L., and J. D. Bever. 2012. "Inoculation with a native soil community advances succession in a grassland restoration." *Restoration Ecology* 20: 218–226.

Millar, C. I., and W. J. Libby. 1989. "Restoration: Disneyland or a native ecosystem?" *Restoration and Management Notes* 7 (1): 18–24.

Miller, J. R., and R. J. Hobbs. 2007. "Habitat restoration—do we know what we're doing?" *Restoration Ecology* 15 (3): 382–390.

Milne, L. J., and M. Milne. 1960. *The Balance of Nature*. New York: Alfred A. Knopf.

Minnesota Department of Health. 2015. *Minnesota Drinking Water 2015 Annual Report for 2014*.

Moncada, K. M., N. J. Ehlke, G. J. Muehlbauer, C. C. Sheaffer, D. L. Wyse, and L. R. Dehaan. 2007. "Genetic variation in three native plant species across the state of Minnesota." *Crop Science* 47: 2379–2389.

Moranz, R. A., D. M. Debinski, D. A. McGranahan, D. E. Engle, and J. R. Miller. 2012. "Untangling the effects of fire, grazing, and land-use legacies on grassland butterfly communities." *Biodiversity Conservation* 21: 2719–2746.

Moranz, R. A., S. D. Fuhlendorf, and D. M. Engle. 2014. "Making sense of a prairie butterfly paradox: the effects of grazing, time since fire, and sampling period on regal fritillary abundance." *Biological Conservation* 173: 32–41.

Mortlock, W. 2000. "Local seed for revegetation: where will all that seed come from?" *Ecological Management and Restoration* 1 (2): 93–101.

Muir, J. 1911. *My First Summer in the Sierras*. Boston: Houghton Mifflin Co.

———. 1913. *The Story of My Boyhood and Youth*. Boston: Houghton Mifflin Co.

Mutel, C. F. 2008. *The Emerald Horizon: A History of Nature in Iowa*. Iowa City: University of Iowa Press.

Nelson, D. M., and F. S. Hu. 2008. "Patterns and drivers of Holocene vegetational change near the prairie-forest ecotone in Minnesota: revisiting McAndrews' Transect." *New Phytologist* 179: 449–459.

Nelson, D. M, F. S. Hu, E. C. Grimm, B. B. Curry, and J. E. Slate. 2006. "The influence of aridity and fire on Holocene prairie communities in the eastern tallgrass prairie peninsula." *Ecology* 87: 2523–2536.

Nemec, K. T., and T. B. Bragg. 2008. "Plant-feeding Hemiptera and Orthoptera communities in native and restored mesic tallgrass prairie." *Restoration Ecology* 16: 324–335.

Nicollet, J. 1838. *Joseph Nicollet on the Plains and Prairies*. Edited by E. C. Bray and M. C. Bray. St. Paul: Minnesota Historical Society.

Norris, K. 1993. *Dakota: A Spiritual Geography*. New York: Ticknor and Fields.

Noss, R. 1994. "Cows and conservation biology." *Conservation Biology* 8: 613–616.

Nuttall, T. 1821. *Travels into the Arkansas Territory, 1819*. Philadelphia: Thos H. Palmer.

Oliver, W. 1843. *Eight Months in Illinois with Information to Immigrants*. N.p: W. A. Mitchell.

Orr, C. C., and O. J. Dickerson. 1966. "Nematodes in true prairie soils of Kansas." *Transactions of the Kansas Academy of Science* 69 (3/4): 317–334.

Ott, J. P., and D. C. Hartnett. 2015. "Vegetative reproduction and bud bank dynamics of the perennial grass Andropogon gerardii in mixedgrass and tallgrass prairie." *American Midland Naturalist* 174 (1): 14–32.

Palliser, J. 1853. *Solitary Rambles and Adventures of a Hunter in the Prairies*. Rutland: Charles E. Tuttle Co.

Panzer, R. 1988. "Managing prairie remnants for insect conservation." *Natural Areas Journal* 8: 83–90.

———. 2002. "Compatibility of prescribed burning with conservation of insects in small, isolated prairie reserves." *Conservation Biology* 16: 1296–1307.

Parker, J., ed. 1976. *The Journals of Jonathan Carver and Related Documents, 1766–1770*. Minneapolis: Minnesota Historical Society Press.

Patten, M. A., E. Shochat, D. L. Reinking, D. H. Wolfe, and S. K. Sherrod. 2006. "Habitat edge, land management, and rates of brood parasitism in tallgrass prairie." *Ecological Applications* 16: 687–695.

Peattie, D. C. 1938. *A Prairie Grove*. New York: Literary Guild of America.

Petty, R. O. 1973. "Where have all the prairies gone?" In *Wilderness USA*, 185–206. Washington, DC: National Geographic Society.

Petty, R. O., and M. T. Jackson. 1966. "Plant communities." In *Natural Features of Indiana. A Symposium Held April 22–23, 1966, at Wabash College, Crawfordsville, Indiana*, edited by A. A. Lindsey, 264–296. Indianapolis: Indiana Academy of Sciences.

Pickett, S. T. A., and P. S. White. 1985. *The Ecology of Natural Disturbance and Patch Dynamics*. San Diego: Academic Press.

Pielou, E. C. 1991. *After the Ice Age: The Return of Life to Glaciated North America*. Chicago: University of Chicago Press.

Pike, A. (1832) 1969. *Journeys in the Prairie*. Edited by J. E. Haley. Canyon: Panhandle-Plains Historical Society.

Pillsbury, F. C., J. R. Miller, D. M. Debinski, and D. M. Engle. 2011. "Another tool in the toolbox? Using fire and grazing to promote bird diversity in highly fragmented habitats." *Ecosphere* 2: 1–14.

Pitman, J. C., C. A. Hagen, R. J. Robel, T. M. Loughin, and R. D. Applegate 2005. "Location and success of lesser prairie-chicken nests in relation to vegetation and human disturbance." *Journal of Wildlife Management* 69: 1259–1269.

Plumb, G. E., and J. L. Dodd. 1993. "Foraging ecology of bison and cattle on a mixed prairie: implications for natural areas management." *Ecological Applications* 3: 631–643.

———. 1994. "Foraging ecology of bison and cattle." *Rangelands* 16: 107–109.

Poiani, K. A., M. D. Merrill, and K. A. Chapman. 2001. "Identifying conservation-priority areas in a fragmented Minnesota landscape based on the umbrella species concept and selection of large patches of natural vegetation." *Conservation Biology* 15: 513–522.

Pruett, C. L., M. A. Patten, and D. H. Wolfe. 2009a. "Avoidance behavior by prairie grouse: implications for development of wind energy." *Conservation Biology* 23 (5): 1253–1259.

———. 2009b. "It's not easy being green: wind energy and a declining grassland bird. *Bioscience* 59 (3): 257–262.

Quayle, W. A. 1905. *The Prairie and the Sea*. Cincinnati: Jennings and Graham.

Quick, H. 1925. *One Man's Life*. Indianapolis: The Bobbs-Merrill Co.

Rabinowitz, D., and J. K. Rapp. 1985. "Colonization and establishment of Missouri prairie plants on artificial soil disturbances. III. Species abundance distributions, survivorship, and rarity." *American Journal of Botany* 72: 1635–1640.

Ransom, M. D., C. W. Rice, T. C. Todd, and W. A. Wehmueller. 1998. "Soils and soil biota." In *Grassland Dynamics: Long-term Ecological Research in Tallgrass Prairie*, edited by A. K. Knapp, J. M. Briggs, D. C. Hartnett, and S. L. Collins, 48–68. New York: Oxford University Press.

Rapp, J. K., and D. Rabinowitz. 1985. "Colonization and establishment of Missouri prairie plants on artificial soil disturbances. I. Dynamics of forb and graminoid seedling and shoots." *American Journal of Botany* 72: 1618–1628.

Raynor, E. J., A. Joern, and J. M. Briggs. 2015. "Bison foraging responds to fire frequency in nutritionally heterogeneous grassland." *Ecology* 96: 1586–1597.

Reichman, O. J. 1987. *Konza Prairie: A Tallgrass Natural History*. Lawrence: University Press of Kansas.

Ribic, C. A., R. R. Koford, J. R. Herkert, D. H. Johnson, N. D. Niemuth, D. E. Naugle, K. K. Bakker, D. W. Sample, and R. B. Renfrew. 2009. "Area sensitivity in North American grassland birds: patterns and processes." *Auk* 126: 233–244.

Rising, J. D. 1983. "The Great Plains Hybrid Zone." In *Current Ornithology* Volume 1, edited by R. F. Johnston, 131–158. New York: Plenum Press.

———. 1996. *A Guide to the Identification and Natural History of the Sparrows of the United States and Canada*. San Diego: Academic Press.

Risser, P. G., E. C. Birney, H. D. Blocker, S. W. May, W. J. Parton, and J. A. Weins. 1981. *The True Prairie Ecosystem*. Stroudsburg: Hutchinson Ross Publishing Company.

Rogers, W. E., and D. C. Hartnett. 2001. "Vegetation response to different spatial patterns of soil disturbance in burned and unburned tallgrass prairie." *Plant Ecology* 155 (1): 99–109.

Rogers, W. E., D. C. Hartnett, and B. Elder. 2001. "Effects of plains pocket gophers (geomys bursarius) disturbances on tallgrass-prairie plant community structure. *American Midland Naturalist* 145 (2): 344–357.

Rooney, T. P., and M. K. Leach. 2010. "Replacing hay-mowing with prescribed fire restores species diversity and conservation value in a tallgrass prairie sampled thrice: a 59-year study." *American Midland Naturalist* 164 (2): 311–321.

Samson, F. B., and F. L. Knopf. 1994. "Prairie conservation in North America." *Bioscience* 44: 418–421.

Sauer, C. O. 1950. "Grassland climax, fire, and man." *Journal of Range Management* 3: 16–21.

Savage, C. 2004. *Prairie: a natural history.* Vancouver: Douglas and McIntyre Publishing Group.

Schaal, B. A., and W. J. Leverich. 2005. "Conservation genetics: theory and practice." *Annals of the Missouri Botanical Garden* 92: 1–11.

Schilling, K. E., and P. Drobney. 2014a. "Restoration of prairie hydrology at the watershed scale: two decades of progress at Neal Smith National Wildlife Refuge, Iowa." *Land* 3 (1): 206–238.

———. 2014b. "Hydrologic recovery with prairie reconstruction at Neal Smith National Wildlife Refuge, Jasper County, Iowa." N.p.: US Fish and Wildlife Service.

Schlesinger, W. H. 1991. *Biogeochemistry: An Analysis of Global Change.* San Diego: Academic Press.

Schmitz, R. A., and W. R. Clark. 1999. "Survival of ring-necked pheasant hens during spring in relation to landscape features." *Journal of Wildlife Management* 63 (1): 147–154.

Schramm, P. 1990. "Prairie restoration: a twenty-five-year perspective on establishment and management." In *Proceedings of the Twelfth North American Prairie Conference*, edited by D. Smith and C. Jacobs, 169–177. Cedar Falls: University of Northern Iowa.

Schulenberg, R. 1970. "Summary of Morton Arboretum prairie restoration work, 1963 to 1968." In *Proceedings of Symposium on Prairie and Prairie Restoration*, edited by P. Schramm, 45–46. Galesburg: Knox College.

Schuler, K. L., D. M. Leslie, Jr., J. H. Shaw, and E. J. Maichak. 2006. "Temporal-spatial distribution of American bison (*Bison bison*) on a tallgrass prairie fire mosaic." *Journal of Mammalogy* 87: 539–544.

Schulte, L. A., J. Niemi, M. J. Helmers, et al. 2017. "Prairie strips improve biodiversity and the delivery of multiple ecosystem services from corn–soybean croplands." *Proceedings of the National Academy of Sciences* 114 (2): 11247–11252.

Schwartz, C. W. 1945. *The Prairie Chicken in Missouri.* Columbia: University of Missouri Press.

Seastedt, T. R. 1995. "Soil systems and nutrient cycles of the North American prairie." In *The Changing Prairie: North American Grasslands*, edited by A. Joern and K. H. Keeler, 157–176. New York: Oxford University Press.

Seastedt, T. R., and A. K. Knapp. 1993. "Consequences of nonequilibrium resource availability across multiple time scales: the transient maxima hypothesis." *American Naturalist* 141: 621–633.

Seton, E. T. 1929. *Lives of Game Animals.* New York: Doubleday, Doran, and Company, Inc.

Shaw, J. H. 1995. "How many bison originally populated western rangelands?" *Rangelands* 17 (5): 148–150.

Shea, M. E., L. A. Schulte, and B. J. Palik. 2014. "Reconstructing vegetation past: pre-Euro-American vegetation for the Midwest Driftless Area, USA." *Restoration Ecology* 32 (4): 417–433.

Shelford, V. E. 1913. *Animal Communities in Temperate North America as Illustrated in the Chicago Region.* Chicago: University of Chicago Press.

Shimek, B. 1911. "The Prairies." *Bulletin from the Laboratories of Natural History of the State University of Iowa* 6 (2): 169–241.

———. 1925. "The persistence of prairies." *University of Iowa Studies in Natural History* 11: 3–29

———. 1931. "The relation between the migrant and native flora of the prairie region." *University of Iowa Studies in Natural History* 14: 10–16.

Short, C. W. 1845. "Observations on the botany of Illinois, more specifically with reference to autumnal flora of the prairies." *Western Journal of Medicine and Surgery,* New Series 3: 185–198.

Shuman, B., A. K. Henderson, C. Plank, I. Stefanova, and S. S. Zeigler. 2009. "Woodland-to-forest transition during prolonged drought in Minnesota after ca. AD 1300." *Ecology* 90 (10): 2792–2807.

Siemann, E., J. Haarstad, and D. Tilman. 1999. "Dynamics of plant and arthropod diversity during old field succession." *Ecography* 22: 406–414.

Siemann, E., D. Tilman, J. Haarstad, and M. Ritchie. 1998. "Experimental tests of the dependence of arthropod diversity on plant diversity." *American Naturalist* 152 (5): 738–750.

Simberloff, D. 2014. "The 'Balance of Nature'—evolution of a panchreston." *PLoS Biol* 12 (10): e1001963.

Smeins, F. E., and D. E. Olsen. 1970. "Species composition and production of a native northwestern Minnesota tallgrass prairie." *American Midland Naturalist* 84: 398–409.

Smith, D. 2010. "Introduction: Returning prairie to the Midwest." In *The Tallgrass Prairie Center Guide to Prairie Restoration in the Upper Midwest,* edited by D. Smith, D. Williams, G. Houseal, and K. Henderson, xvii–xxi. Iowa City: University of Iowa Press.

Smith, D. 2019. "2019 Upland Gamebird hunting forecast." *Retriever Journal* Oct/Nov: 18–25.

Smith, M. D. 2011. "The ecological role of climate extremes: current understanding and future prospects." *Journal of Ecology* 99: 651–655.

Smith, R. C. 1932. "Upsetting the balance of nature, with special reference to Kansas and the Great Plains." *Transactions of the Kansas Academy of Science* 35: 31–33.

Smolik, J. D., and J. K. Lewis. 1982. "Effects of range condition on density and biomass of nematodes in mixed prairie ecosystems." *Journal of Range Management* 35 (5): 657–663.

Sperry, T. M. 1935. "Root systems in Illinois prairie." *Ecology* 16 (2): 178–202.

Stegner, W. 1962. *Wolf Willow.* New York: Viking Press.

———. 1969. *Sound of Mountain Water.* New York: Doubleday & Company, Inc.

Steinauer, E. M., and S. L. Collins. 1995. "Effects of urine deposition on small-scale patch structure on prairie vegetation." *Ecology* 76: 1195–1205.

———. 2001. "Feedback loops in ecological hierarchies following urine deposition in tallgrass prairie." *Ecology* 82 (5): 1319–1329.

Steuter, A. A., and L. Hidinger. 1999. "Comparative ecology of bison and cattle on mixed-grass prairie." *Great Plains Research* 9: 329–342.

Stewart, O. C. 1955. "Why were the prairies treeless?" *Southwestern Lore* XX (4): 59–64.

Stuble, K. L., S. E. Fick, and T. P. Young. 2017. "Every restoration is unique: testing year effects and site effects as drivers of initial restoration trajectories." *Journal of Applied Ecology* 54: 1051–1057.

Swenson, S. 2009. *My Healthy Woods.* Washington, DC: Aldo Leopold Foundation and American Forest Foundation.

Taft, J. B. 2016. "Are small, isolated prairie remnants effectively smaller than they look and getting smaller?" *Journal of the Torrey Botanical Society* 143 (3): 207–223.

Tansley, A. G. 1935. "The use and abuse of vegetational concepts and terms." *Ecology* 16 (3): 284–307.

Thomas, D. 1819. "Travels through the western country in the summer of 1816." In *Indiana as Seen by Early Travelers (1916)*, edited by H. Lindley, 42–135. Indianapolis: Indiana Historical Commission.

Thompson, P. W. 1983. "Composition of prairie stands in southern Michigan and adjoining areas." In *Proceedings of the Eighth North American Prairie Conference*, edited by R. Brewer, 105–111. Kalamazoo: Western Michigan University.

Thompson, S. J., T. W. Arnold, and C. L. Amundson. 2014. "A multiscale assessment of tree avoidance by prairie birds." *Condor* 116: 303–315.

Thomson, J. W. 1940. "Relic prairie areas in central Wisconsin." *Ecological Monographs* 10: 685–717.

Tomer, M. D., K. E. Schilling, C. A. Cambardella, P. Jacobson, and P. Drobney. 2010. "Groundwater nutrient concentrations during prairie reconstruction on an Iowa landscape." *Agriculture, Ecosystems, and Environment* 139: 206–213.

Tonietto, R. K., J. S. Ascher, and D. J. Larkin. 2017. "Bee communities along a prairie restoration chronosequence: similar abundance and diversity, distinct composition." *Ecological Applications* 27 (3): 705–717.

Towne, E. G., D. C. Hartnett, and R. C. Cochran. 2005. "Vegetation trends in tallgrass prairie from bison and cattle grazing." *Ecological Applications* 15: 1550–1559.

Towne, E. G., and K. E. Kemp. 2003. "Vegetation dynamics from annually burning tallgrass prairie at different seasons." *Journal of Range Management* 56: 185–192.

Towne, E. G., and A. K. Knapp. 1996. "Biomass and density responses in tallgrass prairie legumes to annual fire and topographic position." *American Journal of Botany* 83: 175–179.

Towne, E. G., and C. Owensby. 1984. "Long-term effects of annual burning at different dates in ungrazed Kansas tallgrass prairie." *Journal of Range Management* 37: 392–397.

Transeau, E. N. 1935. "The prairie peninsula." *Ecology* 16: 423–437.

Van Tramp, J. 1868. *Prairie and Rocky Mountain Adventures or Life in the West.* Columbus, OH: Segner and Condit.

Vermeire, L. T., R. B. Mitchell, S. D. Fuhlendorf, and R. L. Gillen. 2004. "Patch burning effects on grazing distribution." *Journal of Range Management* 57: 248–252.

Vestal, A. G. 1914. "A black-soil prairie station in northeastern Illinois." *Bulletin of the Torrey Botanical Club* 41: 351–363.

Vinton, M., D. C. Hartnett, E. J. Finck, and J. M. Briggs. 1993. "Interactive effects of fire, bison (*Bison bison*) grazing and plant community composition in tallgrass prairie." *American Midland Naturalist* 129: 10–18.

Vogel, J. A., D. M. Debinski, R. R. Koford, and J. R. Miller. 2007. "Butterfly response to prairie restoration through fire and grazing." *Biological Conservation* 140: 78–90.

Volney, C. F. 1804. "A View of the Soil and Climate of the United States of America." In *Indiana as Seen by Early Travelers (1916),* edited by H. Lindley, 17–24. Indianapolis: Indiana Historical Commission.

Walk, J. W., E. L. Kerschner, T. J. Benson, and R. E. Warner. 2010. "Nesting success of grassland birds in small patches in an agricultural landscape." *Auk* 127 (2): 328–334.

Walk, J. W., and R. E. Warner. 1999. "Effects of habitat area on the occurrence of grassland birds in Illinois." *Journal of Wildlife Management* 63 (3): 956–963.

Weaver, J. E. 1947. "Rate of decomposition of roots and rhizomes of certain range grasses in undisturbed prairie soil." *Ecology* 28: 221–240.

———. 1954. *North American Prairie.* Lincoln: Johnsen Publishing Co.

———. 1968. *Prairie Plants and Their Environment: A Fifty-Year Study in the Midwest.* Lincoln: University of Nebraska Press.

Weaver, J. E., and F. E. Clements. 1938. *Plant Ecology.* New York: McGraw-Hill Book Company, Inc.

Weidman, T., and J. A. Litvaitis. 2011. "Are small habitat patches useful for grassland bird conservation?" *Northeastern Naturalist* 18 (2): 207–216.

Wells, P. V. 1970. "Historical factors controlling vegetational patterns and floristic distribution in the Central Plains Region of North America." In *Pleistocene and Recent Environments of the Central Great Plains.* Special publication 3, edited by W. Dort and J. Jones, 211–221. Lawrence: University Press of Kansas.

Wells, R. W. 1819. "On the origins of prairies." *American Journal of Science* 1: 331–337.

White, J. A., and D. C. Glenn-Lewin. 1984. "Regional and local variation in tallgrass prairie remnants of Iowa and eastern Nebraska." *Vegetatio* 57: 67–78.

White, P. S., and J. Walker. 1997. "Approximating nature's variation: selecting and using reference information in restoration ecology." *Restoration Ecology* 5 (4): 338–349.

Whitford, P. B. 1958. "A study of prairie remnants in southeastern Wisconsin." *Ecology* 39: 727–733.

Whitman, W. 1882. *Specimen Days.* Philadelphia: Rees Welsh and Company.

Whitney, J. D. 1876. "Plain, prairie, forest." *The American Naturalist* 10: 656–667.

Whittaker, R. H. 1951. "A criticism of the plant association and climatic climax concepts." *Northwest Science* 25: 17–31.

Wilder, L. I. 1935. *Little House on the Prairie.* New York: Harper Collins.

Williams, D. W., L. L. Jackson, and D. D. Smith. 2007. "Effects of frequent mowing on survival and persistence of forbs seeded into a species-poor grassland." *Restoration Ecology* 15 (1): 24–33.

Wilsey, B. J., and L. M. Martin. 2015. "Top-down control of rare species abundance by native ungulates in a grassland restoration." *Restoration Ecology* 23: 465–472.

Wilson, G. W. T., and D. C. Hartnett. 1997. "Effects of mycorrhizae on plant growth and dynamics in experimental tallgrass prairie microcosms." *American Journal of Botany* 84: 478–482.

———. 1998. "Interspecific variation in plant responses to mycorrhizal colonization in tallgrass prairie." *American Journal of Botany* 85: 1732–1738.

Winder, V. L., L. B. McNew, A. J. Gregory, L. M. Hunt, S. M. Wisely, and B. K. Sand-
ercock. 2014. "Effects of wind energy development on survival of female greater
prairie-chickens." *Journal of Applied Ecology* 51 (2): 395–405.

Winter, M., and J. Faaborg. 1999. "Patterns of area sensitivity in grassland-nesting
birds." *Conservation Biology* 13: 1424–1436.

Winter, M., D. H. Johnson, and J. Faaborg. 2000. "Evidence for edge effects on
multiple levels in tallgrass prairie." *Condor* 102 (2): 256–266.

Winter, M., D. H. Johnson, and J. A. Shaffer. 2006a. "Does body size affect a bird's
sensitivity to patch size and landscape structure?" *Condor* 108: 808–816.

Winter, M., D. H. Johnson, J. A. Shaffer, T. M. Donovan, and W. D. Svedarsky.
2006b. "Patch size and landscape effects on density and nesting success of
grassland birds." *Journal of Wildlife Management* 70 (1): 158–172.

Wolfe-Bellin, K. S., and K. A. Moloney. 2001. "Successional vegetation dynamics
on pocket gopher mounds in an Iowa tallgrass prairie." In *Proceedings of the 17th
North American Prairie Conference,* edited by N. Bernstein and L. Ostrander,
155–163. Mason City: North Iowa Area Community College.

Woodard, J. 1924. "Origins of prairie in Illinois." *Botanical Gazette* 77: 241–261.

Worster, D. 1990. "The ecology of order and chaos." *Environmental History Review*
14 (1/2): 1–18.

Wright, C. K., and M. C. Wimberly. 2013. "Recent land use change in the western
corn belt threatens grasslands and wetlands." *PNAS* 110 (10): 4134–4139.

Wright, H. E. 1970. "Vegetational history of the Great Plains." In *Pleistocene and
Recent Environments of the Central Great Plains.* Special publication 3, edited by
W. Dort and J. Jones, 157–172. Lawrence: University Press of Kansas.

Wu, J., and O. L. Loucks. 1995. "From balance of nature to hierarchical patch dynamics: a paradigm shift in ecology." *Quarterly Review of Biology* 70: 439–466.

Yang, Y., D. Tilman, G. Furey, and C. Lehman. 2019. "Soil carbon sequestration
accelerated by restoration of grassland biodiversity." *Nature Communications.*
https://doi.org/10.1038/s41467-019-08636-w.

Zettler, L. W., and K. A. Piskin. 2011. "Mycorrhizal Fungi from protocorms,
seedlings and mature plants of the Eastern Prairie Fringed Orchid, Platanthera
leucophaea (Nutt.) Lindley: A comprehensive list to augment conservation."
American Midland Naturalist 166 (1): 29–39.

Zimmerman, J. L. 1993. *The Birds of Konza.* Lawrence: University Press of Kansas.

Index

Selected Bur Oak Books of Interest

Booming from the Mists of Nowhere
by Greg Hoch

A Country So Full of Game
by James J. Dinsmore

Ecological Restoration in the Midwest
edited by Christian Lenhart
and Peter C. Smiley Jr.

*The Ecology and Management of
Prairies in the Central United States*
by Chris Helzer

The Emerald Horizon
by Cornelia F. Mutel

Fragile Giants
by Cornelia F. Mutel

Hidden Prairie
by Chris Helzer

*An Illustrated Guide to Iowa
Prairie Plants*
by Paul Christiansen and Mark Müller

Landforms of Iowa
by Jean C. Prior

Of Men and Marshes
by Paul L. Errington

Of Wilderness and Wolves
by Paul L. Errington

Out Home
by John Madson
and Michael McIntosh

*A Practical Guide to Prairie
Reconstruction*
by Carl Kurtz

Restoring the Tallgrass Prairie
by Shirley Shirley

Sky Dance of the Woodcock
by Greg Hoch

Stories from under the Sky
by John Madson

The Tallgrass Prairie Reader
edited by John T. Price

Up on the River
by John Madson

Where the Sky Began
by John Madson

With Wings Extended
by Greg Hoch